INSTITUTIONS AND THE EVOLUTION OF MODERN BUSINESS

T0348038

Books of related interest

Banks, Networks and Small Firm Finance
edited by Andrew Godley and Duncan M Ross

Nordic Business in the Long View
On Control and Strategy in Structural Change
edited by Kersti Ullenhag

Organisational Capability and Competitive Advantage
edited by Charles Harvey and Geoffrey Jones

Labour and Business in Modern Britain
edited by Charles Harvey and John Turner

Business History
Concepts and Measurement
edited by Charles Harvey

International Competition and Industrial Change
edited by Charles Harvey and Jon Press

International Competition and Strategic Response int he Textile Industries since 1870
edited by Mary B Rose

Banks and Money
International and Comparative Finance in History
edited by Geoffrey Jones

Capital, Entrepreneurs and Profits
edited by R P T Davenport-Hines

Institutions and the Evolution of Modern Business

edited by

MARK CASSON and MARY B. ROSE

FRANK CASS

LONDON • PORTLAND , OR

First published in 1998 in Great Britain by
FRANK CASS AND COMPANY LIMITED
Newbury House, 900 Eastern Avenue
London IG2 7HH, England

and in the United States of America by
FRANK CASS
c/o International Specialized Book Services, Inc.
5804 N.E. Hassalo Street, Portland, Oregon 97213-3644

Copyright © 1998 Frank Cass & Co. Ltd

British Library Cataloguing in Publication Data

Institutions and the evolution of modern business
  1. Business enterprises 2. Organizational change – Histor
  I. Casson, Mark, 1945 – II. Rose, Mary B.
  338.8'8

ISBN 0 7146 4854 0 (hbk)
ISBN 0 7146 4400 5 (pbk)

Library of Congress Cataloging-in-Publication Data

Institutions and the evolution of modern business / edited by Mark
Casson and Mary B. Rose.
    p.   cm.
  "This group of studies first appeared in a special issue of Business
History, vol. 39, no. 4 (October 1997), [Institutions and the evolution of
modern business]" – t.p. verso.
  Includes bibliographical references and index.
  ISBN 0-7146-4845-0 (hb). – ISBN 0-7146-4400-5 (pb)
  1. Industrial organization – Great Britain – History. 2. Industrial
organization – History. 3. Business enterprises – Great Britain – History.
4. Business enterprises – History. 5. Institutional economics – History. I.
Casson, Mark, 1945-   . II. Rose, Mary B. HD70.G7157 1997
338.7'0941– dc21   97-28112
                                                              CIP

This group of studies first appeared in a Special Issue of *Business History*,
Vol.39, No.4 (October 1997), [Institutions and the Evolution of Modern Business]

Printed in Great Britain by
Antony Rowe Ltd., Chippenham, Wilts.

Contents

Institutions and the Evolution of Modern Business: Introduction

MARK CASSON and MARY B. ROSE

University of Reading

Lancaster University

For more than 30 years a symbiosis has developed between the 'new institutionalists' and business historians, which stems from synergies in the interests of both groups. The central questions posed by Coase and Williamson, of why firms exist and grow, have found echoes in the historical work of Chandler on the forces leading to the rise of big business first in the United States and then in Europe.[1] Conversely Williamson used Chandler's historical evidence to give foundation to his development of transaction cost economics.[2]

Transaction cost economics is embedded in an institutional model of economic activity which explains why some, but not all, activities are organised in firms, rather than being co-ordinated by markets. A critical appraisal of transaction cost economics is to be found in Jones' essay in this volume. This shows the way in which transaction cost economics evolved to fill some of the gaps in neoclassical economic theory, with respect to the firm, and highlights its strengths and weaknesses as a tool for business historians. Consequently this evolution needs no repetition here. The dialogue between the new institutionalists and business historians has been difficult because of their very different methodological starting points. Williamson's analysis, like that of neoclassical economics, has to be applied using the method of comparative statics. His analysis explains how, following an exogenous change in the economic environment, the configuration of firms and markets adjusts, through changes in the boundaries of firms, from one equilibrium to another. The process by which this change is accomplished is assumed to be of no consequence: thus the equilibrium *from* which the system adjusts has no impact on the equililibrium *to* which it adjusts. By contrast, Chandler's 'stages approach', to the development of the business corporation, highlights the complex, dynamic interaction between the innovative growth strategies of firms and the subsequent development of professionally managed hierarchical structures. Indeed Williamson has been accused of abusing Chandler's historical evidence as a result of a combination of an ahistorical methodology and a neoclassical if not ideological attachment to the market.[3]

The 'new institutionalism' does not end with transaction costs, however, any more than business historians are interested only in the organisation of firms. Their interests in both innovation and competitive advantage and the origins of economic decline in mature economies has meant that the theoretical underpinning of business history has widened, whilst there have been increasing opportunities for institutional theory to draw on business history. Developed partly as a result of some of the shortcomings of transaction cost economics, evolutionary theory drew on the behaviouralists such as Cyert and March, Edith Penrose's *Theory of the Growth of the Firm* and Schumpeter's work on entrepreneurship.[4] With its emphasis on the development of organisational capabilities it is potentially extremely fruitful for business historians.[5] By highlighting the path dependency of innovation it demonstrates the impact of firm-specific routines on the choice of technology and as such is invaluable in the explanation of divergent as opposed to convergent business developments. Recently it has been successfully used with a combination of transaction cost theory and historical methodology in a 'dynamic theory of business institutions'. In *Firms, Markets and Economic Change: A Dynamic Theory of Business Institutions,* Langlois and Robertson demonstrate that, since the late nineteenth century, the large and centralised corporate enterprise is but one route to innovation and economic growth. Whether loose networks of small firms, coalitions or joint ventures are preferred and form the basis of competitive advantage depends upon 'the nature of the problem ... the stage in the product life cycle and the availability of information'.[6]

The notion that, in certain circumstances, networks represent a competitive alternative to integration is an important conclusion for business historians and marks a departure from both Williamson and Chandler. Williamson, for example, whilst exploring the circumstances which make intermediate forms of organisation more suitable than the two extremes of markets and firms, clearly sees them as exceptional. Chandler, in similar vein, believed that coalitions of firms existed but were transient while Kogut has demonstrated that joint ventures were highly unstable.[7] The implication is that groupings are merely a stage along the way to more efficient integrated firms. It is a conclusion which is in line with that in the development economics literature where the existence of business groups are seen as a sign of market failure in young economies.[8]

The view that networks are little more than an intermediate form of organisation has left both Chandler and Williamson open to the criticism of concentration on the Western – if not the American – economic system. In East Asian economies, however, it is impossible to separate the family firm from its networks. In societies like Taiwan and Hong Kong networks are so embedded as to be viewed as economic institutions, in their own right, rather than just a stage between market and firm.[9] However, internationally comparative research has increasingly demonstrated that loose networks persist in the twentieth century and form an important basis of international competitive advantage in the Western world, as well as in the Far East. In the United States, for example, interlocking directorships create vertical social ties in big business and especially between big business and finance. In the 'Third Italy', on the other hand, more formal clusters in the textile and clothing industries have formed the basis of their international competitive advantage since 1980.[10]

One of the reasons Williamson sees networks as merely an intermediate form of organisation lies in his concentration on the contractual underpinnings of institutions. This has led him to reject the idea that power and authority, and indeed cultural forces, are significant variables in economic organisation.[11] However, some new institutionalists have evolved theories, based upon family and family-like firms, which provide a partial theoretical underpinning to the study of networks both within and between firms. Theorists such as Ben-Porath and Pollak have, for example, applied transaction cost theory to family behaviour whilst complementary analysis has highlighted those circumstances which make informal 'clan-like' control arrangements, within firms, more successful than formal bureaucracies.[12] Implicit in the transaction cost approach is the idea that where regular transactions are conducted in a hazardous environment bureaucratic arrangements, by reducing uncertainty, will increase efficiency. It has been suggested, however, that some circumstances are so hazardous that they cannot be regulated either by the market or the firm. As a result, transaction costs will be reduced within firms when control is on the basis of shared attitudes, goals and aspirations, either through a shared background or the creation of a business culture, rather than rules and regulations. Therefore: 'In the clan form, with its lower demands on formalised, sophisticated information – common ideas, beliefs and values instead function as information carriers – yielding sufficient guidance for action, providing sufficiently good measures of the values to be exchanged.'[13]

Understanding of the development and success of networks clearly, therefore, requires an understanding of the way in which power and trust relationships develop and the impact which they have upon business behaviour. Inevitably, sociology provides invaluable insights on such issues whilst comparative management theorists such as Hofstede and Hampden-Turner and Trompenaars allow for culturally based comparisons of business behaviour.[14]

New institutionalism is not, however, always acultural. Casson has claimed that by linking the notion of transaction costs to that of trust it is possible to provide insights into both entrepreneurial behaviour and the formation of networks within and between firms. He has proposed that this theoretical framework should be adopted by business historians.[15] This approach appears to be especially relevant to the study of the boundaries of the family firm, which can be viewed as encompassing not only the partners and employees, but also the extended kinship group of cousins and in-laws, social connections in the business community and members of the family's religious group. The family consequently represents more than just a reservoir of skill, labour and finance. It is a network of trust, the use of which reduced the transaction costs and the dangers and uncertainties of business activity. Thus, although the family might represent an internal market for managerial labour, a source of funds for establishment and expansion and of market information, the boundaries of the family business have usually lain within a rather wider group with a shared culture and values.

If trust is synonymous with low transaction costs, information costs are incurred irrespective of whether the sources of information are trustworthy. By focusing on the flow of information, which he sees as the most important element of economic activity, Mark Casson explores in this volume the evolution of methods of intermediation. With choice determined by a combination of technological, entrepreneurial and cultural forces, such methods of 'market making' have evolved through time in response to changing circumstances. By shifting the emphasis from the organisation of product to the organisation of information, Casson emphasises the interaction between firms and other types of economic institution. His analytical techniques combine elements of transaction cost theory with evolutionary theory and the theory of entrepreneurship. Using these techniques, he attempts to chart a 'middle road' along which instituional theory can develop.

The organisation of information is a theme that is developed further in Oliver Westall's essay, which analyses organisational change and innovation in general insurance. Westall demonstrates that the very essence of the business of insurance is the processing of information. Consequently, the revolution in information technology transformed the relationship between policy holders and insurers and effectively rendered traditional methods redundant. In so doing information technology encouraged new entrants to the industry and changed its competive structure for ever. Caunce, on the other hand, analyses the development of a localised cluster of dynamic sectors in the Yorkshire woollen industries. He demonstrates that the social and economic institutions, which processed market information, became inseparable from the community's culture and were instrumental in the creation of effective innovative production strategies. Equally, Matthias Kipping, in his comparative analysis of the development of management consultancy in Europe, demonstrates the vital place which intermediating institutions played in the transfer of managerial know-how, highlighting their role in information transfer.

In his theory of relative economic backwardness, Gerschenkron pointed to the importance of the wider institutional environment in overcoming the obstacles to spontaneous industrialisation in developing economies.[16] Equally, Davis and North demonstrated the link between institutional change and the pattern of American economic growth and industrial development. They concluded that the 'wedding of economic theory with an explanation for institutional change is essential for further understanding of the process of economic growth – past, present and future'. In other words, they demonstrated that business reactions and the pattern of development are closely intertwined and shaped by both the legal system and shifts in government policy.[17] It has also become clear that changes in one type of business institution, such as the financial system, will have repercussions for the behaviour and performance of other institutions.

Business historians have demonstrated a growing interest in the development of the institutional environment and in the interaction between differing types of institution.[18] In this volume a number of the contributions explore the significance of this wider environment for business behaviour and the implications of often complex inter-institutional arrangements. Sjögren, in his comparative analysis of financial reconstruction and industrial reorganisation in inter-war Sweden and Britain, demonstrates that the legal framework of financial contracts is embedded in banks, firms and central banks and has implications for their behaviour. Yet he is also able to demonstrate that social relationships, underpinned through interlocking directorships, improved flows of information and reinforced trust relationships within financial groups. This had significant implications for bank–industry relations, especially in Sweden. Knutsen is also concerned with inter-institutional arrangements and demonstrates the extent to which the credit-based state-led system in post-1945 Norway became the basis for the government's industrial policy. In so doing he highlights the importance of a combination of the historical development of the Norwegian banking system and of government–bank relations in the moulding of industrial planning. Finally, Mary Rose, in exploring the 'politics of protection' in the British and American cotton industries, has highlighted the differing bargaining powers of cotton manufacturers over the protection of their industry. She demonstrates that the success or failure of campaigns for protection were critically dependent upon the surrounding political, social and economic environment and the potential of interest groups to influence the outcome of elections. Her analysis demonstrates that the boundaries of the firm have important implications, not only for the efficiency of production and marketing, but for the success of rent-seeking lobbying as well.

The essays in this volume demonstrate that it can be fruitful to apply institutional theory to business history. In addition, the volume shows that the wider study of the institutional environment is inseparable from the study of business. It is clear, however, that although 'institutionalism' in business history has a long pedigree, many areas of research and potential interraction with theory remain to be explored . The extent to which this will occur inevitably depends upon the degree to which the interests of theoreticians serve the needs of historians and vice versa.

This volume demonstrates, on the one hand, that the processing of information within or between institutions is the basis of business strategy, while showing, on the other, the importance of social and political networks to inter-institutional relations. This highlights the need for a theory of business organisation which makes the institutional environment endogenous rather than exogenous. This would involve a movement away from an exclusive emphasis on contractual arrangements to one which highlights the impact which decisions within one institution or group of institutions have upon the rest of the system. Such theoretical development would involve the combination of existing theories of the firm with, for example, theories of economic policy formulation. It would then be possible to show how interactions between economic and political actors can impact on the organisation, strategy and performance of both business and government.[19]

One of the consequences of making the institutional environment endogenous would be that networks and their social underpinnings would move from the periphery to the core of institutional theory. Moreover, it would ensure that the links with the other social sciences, which many theoretical economists look set to sever, would be strengthened. Business history, on the other hand, would be well served by such a development. It would provide an additional tool to help business historians build their own conceptual models to make sense of the complexities of the past and the present.

NOTES

1. R.H. Coase, 'The Nature of the Firm', *Economica*, Vol.4 (1937), pp.386–485; O.E. Williamson, *Markets and Hierarchies; Analysis and Anti-Trust Implications* (New York, 1975); idem, 'The Modern Corporation: Origins, Evolution, Attributes', *Journal of Economic Literature*, Vol.19 (1981), pp.1537–68; idem, *The Economic Institutions of*

Capitalism (New York, 1988); A.D. Chandler, Jr., *Strategy and Structure: Chapters in the History of Business Enterprise* (Cambridge, MA, 1962); idem, *The Visible Hand: The Managerial Revolution in America* (Cambridge, MA, 1977); idem, *Scale and Scope: The Dynamics of Industrial Capitalism* (Cambridge, MA, 1977).

2. Williamson, 'The Modern Corporation', pp.1537–68; idem, 'Emergence of the Visible Hand: Implications for Industrial Organization', in A.D. Chandler and H. Daems (eds.), *Managerial Hierarchies* (Cambridge, MA, 1980).

3. W. Lazonick, *Business Organization and the Myth of the Market Economy* (Cambridge, 1991), pp.265–6.

4. R.M Cyert and J.G. March, *A Behavioural Theory of the Firm* (New York, 1963); E.T. Penrose, *The Theory of the Growth of the Firm* (Oxford, 1959); J.A. Schumpeter, *The Theory of Economic Development* (Cambridge, MA, 1934).

5. R.R. Nelson and S.G. Winter, *An Evolutionary Theory of Economic Change* (Cambridge, MA, 1982).

6. R.N. Langlois and P.L. Robertson, *Firms, Markets and Economic Change* (London, 1995).

7. O.M. Williamson, 'Comparative Ownership and Control: The Analysis of Discrete Structural Alternatives', *Administrative Science Quarterly*, Vol.36 (1991), pp.269–96; Chandler, *Scale and Scope*, pp.390–91; B. Kogut, 'The Stability of Joint Ventures: Reciprocity and Competitive Rivalry', *Journal of Industrial Economics*, Vol.XXXIII (1989), pp.183–98.

8. N.H. Leff, 'Industrial Organization and Entrepreneurship in the Developing Countries: The Economic Groups', *Economic Development and Cultural Change*, Vol.26 (1978), pp.661–75.

9. S.G. Redding, *The Spirit of Chinese Capitalism* (Berlin, 1990); G.G. Hamilton and R.C. Feenstra, 'Varieties of Hierarchies and Markets: An Introduction', *Industrial and Corporate Change*, Vol.4 (1995), pp.51–6; N.W. Biggart and G.G. Hamilton, 'On the Limits of a Firm-Based Theory to Explain Business Networks: The Western Bias of Neoclassical Economics', in N. Nohria and R.G. Eccles (eds.), *Networks and Organizations: Structure, Form and Action* (Boston, MA, 1992), pp.471–90.

10. M. Mizruchi, *The American Corporate Network 1904–1974* (Beverly Hills, CA, 1982), pp.28–9; M. Porter *The Competitive Advantage of Nations* (London, 1990), pp.442–5.

11. O.E. Williamson, 'Hierarchies, Markets and Power in the Economy: An Economic Perspective', *Industrial and Corporate Change*, Vol.4 (1994), pp.21–49.

12. Y. Ben-Porath, 'The F-Connection: Families, Friends and Firms and the Organization of Exchange', *Population and Development Review*, Vol.6 (1980), pp.1–30; R.A. Pollak, 'A Transactions Cost Approach to Families and Households', *Journal of Economic Literature*, Vol.XXIII (1985), pp.581–608; W.G. Ouchi, 'Markets, Bureaucracies and Clans', *Administrative Science Quarterly*, Vol.25 (1980); M. Alvesson and L. Lindkvist, 'Transaction Costs, Clans and Corporate Culture', *Journal of Management Studies*, Vol.30 (1993), pp.427–52.

13. Alvesson and Lindkvist, 'Transaction Costs', p.430.

14. M. Weber, *Economy and Society* (translated and edited by G. Roth and C. Wittich, Berkeley, CA, 1978); G. Hofstede, *Culture's Consequences* (London, 1984); idem, *Cultures and Organizations* (London, 1991); C. Hampden-Turner and F. Trompenaars, *The Seven Cultures of Capitalism* (London, 1994).

15. M.C. Casson, *The Entrepreneur* (London, 1982), pp.302–7; idem, *The Economics of Business Culture: Game Theory, Transaction Costs and Economic Performance* (Oxford, 1991), pp.69–70; idem, 'Entrepreneurship and Business Culture', in J. Brown and M.B. Rose (eds.), *Entrepreneurship, Networks and Modern Business* (Manchester, 1993), pp.30–54.

16. A. Gerschenkron, *Economic Backwardness in Historical Perspective* (Cambridge, MA, 1966).

17. L. Davis and D.C. North, *Institutional Change and American Economic Growth* (Cambridge, 1971), p.270.

18. For example, H. Mercer, 'The State and British Business since 1945', in M. Kirby and M.B. Rose (eds.), *Business Enterprise in Modern Britain* (London, 1994), pp.285–314, provides an up-to-date overview of the literature for Britain and a comprehensive bibliography. See also M. Collins, *Banks and Industrial Finance in Britain, 1800–1939* (London, 1991);

Steven W. Tolliday (ed.), *Government and Business* (Cheltenham, 1991); H. James, H. Lindgren and A. Teichova (eds.), *The Role of Banks in the Interwar Economy* (Cambridge, 1991); P.L. Cottrell, H. Lindgren and A. Teichova (eds.), *European Industry and Banking 1920–1939: A Review of Bank–Industry Relations* (Leicester, 1994).
19. R.E. Baldwin, *The Political Economy of US Import Policy* (Cambridge, MA, 1985).

Transaction Costs and the Theory of the Firm: The Scope and Limitations of the New Institutional Approach

S.R.H. JONES

University of Dundee

I

For much of the twentieth century there have been complaints about the failure of economic theory to provide tools with which to analyse the development of business enterprise. While the neoclassical theory of the firm has enabled scholars to determine the impact of exogenous changes, such as a tax or a subsidy, upon prices and quantities sold, it has provided few insights into the sort of changes that might occur to the structure and organisation of the firm during the equilibrating process. This is not surprising bearing in mind the assumptions underlying the theory and the mechanistic way in which processes are supposed to operate. With all feasible technologies, prices of inputs and production costs assumed to be known by management, as are all future states of the market, then profit maximisation becomes a routine exercise. There is simply no scope for judgement and certainly no role for the innovating entrepreneur. Equilibration is a costless, timeless and riskless process, with the manager of the neoclassical firm no more than an automaton applying known techniques to achieve certain outcomes.

Given the focus of neoclassical theory upon the equilibration of markets rather than the operation of firms, it hardly surprising that it has been regarded by business historians with a degree of frustration. Francis Hyde, writing in the early 1960s, was willing to accept that the use of economic theory might 'lift narrative from the level of the purely descriptive' but at the same time argued that theories that stressed simple profit maximisation as the basis for decision-making could be quite misleading.[1] Barry Supple was rather more positive, pleading for business historians to become more systematic in their approach, suggesting that they ought to 'pose a very rigorous and limited set of questions' and use economic theory to help them 'shuffle the facts of history into meaningful patterns'.[2] But what patterns might there be? The taxonomy employed by the neoclassical theory of the firm is not very helpful in this respect, the categories of perfect and imperfect competition, oligopoly and monopoly being devised to explain equilibration under different market structures rather than the different organisational patterns or structures that might emerge to facilitate equilibration. From the comparative static perspective of the neoclassical economist, how or why firms might change over time and what effect this might have on output is irrelevant.

The new institutional theory of the firm, by way of contrast, is very much concerned with the relationship between organisational structures, resource allocation and the processes of equilibration. Drawing on some of the contextual features of the old institutional economics while retaining the methodological individualism underpinning neoclassical economics, the new institutional theory of the firm seeks to explain what determines the boundaries of the firm and the appropriate system of governance. The focus of analysis is the transaction and the context within which transactions take place. The regularity of the exchange process, the type of assets supporting exchange, uncertainty and the cognitive limits of human actors, and the mores and values of society are all incorporated to generate predictions concerning what institutional or organisational structure might be adopted under a given set of circumstances. The general presumption is that the lower the level of transaction costs *vis-à-vis* other costs, the greater the likelihood that resource allocation will take place within markets rather than firms.

The new institutional theory of the firm has undoubtedly provided business historians with a welcome set of tools with which to 'shuffle the facts of history into meaningful patterns'. It has been applied to the emergence of early chartered companies, the factory system, the organisation of large corporations, the growth of multinationals and questions of franchising and monopoly. Yet while insights have been gained the new theory is subject to a number of limitations. Amongst the more serious are a failure to identify transaction costs in an operationally satisfactory way, an inadequate treatment of innovatory or evolutionary processes, and a disregard for the importance of strategy when selecting organisational modes. The remainder of this essay reviews the development of the new theory, examines some of the methodological and empirical problems encountered, and discusses the ways in which the blending of the transaction costs and capabilities approach of new institutional and evolutionary theorists provides fresh insights into how the boundaries of the firm might change over time.

II

The new institutional economics, of which the new institutional theory of the firm constitutes the core, is regarded by most practitioners as emanating from the work of John R. Commons and Ronald Coase.[3] Commons, a leading institutionalist writing in the 1930s, regarded the transaction as the basic unit of analysis. For him the institution was 'a going concern which engages in a series of transactions within the guidelines of a set of working rules'.[4] Transactions might be rationing transactions concerned with the allocation of benefits within society, managerial transactions or transactions involved in the exchange of property. Production and distribution, within the state or the firm, is harmonised by rule-guided internal governance which constitutes an alternative to court-ordered solutions.[5]

While institutions, of which the firm is a prime example, may be seen as a relatively efficient means of co-ordinating transactions, to what do they owe their origins and scope? Commons argued for an evolutionary process, with collective action on the part of ordinary people, such as businessmen and labourers, resulting in the deliberate creation of institutions designed for particular purposes.[6] For Coase, trained in neoclassical economics, the origins of the firm lay not in collective and purposive action but in the response of individuals to the costs of transacting business. 'The main reason why it is profitable to establish a firm would seem to be that there is a cost of using the price mechanism'.[7] Of course, the internalisation of activities does not completely eliminate the cost of transacting in the market-place, for goods and service still have to be bought and sold, but the producer will enter into far fewer contracts with respect to inputs and outputs. The management or co-ordination of production is not costless, however, and Coase, reflecting the contemporary orthodoxy of the 1930s, couched his argument in a way that was consistent with notions of managerial diseconomies of scale. Consequently, he saw the boundaries of the firm as being determined by the simple application of the marginal rule, with the producer continuing to internalise activities up to that point at which the cost of management equalled the cost of transacting in the market-place.

These early contributions provided the basis for a more realistic theory of the firm in which the development of working rules, incorporating both general and firm-specific cultures, and the evolution of governance structures might help to explain how firms and markets grow. However, for the next two decades neoclassical economists were concerned not with the effect that values, rules and governance structures might have upon the boundaries of the firm but whether firms maximised profits. Empirical research by Hall and Hitch in the late 1930s demonstrated that practical businessmen followed full cost rather than marginal cost pricing and that normal rather than maximum profits were sufficient for them to stay in business.[8] Interest in what businessmen actually did was brief, however, with the famous debate between Alchian and Friedman concentrating on outcomes rather than processes. That businessmen set prices by rules of thumb and did not consciously maximise profits was irrelevant. Striving for profits, Friedman argued, was an instinctive process, and the competitive process would ensure that in the long run only those whose instincts led them to maximise profits would survive.[9]

Dissatisfaction with the theory of the firm and its central postulate of profit maximisation persisted, however, and during the 1950s a number of scholars led by March and Simon began to investigate behaviour in organisations. Once again the concept of the firm as a collective organisation was introduced, with attention paid to the ways in which conflicting objectives might be resolved and transformed into goals. More importantly for subsequent theorising, March and Simon also explored how efforts were made to push back the cognitive limits of the individual by the introduction of systems, structures and rules so that it was possible to assimilate and act on the large amounts of information necessary for the firm to meet goals and adapt to changing circumstances.[10] The work of the behaviouralists, especially the notion that 'the cost of obtaining and processing information meant that satisficing and rule of thumb strategies would be followed', was not well received by an economics profession still wedded to the view that firms which did not maximise profits would not survive.[11]

The traditional view became increasingly difficult to sustain, however, as neoclassical economists began to pay closer attention to the shortcomings of managerial capitalism. A major blow was struck by Baumol in a celebrated work which argued that following the divorce of ownership from control, management was likely to exploit information asymmetries to pursue its own goals, especially the goal of sales maximisation, subject to a minimum profit constraint.[12] The idea that information asymmetries might be exploited was taken further by Marris, who suggested that profits might be diverted by managers to support long-run growth, albeit at the risk of takeover.[13] Yet, true to their neoclassical roots, these writers did not delve deeply into the workings of large corporations and ask whether their governance structures were capable of supporting growth. For most managerial theorists, it was sufficient that the discipline of the capital market worked effectively, with wayward managements being subject to ejection via hostile takeovers.[14]

Few would regard the capital market as other than a blunt instrument limited in scope, and so the question remained as to how the principals of firms effectively controlled their agents. Control took on two dimensions, for it was important that principals not only prevented agents from using resources for their own ends but they also ensured that resources were used efficiently. For Alchian and Demsetz, the problem was sufficiently important for them to argue that shirking – rather than transaction cost minimisation – provided the rationale for the firm. To ensure that the gains from team (firm) production were not dissipated, they argued that it would pay team members to appoint a monitor with the power to negotiate input contracts and discipline those who shirked. In recompense, the monitor would receive the residual profit stream after input suppliers had been paid, effectively becoming the owner of the firm.[15]

The proposition that the firm was little more than a nexus of contracts afforded an interesting, if ahistorical, perspective on the origins of the owner-managed firm. It also took the debate back to the work of Commons, who saw the going concern as an institution that harmonised individual transactional activity through collective action that was based on rules, both formal and informal. Yet Alchian and Demsetz had little new to say about the internal workings of the firm, merely offering brief comments about the rules, values and routines necessary to support efficient contracts and the need for control systems to be modified if owner-managed firms were to grow. Not that the concept of growth would appear to be terrribly meaningful, given their view of the firm as nothing more than a particularly dense intersection of contracts with necessarily fuzzy boundaries.[16] More seriously, their presumption that efficient contracts providing for all contingencies (including re-contracting) might be written without too much difficulty and that enforcement would be unproblematical led them to minimise the effects that transaction costs might have upon the scope and structure of business enterprise.

That Alchian and Demsetz should fail to consider how contracting difficulties might affect the boundaries of the firm seems a little surprising, given Coase's 1960 article concerning social costs and the substantial literature on the role of institutions in the presence of market failure that ensued.[17] Indeed, they explicitly rejected imperfect knowledge and unforeseen circumstances as providing any rationale for the existence and organisation of the 'classical firm'.[18] The new institutional theory of the firm that was to follow turned this position on its head, arguing that in many instances the growth of the firm was designed precisely to overcome market failures, especially the costs and difficulties of transacting in markets under conditions of uncertainty.

III

The theoretical framework for much of the new institutional economics was first developed by Oliver Williamson in *Markets and Hierarchies*, published in 1975 and refined in *The Economic Institutions of Capitalism*, which appeared ten years later.[19] Williamson, following Commons, viewed economic activity as a series of transactions taking place within a framework of working rules and, following Coase, saw the locus of transactions moving out of the market-place and into the firm when the cost of contracting in the former was relatively high. Yet to raise Coase's observations beyond the level of tautology, it was important to identify those factors that raised the search, negotiation and enforcement costs incurred in a market transaction.

Williamson, drawing on the work of Simon and other behaviouralists, attributed the existence of high transaction costs to the existence of two behavioural characteristics, bounded rationality and opportunism, together with two environmental features, small numbers bargaining and complexity linked with uncertainty. Bounded rationality comes about because 'the capacity of the human mind for formulating and solving complex problems is very small compared with the size of problems whose solution is required for objectively rational behaviour in the real world'. Opportunism is encouraged by information asymmetries and refers to a lack of candour or honesty in transactions, to include 'self-interest seeking with guile'.[20]

When large numbers of repeat transactions take place in a competitive market-place opportunism poses little risk, as the competitive process is inimical to opportunistic behaviour. However, when repeated contracting results in multilateral trades being transformed into bilateral trades engendering semi-permanent relationships, opportunism may become a problem if one party seeks to gain advantage over the other. If rationality were unbounded, then all contingencies, including opportunistic behaviour, might be addressed through appropriately written contracts. In the absence of opportunistic behaviour, problems arising because of complexity and uncertainty might be adequately dealt with by re-contracting as they occur. It is the linking of bounded rationality with opportunism that provides the critical spur for bringing transacting parties within the ambit of one firm, with opportunism being put aside in the pursuit of joint profit maximisation.

The problems of bounded rationality and opportunistic behaviour are not magically solved by internalisation, however, as the work of behavioural and managerial theorists makes abundantly clear. Williamson, building on Chandler's empirical work,[21] argued that divisionalisation and the development of other control systems help to mitigate internal market failures. Moreover, the pursuit of sub-goals by divisional management might be constrained by appropriate adjustments to governance structures. In many cases the multi-divisional corporation acts as a mini-capital market, the creation of divisions as profit centres providing both a monitoring mechanism and a yardstick by which head office can allocate resources. Head office, having intimate knowledge of a particular sector and detailed knowledge of its own operations, is better able to make an informed and expeditious decision with respect to investment, both routine and strategic, than external capital markets.[22] Failure by head office to ensure efficient resource allocation will result in takeover as the capital market disciplines errant management.

The theoretical propositions advanced in *Markets and Hierarchies* were supported with examples drawn from economic history, although the hypothesis that the locus of economic activity was determined by the comparative transaction cost properties of firm and market was not systematically tested. Empirical support was ultimately forthcoming in Williamson's 1980 article, which sought to demonstrate that the triumph of Adam Smith's pin factory over putting-out was due to its superior transaction cost properties.[23] The inability to develop a methodology that allowed the costs of firm and market to be compared, together with questionable interpretation of historical data, weakened Williamson's case.[24] More seriously, the article demonstrated that the transactions cost hypothesis was still no more than a tautology, for it lacked the elements that might indicate, in advance, whether putting-out or the factory was likely to be preferred.

In 1981 Williamson added a new condition to provide his model with predictive capabilities.[25] The condition, asset specificity, refers to the extent to which a particular investment might be used for alternative purposes, the lack of alternative uses raising the scope for opportunistic behaviour amongst contracting parties. Asset specificity initially referred to physical assets, but by 1988 had been refined to include investments in sites, additional plant, brands and human capital.[26] Contracts providing employment for such investments can be written *ex ante* although *ex post* opportunistic activities on the part of either buyer or seller, especially a refusal to transact unless contract conditions are renegotiated, might discourage *ex ante* investment. Consequently, 'where asset specificity is great, buyer and seller will make special efforts to design an exchange relation that has continuity properties'.[27] The ability to identify degrees of asset specificity enabled Williamson to specify the occasions when markets, firms, or some intermediate governance structure, such as a joint venture (trilateral governance), are likely to be preferred. As a rule non-specific investment will result in market governance while specific or idiosyncratic investment and recurrent transacting will result in firm (or unified) governance. Where transactions are infrequent and the level of asset specificity mixed or high, such as purchasing customised equipment or constructing a plant, trilateral governance might be optimal with disputes between contracting parties going to arbitration (see Figure 1).

FIGURE 1
EFFICIENT GOVERNANCE

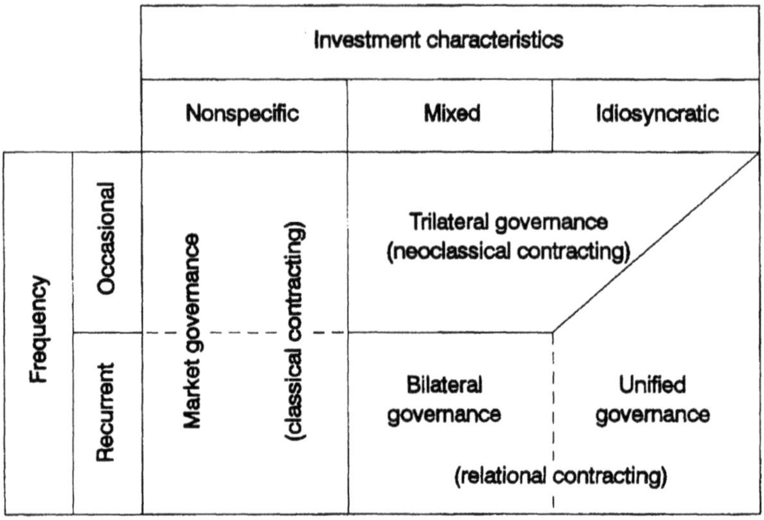

Investment characteristics		
Nonspecific	Mixed	Idiosyncratic

Source: O.E. Williamson, *The Economic Institutions of Capitalism* (New York, 1985), p.79.

From the preceding argument it follows that, in the absence of asset specificity, bounded rationality and opportunism no longer constitute a problem, as re-contracting can take place relatively costlessly. The implications are far-reaching, for it would now appear that in most types of exchange there is little reason for the firm to supplant the market. Asset specificity, therefore, adds significantly to the predictive power of the new theory of the firm although at the cost of general applicability, for the revised theory now focuses not on why firms exist, but why large, capital intensive firms might be vertically integrated.

IV

The old institutional economics was concerned with the processes of change, the way in which working rules adapt to changes in values and environment to give expression to new institutional forms. Despite adopting the label 'institutional', it is clear that the Williamsonian brand of the new institutional economics draws its inspiration not so much from the evolutionary approach of Commons as from the choice theoretic method of Ronald Coase. The choice of organisational mode, be it firm, market or some intermediate transactional form, is essentially an exercise in comparative statics in which all feasible modes – and their cost implications –

can be identified in advance. Thus presented, the new institutional theory is merely an extension of the neoclassical theory of the firm in which the choice of mode may be incorporated as part of a mathematical optimisation exercise.[28]

For optimisation to occur it is essential that transaction costs are identified and measured in advance, a task not easily accomplished. Williamson accepts that transaction costs have 'a well deserved bad name as ... there is a suspicion that almost anything can be rationalised, by involving suitably specified transaction costs'.[29] Typically transaction costs have been identified as the *ex ante* costs of search and negotiation and *ex post* costs of enforcement. The costs of using markets might be relatively easily identified even if *ex post* costs can only be roughly estimated. It is far more difficult to estimate the costs of firm governance since the costs of utilising internal markets have to be identified, broken down and evaluated in such a way as to make valid comparisons possible.

A major problem faced when identifying the costs of utilising internal markets (which are referred to in the literature as governance, management and co-ordination costs) is that resources, both staff and plant, are frequently employed in co-ordinating flows between technologically separable stages (a quasi-market function) and production. Functional specialisation and divisionalisation in multi-product firms may help to identify costs, but questions concerning matters such as the apportionment of overheads, and whether adaptive activities such as reconfiguring product flows and characteristics to meet customers' needs is a management or production activity, still remain. In any event, internalisation does not do away with transaction costs in their entirety, as a firm still has to purchase inputs and sell outputs. Embodied in purchased inputs are the supplying firms' own management and production costs, and a comparative assessment of these also should also be factored into the decision making process.[30] Thus it is conceivable that even with zero transaction costs it might still be cheaper for a firm to integrate backwards if its internal management and production costs are lower than those of suppliers. Similarly, a firm might integrate downstream if it possesses a comparative advantage in management and production costs when compared to downstream establishments.

Transaction, management and production costs are therefore incurred to a greater or lesser extent whether a product is made, bought or sold, the choice of organisational mode being in the nature of a trade-off between various costs. Sometimes the choice between buying or making will be straightforward, but on many occasions there will be difficulties in measuring and identifying relevant costs. Indeed, it has been argued that, given the existence of complexity and uncertainty in conjunction with bounded rationality, decision makers are necessarily incapable of making a fully informed choice between alternative organisational modes.[31] They will, in any case, wish to incorporate in their decisions expectations concerning future costs, demand shifts, capacity utilisation, the prospect of new technology, factor availability and other elements excluded by the comparative static model. The decision whether to internalise or not is therefore not a nice matter of calculation, but a function of judgement and experience, which will include both an estimate of comparative costs and levels of risk involved. What is required for action under these circumstances are a set of decision rules that have evolved over time and an entrepreneur prepared to bear risk under conditions of uncertainty and able to devise innovatory solutions when opportunities arise. The enterpreneur, however, is necessarily excluded from Williamson's well specified comparative static world.

The movement from the richer, if somewhat descriptive, model of Williamson's earlier years to the more parsimonious and predictive model characterised by asset specificity does away with some of the problems of identifying and computing costs. As we have seen, without high levels of asset specificity there is no rationale for vertical integration as in the event of opportunism asset owners can easily transfer their resources to alternative uses. Alternatively, 'where asset specificity is great, buyer and seller will make special efforts to design an exchange relation that has continuity properties'.[32]

Yet how does one measure the degree of asset specificity, especially where human asssets are involved, what level do potential losses have to reach before integration is warranted, and what is the relationship between the degree of asset specificity and losses sustained? While any competent accountant might be able to compare the salvage value of a physical asset with its book replacement value, it is rather less straightforward to estimate the difference between a hypothetical income stream that might eventuate were such assets to be placed in their next best use and the income stream forgone. The losses involved in redeploying less tangible types of asset would necessarily be more difficult to assess. In any event, redeployment would represent a last resort and losses sustained would constitute an absolute limit. If the management believed that hold-up was likely to take place irregularly and/or be of short duration, losses might be both trivial and sustainable, obviating any need for integration. Certainly there would appear to be many instances of industries where the degree of asset specificity would appear to be great, yet vertical integration is not the norm.[33] Indeed, Williamson recognises that the predisposition to buy rather than make is greater in Japan than the United States, but has little to say about the system of business networks, cultural values and organisational practices that significantly reduce problems of intentional or unintential hold-up.[34]

V

Despite the limitations of the asset-specificity approach, the traditional view that the boundaries of the firm are essentially determined by technological non-separabilities has nevertheless been successfully overturned by Williamson, who has rightly insisted that one has to take account of transaction and governance costs as well as the physical characteristics of the productive process. Yet it is clear from our previous discussion that, even in the short run, the choice between markets and hierachies is far from clear-cut, while the mix of organisational forms to be adopted in the long run is outside the purview of the Williamson model. Necessarily, his comparative static approach is incapable of providing insights as to how the interplay of strategy and structure might affect the future boundaries of the firm or what might be done to preserve and enhance competitive advantage. This inability to deal with process reflects the neoclassical roots of Williamson and the agency theorists whose ideas provide the underpinning for much of the new institutional economics.

Like the old institutional economics, however, the new institutional economics is a far from unified school of thought. Thus, at the same time that Williamson was developing his transactions cost approach, G.B. Richardson began to explore the boundaries of the firm by relating it to the capabilities or resources available to each enterprise. From the start, Richardson rejected the market and hierarchies dichotomy as a gross oversimplification, arguing that it was far more realistic to view industrial activity as 'a dense network of co-operation by which firms are interrelated'.[35] Co-operation, sustained by shareholding, long-term contracts, or merely goodwill, is the norm as far as Richardson is concerned, with notions of obligation and assurance permeating and supporting large networks of suppliers and customers in all but the most impersonal of markets. This is not to say that opportunism and hold-up are absent, but given the social context of economic activity, a combination of existing mores and values and the need to maintain reputation reduces the need for any permanent association to mitigate the effects of opportunism, and so on.

Far more important for Richardson in determining the boundaries of the firm are capabilities or resources available to a particular enterprise. Production requires access to an appropriate bundle of capabilities if a firm is to operate competitively, with the scope for expansion circumscribed by the nature of those capabilities and the extent to which they are utilised. In this respect, Richardson's view of the firm is similar to that of Penrose, his notion of capabilities including the knowledge, skill and experience embedded in an enterprise, as well as a command over the necessary material and technical resources. Firms specialise in those 'activities for which their capabilities offer some comparative advantage', buying from or selling to firms with a different bundle of capabilities. Where the activities of firms are closely complementary but the capabilities required dissimilar, then it makes sense to match complementary activities not by integration but by co-operation. Co-operation may come close to direction where one firm is the dominant partner, but in terms of ownership the two enterprises remain distinct. Only where large numbers of buyers or sellers provide a stability of demand or supply might transactors eschew co-operation and rely solely upon the operation of impersonal markets.

VI

Richardson believed a special type of co-operation or co-ordination to be necessary where the transfer of technology is concerned, not only so that a licensee is able to receive assurances about the future use of a proprietary technology by the licensor and others, but also to ensure that the technology is used effectively. Thus technological transfer might require not only possession of a licence and blueprints, but also technical assistance in the form of essentially idiosyncratic knowledge fundamental to successful plant operation.

The difficulties inherent in the transfer of idiosyncratic proprietary knowledge was first raised by Hymer, who suggested that the emergence of American-owned plants in Britain was due to problems associated with effectively transferring technical knowledge via the licensing process.[36] However, it was left to scholars such as Buckley and Casson to develop a more general theory of internalisation, the central thrust of which is that idiosyncratic knowledge, that is, the skills, knowledge and experience that often constitute the core capabilities of a firm, is sometimes impossible to codify, transfer and control via normal contractual means.[37] Because of the high transaction costs involved in the transfer of idiosyncratic knowledge, firms wishing to expand in different countries might be obliged to establish subsidiaries abroad if they wish to maximise the firm-specific rents generated by their particular bundle of capabilities.

Transaction cost considerations, therefore, are an important factor in determining whether it is appropriate for a firm to export, license abroad, or establish foreign subsidiaries. Generally speaking, the problems involved in transferring idiosyncratic knowledge are likely to be greatest in high-technology industries, although it is clear from the number of low-technology and service multinationals that non-tangible capabilities embedded in the routines and culture of such enterprises constitute important rent-yielding assets. Such routines and culture offer a guarantee of quality which, when associated with brands or reputation, generate custom and enhance rents. Moreover, given the ease with which low-technology processes might be emulated abroad and the fact that such processes and their products might not be adequately protected by patent or trademark law, low-technology corporations have every incentive to supply overseas markets via foreign subsidiaries in order to exploit first-mover advantage.

Of course, difficulties in codifying and licensing know-how do not constitute the only rationale for multinationals, especially for vertically integrated operations where activities at different stages of production may require complementary rather than similar capabilities. Teece has suggested that vertical integration might be appropriate if the development of a transaction-specific asset in country X occurs at a time when the asset owner believes there is limited scope for judicial redress or re-contracting in the event of hold-up by a sole supplier in country Y.[38] Nevertheless, it has to be recognised that vertical integration may take place to accommodate other institutional features, such as international differences of taxation, tariffs and barriers to the repatriation of foreign-held funds, as well as subsidies and joint venture incentives offered by host nations. These institutional features, together with relative production, transaction and transportation costs, are all variables that have to be considered when deciding whether internalisation is an appropriate strategy.

VI

The internalisation approach of trade theorists, which combines the concepts of capabilities, transaction costs and other institutional features in a decidedly eclectic manner, provides a far more comprehensive framework for analysing the processes of horizontal and vertical integration than Williamson's. Yet while possible future states of the world may be considered when strategic decisions are being taken, internalisation theory has little to say about the way in which the capabilities of firms may change over time, or how such changes might affect the decision set facing management.

The activities open to a firm are necessarily constrained by the bundle of capabilities or resources available to a firm at any particular time. As we have seen, capabilities are made up of the tangible assets of the firm, which might easily be replicated elsewhere, together with the intangible and idiosyncratic assets in the form of the skills and knowledge embedded in the routines, culture and collective memories of employees. Capabilities are synergistically related in that, together, they are able to produce an output at lower cost than if deployed separately, and it is this that provides the firm with its competitive advantage. However, as Richardson has observed, no firm is an island, and to operate effectively an enterprise requires regular and convenient access to complementary assets supplied by other firms, each of which has its own particular bundle of capabilities. In certain instances the activities or output of a firm may be highly circumscribed by its resource base, although in practice many firms can produce a wide range of outputs, as wartime redeployment amply demonstrates.[39] What the firm actually produces is open to the discretion of owners and management, although rationally output decisions should be based on matching capabilities with demand conditions.

Capabilities, however, are rarely stable for any length of time, because as time passes people in organisations learn how to perform their tasks more efficiently, with processes of trial and error in discharging certain functions being replaced by known routines which are subsequently refined and adapted according to need. The result of organisational learning, as Penrose stressed many years ago, is that fewer managerial and other resources are required to produce a given output, thereby enhancing the overall capabilities of the firm.[40] Whether the firm reinvests surplus resources in existing lines of business, diversifies, or attempts to sell the services of surplus assets to other firms depends on the state of demand in existing markets, whether its capabilities can be profitably deployed in new industries, and its ability to conclude contracts effectively and economically for highly idiosyncratic and intangible resources. Where routines are separable then the transfer of intangible resources via an individual or teams may be feasible, but there will be occasions when 'external transfer beyond an organization's boundaries may be difficult if not impossible, since taken out of context an individual's knowledge of a routine may be quite useless'.[41] Faced with high transaction costs, the owners of a firm must consider whether they should use surplus resources by extending the boundaries of their firm or shed those resources with or without recompense to themselves.

The boundaries of the firm may also change as additional core organisational capabilities are developed as part of a strategy to maintain competitive advantage. This is essential for survival because, as Robertson and Langlois point out, while individual firms may become increasingly capable over time, other firms will also become more capable as techniques pioneered and translated into routines by innovators are learnt and adapted by imitators. Idiosyncratic core activities that, in the short run, are incontestable, thus become completely contestable in the long run, with capabilities diffusing 'completely into the market, leading to full specialisation and vertical disintegration'.[42] In other words, transaction costs, which initially helped to determine the boundaries of the firm, progressively diminish over time as routinised capabilities which hitherto conferred firm-specific advantages become ever more widely distributed through industry.

The successful firm must therefore develop new strategies and generate new capabilities if it is to retain its competitive advantage and continue to extract rents. The choice of new strategies is almost inevitably conditioned by the original resource base of the firm together with the structures and routines that have developed to accommodate past strategies. There is consequently an element of path dependency in the way in which strategy usually evolves. Successful firms, however, are also learning firms, with routines established to ensure that not only does an enterprise move quickly along its learning curve so as to exploit its current capabilities but that it also remains alert to the possibility of exploiting new opportunities where they arise. In high-technology enterprises the bulk of such activity might take place in R & D departments, but to make the most of such opportunities both the structure and culture of the firm have to be supportive of learning and change.

The creation of new firm-specific advantages may require not only the development of capabilities within an enterprise, however, but also the parallel development of the capabilities of suppliers and distributors if the full fruits of technical or organisational innovation are to be appropriated. Such systemic change might be achieved relatively costlessly through close co-operation within a well functioning network, but the possibility exists that a firm either inside or outside the existing network will be unwilling to or incapable of developing the requisite ancilliary assets. Part of the resistance may be the result of the innovator being unable to communicate the new requirements to a potential supplier or distributor in an easily comprehensible way, due to the novel or highly idiosyncratic nature of the changes called for. Given this transactional bottleneck, the innovator may be obliged to enlarge the boundaries of the enterprise and undertake the requisite activity itself. In addition, the innovator may take further positions in complementary and co-specialised assets to ensure that newly created rents are not appropriated either by imitators or through hold-up. The costs of acquiring these ancilliary capabilities, together with the 'costs of persuading, negotiating, coordinating and teaching outside suppliers', have been termed 'dynamic transaction costs' by Langlois and Robertson.[43] A capability that allows an enterprise to economise on dynamic transaction costs has obvious implications for competitive advantage, the growth of the firm and the return on funds.

VII

The new institutional theory of the firm has been hailed as a welcome attempt to prize open the black box of the neoclassical firm, showing conclusively that organisation matters. Certainly the concepts of transaction costs, bounded rationality, opportunism and asset specificity, moved to the centre-stage of industrial organisation by Oliver Williamson, have proved helpful to business historians in their attempts to analyse and understand the economic behaviour of firms. The main deficiency of his work, however, is that the comparative static neoclassical approach is both too ahistorical and too limited to explain all but a small proportion of business behaviour. The choice theoretic framework which focuses on transaction cost economising under given circumstances ignores the processes of growth or the way in which new choice sets evolve. As Lazonick has observed, Williamson conspicuously fails to comprehend the dynamic interaction between organisation and technology so crucial to an understanding of strategic development and structural change.[44]

By way of contrast, the linking of transaction cost economics to the notion of firm-specific advantages by trade theorists, and the view of the more Austrian wing of the new institutional economists that firm-specific advantages are derived from a bundle of capabilities, has provided valuable insights into what firms are and how they might grow.[45] An appreciation of transaction costs is central to an understanding of these processes, being a key factor in determining the boundaries of the firm and the way in which firm-specific advantages might be preserved or dissipated over time.

NOTES

1. F.E. Hyde, 'Economic Theory and Business History', *Business History*, Vol.V (1962), p.22.
2. B.E. Supple, 'The Uses of Business History', *Business History*, Vol.IV (1961), pp.87–8.
3. O.E. Williamson, *The Economic Institutions of Capitalism* (New York, 1985), pp.3–4.
4. W.M. Dugger, 'Methodological Differences between Institutional and Neo-classical Economics', *Journal of Economic Issues*, Vol.XIII (1979), p.901.
5. J.R. Commons, *Institutional Economics* (Madison, 1934), p.6.
6. D. Seckler, *Thorstein Veblen and the Institutionalists* (London, 1975), pp.128–9.
7. R.H. Coase, 'The Nature of the Firm', *Economica*, Vol.4 (1937), p.390.
8. R.L. Hall and C.J. Hitch, 'Price Theory and Business Behaviour', in T. Wilson and P.W.S. Andrews (eds.), *Oxford Studies in the Price Mechanism* (Oxford, 1951), p.113.
9. M. Friedman, 'The Methodology of Positive Economics', in *Essays in Positive Economics* (Chicago, 1953), p.22.
10. J. March and H. Simon, *Organisations* (Oxford, 1958), pp.137–45.
11. J.E. Stiglitz, 'Symposium on Organisations in Economics', *Journal of Economic Perspectives*, Vol.5 (1991), p.16.
12. W.J. Baumol, *Business Behaviour, Value and Growth* (New York, 1959), pp.45–53.
13. R. Marris, *The Economic Theory of Managerial Capitalism* (London, 1964), pp.29–45.
14. H. Manne, 'Mergers and the Market for Corporate Control', *Journal of Political Economy,*

Vol.73 (1965), pp.112–13.
15. A.A. Alchian and H. Demsetz, 'Production, Information Costs and Economic Organisation', *American Economic Review*, Vol.62 (1972), pp.777–95.
16. R.N. Langlois and P. Robertson, *Firms, Markets and Economic Change* (London, 1995), p.10.
17. R.H. Coase, 'The Problem of Social Cost', *Journal of Law and Economics*, Vol.3 (1960), pp.1–44.
18. Alchian and Demsetz, 'Production, Information Costs', pp.784–5.
19. O.E. Williamson, *Markets and Hierarchies: Analysis and Antitrust Implications* (New York, 1975); *The Economic Institutions of Capitalism* (New York, 1985).
20. Williamson, *Economic Institutions*, p.30.
21. A.D. Chandler, *Strategy and Structure* (Cambridge, MA, 1962).
22. Williamson, *Markets and Hierarchies*, p.162.
23. O.E. Williamson, 'The Organization of Work', *Journal of Economic Behaviour and Organization*, Vol.1 (1980), pp.5–38.
24. S.R.H. Jones, 'The Organization of Work: A Historical Dimension', *Journal of Economic Behaviour and Organization*, Vol.3 (1982), pp.117–38.
25. O.E. Williamson, 'The Modern Corporation: Origins, Evolution, Attributes', *Journal of Economic Literature*, Vol.19 (1981), pp.1537–68.
26. O.E. Williamson, 'Technology and Transaction Cost Economics', *Journal of Economic Behaviour and Organization*, Vol.10 (1988), pp.358–9.
27. Williamson, 'Modern Corporation', p.1546.
28. Ibid., p.1551.
29. O.E. Williamson, 'Transaction Cost Economics: The Governance of Contractual Relations', *Journal of Law and Economics*, Vol.22 (1979), p.233.
30. H. Demsetz, *Ownership and Control of the Firm: The Organization of Economic Activity*, Vol.1 (Oxford, 1988), pp.150–51.
31. G.M. Hodgson, 'Transaction Costs and the Evolution of the Firm', in C. Pitelis (ed.), *Transaction Costs, Markets and Hierarchies* (1993), p.86.
32. Williamson, 'Modern Corporation', p.1546.
33. Demsetz found there was little correlation between vertical integration and his measure of asset specificity although he accepted that his empirical work might 'be carrying a heavy load of garbage'. See *Ownership and Control*, p.174.
34. On this subject see M. Casson, *Enterprise and Competitiveness* (Oxford, 1990), especially ch.4.
35. G.B. Richardson, 'The Organization of Industry', *Economic Journal*, Vol.82 (1972), pp.883–96.
36. S. Hymer, 'The Efficiency Contradictions of Multinational Corporations', *American Economic Review*, Vol.60 (1970), pp.441–8.
37. M. Casson, *The Firm and the Market* (Oxford, 1987), pp.5–7.
38. D.J. Teece, 'Technological and Organisational Factors in the Theory of the Multinational Enterprise', in M. Casson (ed.), *The Growth of International Business* (London, 1983), p.56.
39. D.J. Teece, 'Towards an Economic Theory of the Multiproduct Firm', *Journal of Economic Behaviour and Organization*, Vol.3 (1982), reprinted in L. Putterman and R.S. Krosner (eds.), *The Economic Nature of the Firm* (Cambridge 1996), p.178.
40. E.T. Penrose, *The Theory of the Growth of the Firm* (Oxford, 1959).
41. Teece, 'Multiproduct Firm', p.178.
42. Langlois and Robertson, *Firms*, p.32.
43. Ibid., p.35.
44. W. Lazonick, *Business Organization and the Myth of the Market Economy* (Cambridge, 1993), pp.196–7.
45. The neoclassical/Austrian characterisation of the two main branches of the new institutional economics is suggested by M. Rutherford, *Institutions in Economics* (Cambridge, 1996), p.3.

Complexity, Community Structure and Competitive Advantage within the Yorkshire Woollen Industry, c.1700–1850

S.A. CAUNCE

Leeds University Business School

Although the British industrial revolution has been the subject of immense debate, there is much that we do not understand about the actual experience of key regions like the textile district of the West Riding of Yorkshire.[1] While economic development is now usually seen as an evolutionary process rather than a series of largely autonomous revolutions, the remarkable performance of areas like Yorkshire in the eighteenth and early nineteenth centuries still leaves a sense of rapid and far-reaching upheaval that has no generally accepted explanation. In 1700 the modern county of West Yorkshire was a relatively backward producer of poor quality woollen cloth, and its main English rivals, East Anglia and the West of England, seemed to be increasing their dominance of the industry. By 1850 Yorkshire had won undoubted world leadership in most wool textile sectors, and had done so with no apparent factor cost advantage.[2] It is a classic example of what Mokyr has called a 'technologically creative' society,[3] but during most of the eighteenth century its competitive advantage was based on combining the best of its own traditions with copying and borrowing new products and processes from any available source rather than on new technology.

In the long run the woollen sector was the most consistently successful sector of the industry, yet technology was introduced particularly slowly here, the domestic system remained important, and products stayed close to traditional norms. Worsteds achieved enormous growth in the mid-nineteenth century, but thereafter struggled to cope with international competition and protective tariffs, while woollens quietly and unspectacularly continued to increase production and win markets around the world.[4] Technology and factories were thus part of a more broadly based dynamism, not a prime cause of success in their own right, something which is typical of modern industrial districts.[5] Porter has pointed out that competitive advantage today derives largely from highly localised clusters of dynamic industries, and that their success cannot be understood by analysing national accounts.[6] A close examination of the structure of the Yorkshire woollen industry between 1700 and 1850 is therefore worthwhile

FIGURE 1

THE ANCIENT PARISH OF BIRSTALL AND THE WEST YORKSHIRE TEXTILE DISTRICT

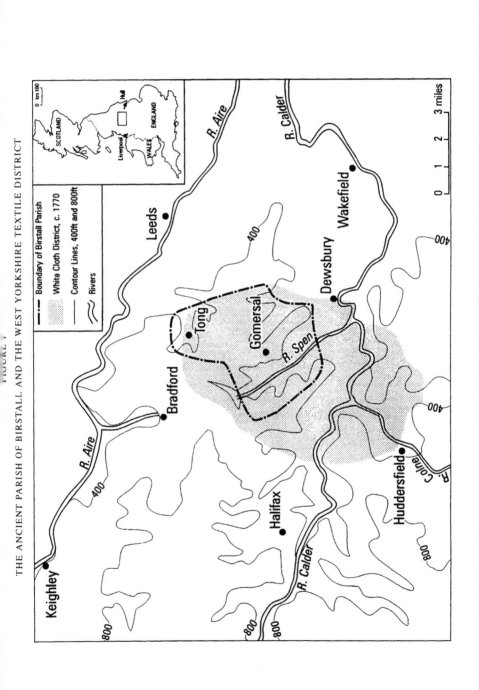

both for its own sake and for the light it may cast on the nature of dynamic clusters in general. Certainly it was not a model which depended on some special local factors, for the striking resemblance it bears to the Philadelphia textile industry of the nineteenth century is no coincidence. The main study of this neglected industry takes as a prime example of American entrepreneurship the Schofield family, who were emigrants from the Yorkshire woollen manufacturing parish of Saddleworth.[7] Heaton has recorded many strong and direct links that existed between America and the Yorkshire woollen area in general (and Saddleworth in particular) around 1800, and such men as the Schofields seem to have felt equally at home on either side of the Atlantic.[8]

Recent work on the Italian industrial districts stresses the central role played by communities and the deep-rooted cultural matrices they supported among entrepreneurs.[9] The central issue of this study is the similar role played by social and economic institutions in Yorkshire. They supported, shaped, helped to spread, and yet also limited organisational and technological change. Above all else they facilitated the processing of market information to create highly effective production strategies. The key to this in the eighteenth century was the widespread use of cloth halls controlled by voluntary trusts, which linked an aggressive and effective merchant group to a flexible production network of several thousand independent clothiers working mostly from their own homes. This created an open and apparently atomistic business structure that accepted change while still retaining a strong sense of tradition as a vital part of business. Randall has argued that communities in the West of England industry had a commitment to a traditional moral economy which gave them a strength that Yorkshire textile communities lacked when faced by modernisers eager for innovation.[10] It seems more productive, however, to ask if the West Yorkshire system was flexible rather than weak. The Yorkshire woollen district should be seen as a self-organising system which preserved a modified vision of the older moral economy while rejecting the hierarchical and centrally controlled production and marketing systems which characterised its main English competitors. By doing so it not only stole their trade, but built up its own to unprecedented levels.

Certainly, with neither a sense of outside control nor general immiseration, any version of the conventional proto-industrial route to mass production is untenable, even though rich and powerful merchants, putting-out, and poor families working entirely for wages certainly existed.[11] Indeed, virtually anything that has been identified with failure in other areas can be found somewhere in the West Yorkshire textile area, which draws attention to its complexity and diversity. This has been commented on before, but it is one of those aspects of the area's history which has not been explored in depth, and recent work on complex, non-linear systems in other fields suggests that in itself this may help explain the creativity and dynamism that set the area apart from its southern rivals. Ascertaining whether it is a significant factor is best achieved by building a comparative approach into a local and detailed study and this has been achieved by focusing on the eight townships that made up the ancient parish of Birstall. Tong, Drighlington, Hunsworth, Gomersal, Wyke, Cleckheaton, Livers-edge, and Heckmondwike together covered almost 14,000 acres in the centre of the ring of West Yorkshire textile towns, and they developed in radically different ways despite starting with a shared natural endowment and social structure. Tracing this divergence can help us understand much that is distinctive about West Yorkshire's success.

II

Birstall shows few of the natural features typically associated with textile production in the Pennines, for it is on the coal measures rather than the millstone grit. There is no rugged moorland, and sheep never played a significant part in local agriculture. Underground aquifers provided an ample water supply, but there were few streams and no fast-flowing torrents. Its soil and climate made it unsuitable for extensive arable cultivation, but wheat could be grown in places and the remnants of common field systems still existed in 1800. The typical farm was the compact holding preferred by all West Yorkshire clothiers and it was used to support manufacturing activity rather than for self-sufficiency. Just under the surface was coal, fireclay and iron, all limited in quantity but ample for early-modern needs and of excellent quality. All had been exploited from an early date, so that by the eighteenth century Birstall had a very diversified economy which was led by textiles but not defined by them.[12]

Birstall lay across the main trans-Pennine trade route of the eighteenth century, which linked York and Leeds to Manchester and Liverpool, and it had easy access to several lesser routes. If undue stress is placed on the upland character of the Lancashire and Yorkshire textile regions their location around such natural lines of communication can be overlooked. As there are few crags and the hills are relatively low and rounded, the watersheds between the major valleys (especially those between the rivers Aire and Calder, and the Calder and Colne) form long, continuous ridges that make very effective strategic communication routes between the estuary of the Humber and those of the Mersey and the Dee.[13] At least from Roman times these routes were of great significance, and they still carry all the most important road and rail links across the Pennines today.[14] Thus, far from being isolated, manufacturers in Birstall were linked to York (a primary centre of the medieval cloth industry), to excellent ports, and to rich agricultural areas. Involvement in commercial manufacturing was a natural development which in turn stimulated substantial population growth. A progressive commercialisation of the agricultural areas further and further to the east meant that the industrial workers could always be fed, and since there was no real urbanisation before the nineteenth century, small rural settlements and farmsteads simply multiplied across the extensive commons, wastes and moors.

Though there were many poor people, perhaps a ninth of the population of the clothing districts near Birstall enjoyed modest prosperity and security, a high proportion for the time. This group constituted a well-developed and self-aware 'middling sort' in the early-modern period.[15] There were very few resident gentry or aristocracy because low agricultural productivity had prevented the growth of any such group in medieval times. As manufacturing began to push rent rolls up it was natural for absentee landlords to look tolerantly on the social change that this implied.[16] The normal mechanisms of social control from above thus became highly attenuated in many places, though they were never completely absent.[17] John Smail has shown that deference remained a force in the eighteenth century, but it had to be earned rather than inherited, and over large stretches of the clothing districts the alliance between the local church and state that was so powerful elsewhere in rural areas never materialised.[18]

Parishes had never been divided since medieval times and many were enormous, with Halifax the largest in England. Nonconformity had been strong among enterprising families since the seventeenth century, and since one of the two chapels of ease in Birstall was paid for by its congregation, nonconformist-leaning ministers were often installed at Cleckheaton. Quakers, Congregationalists and Presbyterians all had congregations of long standing and the Moravians located their English headquarters nearby at Fulneck after inheriting many congregations from the Inghamites, a local sect. John Nelson of Birstall village was one of the main Methodist apostles in Yorkshire and he regularly preached to thousands of people.[19] A wave of Anglican church building and parish division in the early nineteenth century came too late to retrieve the conventional social dominance.

Such large parishes also meant that local government was largely conducted at a township level, where clothiers and local merchants naturally tended to take control, though even then it might not be very effective. Gomersal township, for instance, contained three quite separate field systems, each focused on its own settlement, as well as numerous hamlets and isolated farmsteads. Manorial structures were very varied and generally continued to function throughout the early-modern period, but they were often little more than revenue-raising devices. Many manors were far too large to control their inhabitants' lives, and some disintegrated at an early date. The historic boundaries of the manor of Gomersal, in particular, have never been effectively established. Hudson has drawn attention to the large numbers of freeholders to be found in manors like this, but even copyholders were often left largely to their own devices as non-resident landlords in search of higher rent rolls generally were content to break up large holdings into the smaller units favoured by clothiers.[20] Nineteenth-century enclosure mostly brought into private ownership the large commons and moors, for most arable land had long since passed into severalty by mutual agreement. By the eighteenth century it was not the technicalities of tenure but the attitude of landowners which mattered for economic development.

Thus, Tong township was preserved as an agricultural settlement through the explicit policy of its lords, the Tempests, and it remains unindustrialised to this day even though it is only four miles from the centre of Bradford and five from Leeds. It was a compact manor whose lords had always involved themselves in its affairs. Birstall's other chapel of ease stood in the shadow of Tong Hall, and the Tempests effectively turned it into an independent parish church. Manorial, religious and township boundaries thus more or less coincided in Tong, and the result was stagnation. A local nineteenth-century writer enthused that 'the village remains much the same as it has done for generations past, a few neat cottages, with their little plots of garden ground, the old hall and park, the country inn, the village smithy, [which] all add a charm to this beautiful old time village'. Some income came from selling the coal that lay underneath (though it had to be mined from over the boundary), but essentially Tong had become a status symbol for the Plumbe-Tempests, a Liverpool mercantile family who had inherited it.[21] They could afford to forgo the profits of industrialisation in a search for gentry status, and so while the small part of the township left free to develop had a rateable value of £10,481 in 1900, the main estate was only rated at £6,823.[22]

Equally, there are cases where lords actively promoted development. The Ramsdens played a large part in turning Huddersfield from a village into one of the region's leading industrial and commercial towns.[23] Birstall had no real equivalent, but the last effective lords of the manor of Gomersal, the Batts, encouraged enterprise through their commercial attitudes to their rights before the Civil War destroyed their fortunes.[24] Overall, the result was a landscape of extraordinary economic and social diversity, with manufacturing townships intermingling with others which had developed very little, or which relied on mining and quarrying, like Drighlington. Latecomers to industrialisation, like Cleckheaton township, tended to specialise in engineering and other spin-off trades rather than the direct manufacture of wool textiles. Development was thus as patchy within West

Yorkshire as it was nationally, and success also proved as difficult to defend as it did in East Anglia and the West Country, for while Gomersal and Liversedge had set the pace in pre-industrial times, it was Heckmondwike and Cleckheaton which led the way into the factory era. Gomersal today resembles Tong as much as a centre of manufacturing. The explanation for development therefore cannot be the existence of some particular environment, and the sheer variety of environments and their proximity seems more significant. As conditions changed, new responses could be developed in new and more appropriate settings. Moreover, if Tong village was kept out of the process of change, its inhabitants could work outside the village, or move to a more active township. Certainly, as Gomersal began to lose its drive as a manufacturing centre, it was noticeable that merchants looked elsewhere for opportunities, but they did not have to go very far. The Crowthers, for instance, moved about four miles to purchase a fulling mill in Churwell, which they then proceeded to develop. They were one of the most active families in building links with the United States.[25]

Such flexibility might be seen as a recipe for incoherence, but the merchants made the system work very effectively, providing the manufacturers scattered through parishes like Birstall with information about distant markets of which they knew nothing. William Birkhead of Cleckheaton, for instance, was a successful clothier of the late eighteenth century, who built up a thriving manufacturing business on the basis of a modest inheritance and a partnership with his brother. He had no contact with Russia, nor could he have taken advantage of contact if it had been possible, but he helped clothe its people. A relative described him and his family thus:

> far the greater part were in a low situation ... [and] notwithstanding their accidental good fortune in accumulating a little wealth ... [they] were of mean education and low attainments in knowledge ... They bore, indeed, a pretty fair character for honesty in their dealings in common with many of their neighbours, and paid a strict attention to the formalities of their religion; but had no just ground, I conceive, for ... self-importance.[26]

Hard work, honesty and membership of a religious network are here identified as the fundamentals of business success in the area, and the virtue of this arrangement was that it allowed men of ordinary talents and commitment to contribute independently and almost opportunistically to the common effort. No one had to try to pick winners, for they picked themselves. This does not mean that success was easy or automatic, but there were always enough clothiers to make it likely that some of them would be successful.

Wilson's excellent study of Leeds has perhaps obscured the closeness of clothiers and merchants in places like Birstall. In the mid-sixteenth century Thomas Taylor of Great Gomersal had called himself a chapman, or dealer, but his descendants preferred the title of yeoman or clothier. They manufactured, finished and dyed cloth in and around their house, as well as dealing in it at Leeds.[27] In the eighteenth and early nineteenth centuries they consistently styled themselves 'merchants', and they enjoyed uninterrupted if modest success down to 1826.[28] Joshua Taylor (1760–1840) was described as 'very friendly to his workpeople, very good to all who were beneath him, and submitted quietly to be beneath him, but haughty as Beelzebub to whomsoever the world deemed (for he deemed no man) his superior. Revolt was in his blood: he could not bear control; his father, his grandfather before him, could not bear it'.[29] With a few other families they led the economic activity of their community.[30] They built a public fulling and scribbling mill at Hunsworth and installed a very early steam pumping engine to ensure the water supply for its wheel. A coal mine provided fuel and turnpikes were promoted to improve access. They supported plans to build a local cloth hall (which forced improvements in the service offered in Leeds even though it did not succeed),[31] and they opened a bank to facilitate their complex web of activity as old informal credit systems became inadequate.[32] Each of these initiatives made money for them, but also benefited the whole community.

They had no master plan, and nothing they did was startling or unique. What is most remarkable about the Taylors, in fact, is that they personified so precisely the general developments taking place in the area. They were not outsiders exploiting desperate labourers but a part of the community, even though they expected deference from most of its members. Joshua Taylor's bank relied on his reputation, and, after it crashed amid the general crisis of 1825–26, he and his son eventually cleared all the debts as a matter of honour. His house, though not grand, was smart and kept internally up to date. He had been to Italy and France and relatives resided more or less constantly in Brussels. He spoke several languages, including Standard English, but his preference for Yorkshire dialect disconcerted members of the parliamentary committee investigating the woollen industry in 1806.[33] For men like this, innately hostile to the inherited privileges of the Anglican church and the gentry and aristocracy, business was not just one career among many, but literally the only real choice they had. With no Members of Parliament directly representing any part of the Yorkshire textile area before 1832, they felt completely alienated from the national elites and their governments. The great Leeds merchants did exercise influence, and came to be crucial in the selection of at least some Yorkshire county MPs after 1800, but the constituency was uncontested for much of the eighteenth century, and such merchants were distant and unsympathetic figures to Birstall's people.[34]

Joshua's father John had established his own chapel to preach in, and Joshua was a member of the Methodist New Connexion, like many local merchants of his generation.[35] Nonconformist networks were far more than expressions of religious preference in this setting, and they did not create local replacements for an inclusive Anglican establishment. Individuals worshipped where they felt most at home, and congregations were in no doubt that, since they paid the minister, they expected theological pronouncements in tune with their world view. Without adopting Weberian notions, it seems clear that enterprise here was seen to be blessed by God, and young men received advice on business, and sometimes financial help, through their connections.[36] At a deeper level, a common religious belief reinforced a general attitude that success did not spring from cut-throat competition within the community, however fierce individual rivalry might become.[37]

The voluminous and detailed evidence collected between 1802 and 1806 by parliamentary investigations shows a society with rules which were widely acknowledged even if they were less rigid than those applied in the south of England. Joshua Taylor testified that he was opposed to the apprenticeship system as defined by law, but also that he never laid workers off without trying to find them alternative work.[38] Reputation was so essential for success that disowning responsibility for actions taken would be disastrous, and family, community and trade networks were all too important to be disrupted lightly. The network of cloth halls allowed merchants to meet clothiers on an equal footing despite their differing social standings, and this helped prevent individual merchants trying to push clothiers into personal dependence on them.[39] In normal trading conditions, it was impossible to force down the price of labour, and the widespread access to land meant that independent clothiers were not frightened to withdraw completely from trade for a time if cloth prices were low. They might well exploit themselves and their households at such times to keep their businesses going, but this was an expedient, not a permanent state of affairs.

By responding as individuals to the different prices for different types and grades of cloth, as a group they produced the goods that unknown consumers wanted, and at prices they could afford. Yorkshire woollen cloth thus won markets not primarily through exploitation of the manufacturers, but by encouraging them to use their own labour to best effect. New technology had to find a place within this matrix of forces rather than arriving as an endogenous force in its own right, and what is most remarkable about Lancashire and Yorkshire is that it did so. The manufacturing population of West Yorkshire was quite clear that it wanted a thriving industry above most other things, for it knew that a peasant lifestyle was impossible in that environment.

III

The introduction of machines into production undoubtedly improved northern competitiveness, and the Yorkshire clothiers' own efforts deserve more credit than they usually get. Innovations were copied and adapted from cotton where appropriate, but woollen men had begun mechanising independently by adding carding machines to their fulling mills, and whenever the technological requirements of the two regions diverged they continued to solve their own problems. The issue at stake is one of adoption, for the early inventions were not at all revolutionary at the conceptual level, and, without belittling the enormous achievements of converting the classic inventions into reliable working machines, what is most striking about early nineteenth-century textile machinery is its simplicity and crudity. Made largely of wood, often roughly fashioned, and using as little ironwork as possible, it is quite unlike the precision work of clockmakers, or even the clumsier efforts of the early pioneers of steam.[40] The gig mill had been known for centuries, but it had been prohibited by law and by common consent as a threat to the trade. Coleman has argued that by 1750 the conservatism of early-modern wool textile manufacturers had left them far behind the general standard of improvement visible in industry from c.1500, so that merely by catching up they appeared to work wonders.[41] There was no need to re-invent the loom before adding a power drive, for it had already reached a point where, once the warp had been put in, the weaver simply acted as a power source and a co-ordinator of eminently mechanisable and repetitive actions. The spinning jenny was a natural development of the great wheel, and there is no aspect of its construction that would have been technically impossible two centuries before. The wheel itself, and the later addition of a flyer to allow continuous spinning, had both been far more intellectually difficult achievements.[42] Perhaps even more demanding was the development of the complex geometry of the hammer faces of the fulling mill, making them automatically roll and move cloth during milling, and the French development of punched-card programming technology for the jacquard loom.

The Chinese had had much of the necessary knowledge for centuries, but they never implemented it, and, though the Italians began to mechanise silk spinning in the Middle Ages, it did not lead to a continuous and self-sustaining process of innovation.[43] In neither case was there any practical incentive to save on human skills, while taking away work from those who relied on it threatened the structures of their societies. Similarly, European textile manufacturers had traditionally seen the market for their goods as more or less static in total. Trade might be poached from another area, but new demand was very hard to create, and so improving the productivity of individual workers would simply initiate fierce competition as those pushed out tried to re-enter the trade. Economic activity would only be stimulated where there was an alternative use for their labour, or where low prices stimulated an increase in sales so large as to lead to their re-employment at a similar or better levels of earnings. Neither seemed likely before 1750, and such assumptions underlay the whole ethos of guilds, apprenticeship and resistance to machinery.[44]

In the eighteenth century, however, demand did rise perceptibly over the long term. Yorkshire and Lancashire were well positioned to take advantage of growth in European and American populations, and increasing market orientation as their products were positioned towards but not at the bottom end of the market, and Wilson has estimated that Yorkshire wool textiles experienced an eight-fold increase in the value of production in this period.[45] A progressive diversification of product, most obviously into cottons and worsteds, took the pressure off areas like Birstall, which persisted with older lines and the old atomistic business structure simply continued to evolve.[46] Eighteenth-century clothiers adopted jennies for use in their own home and gained access to more expensive technology through public mills like that of the Taylors' at Hunsworth, or even by building their own as joint-stock enterprises. In the nineteenth century, small firms operating with low capitalisations could rent room and power within speculatively built private mills.[47] When their own success threatened to drive up the price of the raw material, grinding machines were developed to recycle the cast-off rags of Europe for re-manufacture as shoddy and mungo.[48] The clothier networks had certainly changed by 1850, but they were the direct descendants of those operating a century earlier, and they still enabled a wide range of people to take part in business in their own right.

The bulk of the population may not have got any long-term rise in living standards out of the new methods, but the sense of widespread opportunity short-circuited fears of the consequences of change.[49] Conservatism had only been put to one side, however, and in 1812 Luddism showed that insensitive innovation would still be rejected. Shearing frames replaced a whole group of skilled men, since croppers worked either for themselves or for small masters or merchants, whereas devices like the jenny had encouraged the re-allocation of labour within a household production system. Most frames in Yorkshire were taken out of use in a matter of a few weeks and a mill owner who persisted was assassinated. The manufacturing centres were occupied by large numbers of troops because a general armed revolt seemed imminent and Birstall was one of the main storm centres, with Rawfolds Mill between Cleckheaton and Liversedge unsuccessfully besieged by armed men for most of a night. The soldiers failed to catch a single West Yorkshire Luddite, apart from those left behind after the mill siege because they were too badly wounded to move, and they refused to incriminate anyone else.[50] This was not a community divided against itself in a fight by progressive elements taking on ignorant workers over the right to install machinery, but a community already committed to change that was more or less united against a minority perceived as rule breakers. War had virtually closed most major markets and threatening livelihoods at such a time was generally perceived as wrong. Coupled to a general sense that the new methods were opening the gate to factories and an end to the old openness, the result was explosive. Though better times ended overt hostilities, this tradition of resistance was not in any sense eradicated. It re-emerged as Chartism and trade unionism, for instance, and what is reputed to be the last cavalry charge in England took place in Cleckheaton during the Plug Plot riots in 1842.[51] Increasingly, the manufacturing population was being dividing into employers and employed, but it was a slow process and in 1850 the entrepreneurial class remained large, diverse, relatively open and locally oriented. In addition, it is one more sign of the complexity of local affairs that the main allies of the radicals were Tories like Richard Oastler.[52]

IV

Institutions in West Yorkshire therefore had a clear and positive role as buffers and channels, making personal activity more effective rather than hindering it. A weakness of institutional explanations of change in general, however, has always been the obscurity of the actual mechanism that drives a process of change. However, Gunnar Myrdal wrote that

> the dynamics of [a] social system are determined by the fact that among all the endogenous conditions there is *circular causation* [author's italics], implying that, if there is a change in one condition, others will change in response. These secondary changes in their turn will cause new changes all around, even reaching back to the initial condition ... There is no one basic factor, but everything is linked to everything else.[53]

Compared to the simple clarity of Pareto equilibrium this may seem hazy, but support for such an approach comes from the discovery of the inherent ability of all types of apparently chaotic systems to generate both order and change spontaneously. Thus, 'interactions in a dynamical system give you an emergent global order ... Such systems may indeed appear complex on the surface, but they can be generated by a relatively simple set of subprocesses'.[54] Adam Smith's idea of the invisible hand in the market-place is a classic statement of such spontaneous self-organisation. This approach effectively excludes equilibria, except as a sort of vanishing point that the system would tend towards if it could operate for long enough under stable conditions, but in the West Yorkshire textile area since 1750 equilibrium states have never been an accurate description of reality.

Evolutionary change occurs best in a complex landscape like West Yorkshire, where a multitude of outcomes are possible. The production patterns of the woollen industry were not planned, but they did have coherence. The interactions of clothiers and merchants continually modified existing patterns according to the market information possessed by the merchants, and the willingness of the manufacturers to respond.[55] While everyone did not use the piece halls, as long as bargaining was generally free and open the effect was much the same. It was the ability to use the halls if necessary rather than universal usage that defined the system, and less formal networking could do the same job though it laid the system open to subversion. Individual acts have little significance in themselves in such a system because it is the reiteration of complex interactions that drives the system. Tracking the activities of the Taylor family allows us to observe the system in action, but multiplying such studies would soon cease to add anything to our understanding.

Since a highly effective long-term strategy emerged from this apparently stochastic process, it seems that clothiers were doing more than simply reacting to immediate opportunities. Collectively they were processing the available information and producing intelligent strategic responses. This is strongly reminiscent of the neural networks which have been developed as part of the search for artificial intelligence. These machines direct their own development towards a preset goal without external programming or other guidance, and they are accepted by many as capable of intelligent action in a strictly limited sense. They are modelled like biological systems rather than computers, and they work by approximation from imprecise data rather than by manipulating precise data sets according to predetermined routines. They start with a high degree of almost random connectivity between all their processing components, and through trial and error the system finds and keeps open those pathways between components which cause the system to move towards its goal. Inevitably the process is slow at first and almost entirely random, but each success provides a lesson that the system retains, a process analogous to social learning through doing.[56] A cellular processing architecture supports flexibility and adaptability, with sub-networks which can specialise in specific tasks. The actual processing occurs in parallel, unlike most computers, and where there is a clash within the system, it is resolved through consensus. In West Yorkshire communities formed specialised sub-networks that similarly worked in parallel with each other, and since none had automatic precedence the shape of manufacturing activity as a whole simply emerged from this dispersed activity. The merchants acted both as connecting nodes within the system and as links to the outside world, while commercial success was a goal everyone shared. As the merchants dealt with clothiers they maintained those connections that paid off and neglected those that did not. As long as there were enough actors, the actual quality of judgement exercised by individuals was not of prime importance, for every chance success helped to shape the system. Apparently intelligent behaviour and decision-making capabilities would then be possible at the system level, without supposing that West Yorkshire society was an integrated organism, nor that it engaged in creative thinking across a broad spectrum. It suggests only that human interaction within the right framework can in itself produce problem-solving behaviour that is apparently intelligent. This is quite separate from individuals' volitional actions, though these have a role as input into the system.

The formation of such a network would in no sense guarantee continuing success. It encouraged evolutionary adaptation of the system, often at a rapid rate, but changes to the outside environment might be beyond its capacity to cope. In addition, since the human component was conscious of its own role, a merchant who wished to push the system in any particular direction could attempt to do so. One individual was unlikely to achieve much, but concerted action could be very effective. On the positive side, Sam Hill and like-minded men brought the worsted trade to Halifax through a refusal to accept initial market verdicts, which were highly unfavourable.[57] On the negative side, merchants might well come to define success differently from the manufacturers, for success can be defined in many ways. Eighteenth-century merchants like the Taylors knew that they were outsiders and that their only hope of winning markets was to satisfy customers. There was every incentive to represent the real world as accurately as possible to the clothiers, but this might change.

Porter has pointed out that the defence of wealth won through competitive advantage soon erodes the advantage.[58] If merchants as a whole became satisfied with the system as it stood, then information suggesting changes were needed would become unwelcome and would be distorted or suppressed. Manufacturers would have no way of detecting the flaws in the picture they received, but consumers' needs would be neglected, creating an opening for a third party to step into. East Anglia and the West Country had both achieved their success through responding to the markets, but then ceased to do so.[59] They sold through old-established, often captive channels, and a turn to landownership meant that they no longer stood or fell in the short term by their performance in trade. Commercial information was not gathered directly, but on their behalf by London merchants for whom cloth was only one line among many, while government contracts could be defended through political channels rather than through superior performance. Wilson says that in the eighteenth century conservatism and high-quality production was 'a vortex from which there was no escape'.[60] However, since the older textile areas only suffered a gentle and at first merely relative decline, they had both the time and the resources to copy West Yorkshire's methods if they had wanted to, and their high quality image would then have been an asset. When they sought to bring about change, however, it was not on a basis of sharing the rewards, and so, instead of mobilising the manufacturing communities to assist in the process, they simply stirred up resentment and resistance.[61]

The older Leeds merchants actually reacted in much the same way after 1800, but they had no power to control the West Yorkshire system.[62] Localities might suffer, however: Gomersal ceased to develop significantly after a wave of bankruptcies had affected most of the local merchants, including the Taylors.[63] Reform had removed most of their sense of exclusion, and the returns from the early factories set up in the township were so poor that there was no temptation to become involved simply as an investor. With the exception of the Burnley family they opted to use the wealth they retained in a relatively risk-free manner.[64] The only one of the Taylors after Joshua who showed the old rebellious energy and drive was his daughter Mary. As a middle-class Victorian woman she still felt excluded from business and she eventually emigrated to New Zealand to be free to use her considerable abilities.[65] Otherwise the family moved steadily towards Anglicanism and Conservatism and by the late nineteenth century it had inherited and was using a fictitious title of lord of the manor of Great Gomersal, while mixing socially with the gentry Joshua (and Mary) despised.[66] The last two male descendants to be born in the area became doctors in the south of England, and their economic links with their ancestral home were reduced to messages to their solicitors to sell the coal rights under the land they still owned, a reminder of the situation in Tong.[67] The dynamism of the Birstall manufacturing system persisted, but this was because of the actions of a new group of factory-based entrepreneurs in Cleckheaton and Heckmondwike.

It is hoped that this essay is only the start of an in-depth investigation of Birstall, and it is not intended as any sort of universal explanation for economic dynamism. However, it helps to account for the variation in fortunes between Yorkshire and the older English textile regions and it also makes the existence of similar variation within Yorkshire a precondition for its success rather than an awkward fact to be explained away. It is consistent both with Porter's theory of competitive advantage, and with work on industrial districts elsewhere. It places the market in a central position in the explanation, but as part of an institutional framework and not as a self-sufficient device. Markets here were subject to regulation and to interaction with other institutions, and in the woollen area they remained part of the moral economy of traditional society even while promoting rapid change. They appear to have been all the more effective because of this, for strong and flexible communities encouraged ordinary people to make direct contributions to the group effort. It was not that any particular place or social group always supported business activity, but rather that one that would was always available. Complexity prevented the ossification of production systems and community values in West Yorkshire during this period, and modernisation was thereby allowed to occur in an evolutionary manner. Internecine conflict was always part of the system, but the fact that it so rarely came to the surface is a testimony to the ability of the system both to mediate conflict through negotiation, and to use it to drive the system.[68]

NOTES

1. The standard history of pre-industrial Yorkshire textiles remains H. Heaton, *The Yorkshire Woollen and Worsted Industries* (Oxford, 1920). More recent detailed studies are M.J. Dickenson, 'The West Riding Worsted and Woollen Industries, 1679–1770: An Analysis of Probate Inventories and Insurance Policies' (unpublished Ph.D. thesis, University of Nottingham, 1974); D. Gregory, *Regional Transformation and Industrial Revolution: A Geography of the Yorkshire Woollen Industry* (London, 1982); P. Hudson, *Genesis of Industrial Capital: A Study of the West Riding Wool Textile Industry, c.1725–1850* (London, 1986).
2. The best comparative studies of the rise of the Yorkshire industry are R.G. Wilson, 'The Supremacy of the Yorkshire Cloth Industry in the Eighteenth Century', in N.B. Harte and K.G. Ponting (eds.), *Textile History and Economic History: Essays in Honour of Miss Julia de Lacy Mann* (Manchester, 1973), pp.225–46, and A. Randall, *Before the Luddites: Custom, Community and Machinery in the Woollen Industry, 1776–1809* (Cambridge, 1991).
3. J. Mokyr, 'The New Economic History and the Industrial Revolution', in J. Mokyr (ed.), *The British Industrial Revolution: An Economic Perspective* (Oxford, 1993), pp.15–16.
4. D.T. Jenkins and J.C. Malin, 'European Competition in Woollen Cloth, 1870–1914: The Role of Shoddy', *Business History*, Vol.32 (1990), pp.66–86.
5. See, for instance, F. Pyke, G. Becattini and W. Sengenburger (eds.), *Industrial Districts and Inter-Firm Co-operation in Italy* (Geneva, 1990), especially chapters 1–4.
6. M.E. Porter, *The Competitive Advantage of Nations* (1990), pp.117–24.
7. P. Scranton, *Proprietary Capitalism: The Textile Manufacture at Philadelphia, 1800–1855* (London, 1983), pp.3–4, 57–71 and 419.
8. H. Heaton, 'Yorkshire Cloth Traders in the United States 1770–1840', *Thoresby Society Miscellanea*, Vol.37 (1944), pp.225–86.
9. G. Becattini, 'The Marshallian Industrial District as a Socio-economic Notion', in Pyke *et al.* (eds.), *Industrial Districts*. See also P. Thompson, A. Wailey and T. Lummis, *Living the*

42   INSTITUTIONS AND THE EVOLUTION OF MODERN BUSINESS

Fishing (London, 1983), part IV, especially chapter 15 which shows that inshore fishing community structures have played a direct role in generating or vitiating change in UK fishing methods and technology.

10. Randall, *Before the Luddites*, chapter 3, especially pp.86–93.
11. R.G. Wilson, *Gentlemen Merchants: The Merchant Community in Leeds* (London, 1971); A. Randall, *Before the Luddites*, pp.7 and 22–3; and P. Hudson, *Genesis*, chapter 3, both argue against the case made in F. Mendels, 'Proto-Industrialization: The First Phase of the Industrialization Process', *Journal of Economic History*, Vol.32 (1972), pp.241–61.
12. R. Thornes, *West Yorkshire: A Noble Scene of Industry* (Wakefield, 1981) is a brief survey of economic activity in pre-industrial times.
13. W.B. Crump, 'Ancient Highways of Halifax', *Transactions of the Halifax Antiquarian Society* (series of nine articles, 1924–28), brings out in detail the relationship of roads to the landscape.
14. I.D. Margery, *Roman Roads in Britain* (1973), chapters 9 and 10.
15. Royal Commission on Historical Monuments of England, *Rural Houses of West Yorkshire* (London, 1986), pp.127–31.
16. Hudson, *Genesis*, p.260.
17. F. Musgrove, *The North of England* (1990), chapters 8–10 give the background to this situation.
18. J. Smail, *The Origins of Middle Class Culture: Halifax, Yorkshire, 1660–1780* (London, 1985), pp.29–40. See chapter 2 for the culture of the middling sort.
19. F. Peel, *Nonconformity in the Spen Valley* (Heckmondwike, 1891).
20. P. Hudson, 'Landholding and the Organisation of Textile Manufacturing in Yorkshire Rural Townships c.1660–1810', in M. Berg (ed.), *Markets and Manufacture in Early Industrial Europe* (London, 1991).
21. J. Parker, *Illustrated Rambles from Hipperholme to Tong* (Bradford, 1900), pp.308–23. The quotation is from p.308. See also H.C. Cradock, *The History of the Ancient Parish of Birstall* (London, 1933).
22. W. Cudworth, *Round About Bradford* (Bradford, 1876), p.517.
23. R. Brook, *The Story of Huddersfield* (1986), chapters 3–11.
24. G. and N. Cookson, *Gomersal: A Window on the Past* (Huddersfield, 1992), chapter 2 for the manor of Gomersal.
25. Heaton, 'Yorkshire Traders', section 4.
26. T. Wright, *The Autobiography of Thomas Wright of Birkenshaw* (London, 1864), pp.249–50.
27. This house is now Red House Museum, Oxford Road, Gomersal. During the Taylors' occupation of three and a half centuries the site and buildings evolved steadily, and reminders of all the stages are still visible.
28. Documents relating to the Taylor family are held by the Yorkshire Archaeological Society, MD292 and MD311, and the West Yorkshire Archive Service, KC52 and KX100–149. C. Bronte, *Shirley* (London, 1842), is a strongly factual novel in which the Taylors appear as the Yorkes, and Red House as Briarmains. A detailed history of the Taylors is in preparation.
29. Bronte, *Shirley*, pp.35–7. Hiram Yorke is generally acknowledged to be Joshua Taylor.
30. Cookson, *Gomersal*, especially pp.77–9, 121–6.
31. Ibid., pp.114–15.
32. W.C.E. Hartley, *Banking in Yorkshire* (Clapham, N. Yorkshire, 1975), pp.43–5.
33. *The Minutes of Evidence Taken Before the Select Committee Appointed to Consider the State of the Woollen Manufacture* (PP. 1806, Vol.3), pp.378–83.
34. See Porter, *Competitive Advantage*, pp.48–9 on the tendency for innovation to come from outsiders. See also Wilson, *Gentlemen Merchants*, chapter 8, especially pp.166–80.
35. J.S. Werner, *The Primitive Methodist Connexion: Its Background and Early History* (London, 1984), pp.22–5.
36. M. Taylor, *Miss Miles, or a Tale of Yorkshire Life Sixty Years Ago* (London, 1890, new edn. 1990), pp.87–9.
37. Wilson, *Gentlemen Merchants*, pp.188–9.
38. *The Minutes of Evidence, Woollen Manufacture*, pp.378–83.
39. Dickenson, 'West Riding', chapter 6; Randall, *Before the Luddites*, pp.35–8; and Hudson,

Genesis, pp.156–80. D. Defoe, *A Tour Through the Whole Island of Great Britain* (London, 1738, Penguin edn. 1971), pp.500–504, describes the tight regulations observed at Leeds cloth market to prevent merchants achieving dominance.

40. G. Cookson, 'Millwrights, Clockmakers and the Origins of Textile Machine-Making in Yorkshire', *Textile History*, Vol.27 (1996), pp.43–57.
41. D.C. Coleman, 'Textile Growth', in N.B. Harte and K.G. Ponting (eds.), *Textile History and Economic History* (London, 1973), p.5. See also T.K. Derry and T.I. Williams, *A Short History of Technology* (London, 1960), pp.108 and 569.
42. Derry and Williams, *Technology*, p.97.
43. D. Landes, 'What Room for Accident in History?: Explaining Big Changes by Small Events', *Economic History Review, 2nd Series*, Vol.47 (1994), pp.637–56. See also W.G. Samuels, *Institutional Economics* (London, 1988), pp.194–9.
44. Coleman, 'Textile Growth', p.4.
45. Wilson, 'Supremacy', pp.227–34 and 241–2, and G.D. Ramsay, *The English Woollen Industry 1500–1750* (London, 1982), p.37.
46. Smail, *Origins*, pp.56–70.
47. Hudson, *Genesis*, pp.76–81; J.F. Goodchild, 'The Ossett Mill Company', *Textile History*, Vol.1 (1968), pp.46–62; J.F. Goodchild, 'Pildacre Mill: An Early West Riding Factory', *Textile History*, Vol.3 (1970), pp.337–49.
48. Jenkins and Malin, 'European Competition'.
49. Randall, *Before the Luddites*, p.93.
50. E.P. Thompson, *The Making of the English Working Class* (London, 1963), chapter 14. See also F. Peel, *The Risings of the Luddites, Chartists and Plug Drawers* (Heckmondwike, 1895, 3rd edn. with introduction by E.P. Thompson, 1968).
51. Peel, *Risings*, chapter 40, esp. pp.342–3.
52. Wilson, *Gentlemen Merchants*, pp.172–4 and 180–82.
53. G. Myrdal, *Political and Institutional Economics* (London, 1978), p.11.
54. Clear introductions to these subjects can be found in R. Lewin, *Complexity; Life at the Edge of Chaos* (London, 1993); and J. Gleick, *Chaos: Making a New Science* (London, 1987).
55. Coleman, 'Textile Growth', p.9.
56. Introductory books are J. Jubak, *The Image of the Brain* (Boston, MA, 1992); and D. Crevier, *Artificial Intelligence* (New York, 1993), especially chapters 2 and 11.
57. Smail, *Origins*, pp.60–61.
58. Porter, *Competitive Advantage*, pp.10–17 and 565–73.
59. Ramsay, *English Woollen Industry*, pp.45 and 72.
60. Wilson, 'Supremacy', pp.237–41. The quotation is from p.237.
61. Randall, *Before the Luddites*, see especially pp.35 and 234–7.
62. Wilson, *Gentlemen Merchants*, p.235; and Heaton, 'Yorkshire Traders'.
63. Cookson, *Window*, chapter 7.
64. Ibid., pp.116–17 and 123–6.
65. J. Stevens, *Mary Taylor, Friend of Charlotte Bronte: Letters From New Zealand and Elsewhere* (London, 1972); J.H. Murray, 'Introduction to the Oxford edition of Miss Miles', in Taylor, *Miss Miles* (1990 edn.).
66. Cookson, *Gomersal*, pp.62–3 for the supposed manor of Great Gomersal.
67. West Yorkshire Archive Service, KC52, box 2; box 3, bundle 21; box 5.
68. That traditional structures could support rather than impede modernisation is a concept developed in S. Caunce, *Amongst Farm Horses: The Horselads of East Yorkshire* (Stroud, 1991), chapters 16–18. It is taken further in S. Caunce, 'Farm Servants and the Development of English Capitalism', *Agricultural History Review*, Vol.45 (1997), pp.49–60.

Invisible, Visible and 'Direct' Hands: An Institutional Interpretation of Organisational Structure and Change in British General Insurance

OLIVER M. WESTALL

Lancaster University

The history of British general insurance provides a fascinating laboratory in which to explore ideas drawn from 'new institutional' and evolutionary economics. The proposition of this essay is that such investigations yield a high return in terms of historical understanding. This should not be surprising. Both approaches emphasise information as a determining element in industrial organisation and insurance has always depended particularly on the transmission and processing of information. Ideas drawn from both theoretical areas will be used to try to understand the way in which various institutional aspects of insurance organisation and practice are not incidental, but can be incorporated into a broader economic analysis of the business. This will include both strategic considerations and an attempt to open up the 'black box' which contains the internal operations of insurers. In fact, using ideas drawn from evolutionary theory, it will be suggested that these two are linked. The strategic changes which have shaped the evolution of the business over the last 200 years can only be understood in the context of the detail of routine internal operation. Yet, through all these changes, there is a striking continuity in the attempts to adjust organisational structures to meet the same fundamental problems of transmitting and processing information efficiently. Indeed, this remains true to the present day, as the investigation of 'direct' marketing which concludes the paper shows.

The 'new institutional economics' has been instructively packaged as the 'contractual paradigm'.[1] This draws attention to the way in which agency theory and transaction cost economics both emphasise the importance of the information available on either side of an exchange. Asymmetric information, bounded rationality and opportunism require contracting parties to pay close attention to the form of the contract, how it can be monitored, and whether the resulting transaction should take place in a market or hierarchical context.

These are precisely the problems that lie at the heart of insurance. For the insurer the contract must fulfil two functions. It must protect him from the implications of information only known to the insured because of superior technical or other knowledge about the risk. And it must protect against the possibility of opportunistic behaviour by the insured perhaps by deliberately entering into the contract, knowing that he will benefit from it – the so-called 'moral hazard' problem. There are also problems from the insured's point of view. There is the question of the financial security of a contract where indemnity follows the payment of the premium. Occasional purchasers may be unable to obtain as good information on appropriate premium rates or contractual terms as is known to the insurer. Much of the institutional structure of insurance is designed to resolve these difficulties.

English law has helped by providing a framework that reduced the uncertainty insurers face. In the late eighteenth century, Lord Mansfield refined the principle of 'utmost good faith' as the basis for insurance contracts.[2] This required a potential insured to disclose all circumstances that might influence a prudent insurer in fixing a premium or deciding whether to accept a risk.[3] Evidence of bad faith or material misrepresentation makes an insurance contract unenforceable at law. As Park, the eighteenth-century insurance authority, put it, 'the purest equity and good faith are essentially requisite ... to render the contract effectual'.[4] Developed initially in marine insurance, 'utmost good faith' became the basis for all insurance contracts. The protection it offered insurers was important in encouraging the expansion of general insurance in the nineteenth century.[5] Here its existence will be assumed, but it is worth noting that the principle goes to the heart of the problems of the 'contractual paradigm' and its development and impact on insurance may therefore repay further study.[6]

While the form of the contract is the essence of agency theory, the emphasis in the transaction costs literature has been on the institutional framework within which economic activity is co-ordinated, and particularly the comparative costs of market transactions and organisational (or hierarchical) control.[7] Transaction costs may be high if market relations inhibit the exchange of information and facilitate opportunism. This will encourage the direct control of activity within an organisation to avoid these problems. Yet organisations involve the costs of monitoring and information transmission that are explored in agency theory and the economics of organisational forms.[8] The balance between transaction and agency costs suggests the boundary between market and organisational activity. This analytical approach is now familiar to economic historians through the symbiotic relationship between the theoretical work of Williamson and the historical work of Chandler.[9]

It has a particular relevance for the study of general insurance. Over 300 years the business has been characterised by a variety of arrangements through which market- and organisation-based means have been used to suggest some subtlety or indeterminacy in competitive advantage between the two institutional forms. This can most easily be focused on the competition between the companies and Lloyd's. From the early eighteenth century the companies have sought to transact business over distances that have posed problems for the transmission of information and control. As a result, from the mid-nineteenth century they moved towards organisational forms to facilitate and control underwriting and marketing. By the early twentieth century vertical control was established (in principle) from the underwriter at head office through to the control of marketing in branch offices which attracted a range of business, including most types of fire and accident insurance, and sometimes marine and life business as well.[10] In contrast, Lloyd's has always offered a specific market-place for all transactions. Within this, the vertical connection is broken by a contract between the underwriter 'within' the institution and the broker who brings the business to Lloyd's through different market channels. In principle, they take no interest in one another's affairs beyond the integrity of the contract. Brokers often involve several underwriters in a risk, increasing the apparent fragmentation of Lloyd's institutional arrangements, however firmly this may in fact be co-ordinated by its market.[11]

The continued existence of both approaches can partly be explained by their comparative advantage in dealing with different types of insurance risk, differentiated by scale, complexity, information availability and marketing channel. For example, marine risks, with a wide variety of complicated risk factors generating a large premium, might be better handled individually, while standard small-scale private household risks with modest premiums might be processed in bulk. This forms no more than a special example of the opportunities for mass production in large markets with homogenous demand, and individual production when markets are highly segmented and where switching imposes costs.

But there has often been direct competition between Lloyd's and the companies across a wide range of similar risks. This is partly because the actual organisation of business has not been as different as the conventional stereotype suggests. Companies have never fully controlled marketing activity through branches. Their marine underwriting has been conducted similarly to Lloyd's. Some Lloyd's brokers have constructed marketing organisations rather like those of the companies. Across the companies and the Lloyd's market there has existed a spectrum of forms of operation. Nonetheless, at their core, the companies and Lloyd's represent stereotypes of organisational and market solutions to the problem of co-ordinating essentially similar insurance activity, and this must intrigue the analytical historian.

Ideas derived from the 'contractual paradigm' can be used to explain these contrasting forms of organisation, including the spectrum sketched above. Yet it provides essentially an equilibrium analysis, at its best providing *ex post* explanations. This does not offer much insight into the actual process of institutional change. This inhibits its capacity to explain the historical record. Beyond that, the course of change may shape the institutional environment in ways that determine the equilibrium which the 'contractual paradigm' then rationalises.

This provides a point of entry for some ideas drawn from evolutionary economics.[12] By emphasising the relationship between a company's past, present and future, these prove especially congenial to the economic historian. They assume that firms possess particular capabilities. These are determined by resources and experience accumulated in the past, which are embodied as technical and organisational expertise (essentially information) and made manifest in particular routines. Firms which reproduce these capabilities reliably over time through an organisational structure that sustains the routines effectively will survive more successfully than those that do not. Yet this inertia will make radical change difficult. When it occurs, it will usually build on or intensify existing routines.[13] These routines and their gradual evolution determine the firm's competitive advantage. If they are suited to the economic environment, the firm will flourish. If not, their inflexibility makes it likely that the firm's prospects will be diminished. In this way, evolutionary economics links the internal operations of a firm with its performance in the external competitive environment.

This essay suggests that these ideas can add to an understanding of strategic change in insurance beyond that possible by relying on conventional industrial economics or the 'contractual paradigm'. Over time routines or capabilities have become embedded in the institutional framework of market- and organisation-based operation, determining their competitive advantage. Locked into these approaches, their development has usually, though not always, taken the form of a consolidation or intensification of these routines. Institutional change has not taken the form of dramatic moves between market and organisational forms, but in a changing balance between the two forms, both of which have survived over the long term. Their relative success has depended on finding ways of making the limited adjustments possible to satisfy market opportunities.

To appreciate the function of the various approaches, the objective of insurance organisation can be sketched.[14] Its efficiency has depended on three relatively intangible resources: information, skill, and effective mechanisms by which the other two can be transmitted and applied. At one end of the process is the underwriter, whose skill is that of accepting risks of an appropriate quality, individual and aggregate scale and number, in relation to the organisation's financial resources and objectives. At the other is the agent, broker, inspector or surveyor, winning risks in the market or able to appraise them directly. The greater the transparency between these two the better, for the more the underwriter can be familiarised with the real circumstances of the risk, the better – in principle – he can do his job. Conversely, the better the inspector understands the underwriter's objectives, the greater his opportunity to focus on desirable risks and critical characteristics, and the less time wasted on risks likely to be rejected.

Some qualifications are required. Few underwriters restrict themselves to 'perfect' risks. They would end up with a tiny account that could not cover overhead costs. In any case, high premium rates can make apparently poor risks profitable. Risks may also be accepted because their acceptance brings other profitable business. Bounds of rationality considerations restrict the transparency of the process. Information must be limited to that which can be processed successfully. Finally, some of the most valuable information is intangible, relating not to physical characteristics, but to the character of ownership and the risk of moral hazard, increasing the difficulty of transmission. For these reasons, transparency is never reached in practice.[15]

The following sections will examine the historical evolution of the institutional forms designed to carry out these tasks. They will distinguish between the role of the market and the organisation in this process and show how the ideas drawn from the 'contractual paradigm' and evolutionary economics can provide an explanation of the process. Then the final section of the essay will look at a more recent dramatic change – the introduction of direct marketing – to understand the sources of this important strategic development in the light of these ideas.

II
MARKET-BASED INTERMEDIATION

The eighteenth-century expansion of fire insurance was achieved through agents supplying risks to companies on the basis of contractual agreements. Insurers bridged the gap created by a lack of information and confidence in distant companies by appointing men of affairs in provincial business communities to handle risks. The companies attached to themselves the goodwill that their agents possessed in local markets.[16] This approach embodied dangers for underwriting. Agents often exhibited a greater loyalty to their neighbours than to a London-based company. This 'distance' meant that agents could not be relied upon to pursue the companies' interests absolutely when accepting risks or settling claims. Furthermore, there were risks implicit in agents holding premiums before settling with companies. Thus agency control (in practical and theoretical terms) created transaction costs for companies. They found it difficult to devise structures that could contain them. Contracts between companies and agents remained unsophisticated and failed to address the problem adequately. Agents received commission on premium income with a flat rate sum for new risks. Profit commission was not a practical alternative, perhaps because it would delay payments.[17] Alongside commission, contract fulfilment was dependent on adherence to an agency rule-book. Insurers might require an agent's bond, related to the scale of business, accompanied by personal guarantors, but this could only be used in cases of obvious malpractice, rather than as a protection against a general run of underwriting skewed against the insurer.[18] When a claim was made, the check was no more than a certificate signed by a clergyman or other representative of local respectability.[19] Companies had no inexpensive way of monitoring this problem. They had no directly controlled local or peripatetic representation before the 1820s. Even then, this was often directed to serious problems apparent to the companies, rather than systematic monitoring. Most inadequate contractual performance by agents must have remained undetectable. The only real direct control was to cancel the appointment of obviously untrustworthy agents. Indirectly, the companies protected themselves in two ways. They often structured the contract in their favour by requiring an under-valuation of the sums insured, to force policyholders to meet a proportion of any claim.[20] And the implicitly collusive nature of eighteenth-century insurance meant that premium rates could be maintained at a level that covered the shared problem of inadequate control. The success of the new provincial offices in the late eighteenth century probably owed something to the opportunities their directors had to select active, honest local agents in their hinterland who were well known to them and could be supervised closely.[21]

These transaction costs associated with the agency system were never entirely resolved, and there was never any radical change in the approach to marketing, but companies did attempt to intensify control. The early inspectors, together with district representatives (agents with exclusive rights in particular regions), who emerged in the early nineteenth century, were gradually transformed into a branch office system through the late nineteenth century.[22] Alongside the potential for more directed marketing, this offered an opportunity for local monitoring of agents and, in principle, a better flow of information for underwriters in ways examined later. However, it never freed companies from transaction costs.

One of the main tasks of the branch office became that of dealing with agents and the emerging brokers (specialists dealing on a larger scale and with more energy), who now revealed their true colours in representing clients' interests. They might argue vigorously for the acceptance of a difficult risk or more generous claim settlements. This was no problem if openly discussed, but this was rare. More frequently, companies had less information than agents and the insured in making critical decisions. The position was complicated by the agent's ambiguous position. He owed 'utmost good faith' to both sides, separate specific duties to the company and the insured, was paid commission by the company, but depended on satisfying policyholders to win business. It is not surprising that companies' interests could be compromised in ways difficult to monitor. Practical considerations sometimes complicated the issue. For example, many prolific motor insurance agents in the inter-war years were garage proprietors, well placed to obtain business when selling cars. But it made them likely beneficiaries of claims for repairs.[23] Companies had to control underwriting without prejudicing revenue in a world of mixed interests and incentives.

The growth of large brokers created another 'market' problem. Their emergence was partly founded on their expertise in advising policyholders on the premium rates and policy terms available and in negotiating claims. They thus balanced the company's otherwise superior knowledge of market rates and terms. Their large accounts with individual insurers also created a countervailing market power. This they used to carve out additional profitability for themselves, and to influence underwriting decisions. Brokers would favour companies willing to take a broad run of good and bad risks or make generous claim settlements. In this context companies could not assume that agents or brokers would place company interests first or even act objectively. The agency/broker market was itself fiercely competitive and its players protected themselves by placing the insured's concerns immediately after their own profitability. Thus, at the end of the line of control from underwriter to branch office inspector, there always remained a market interface that continued to create intractable transaction costs that blurred the clarity of underwriting control.

From its seventeenth-century origins, Lloyd's maintained the traditional practice of operating on the basis of the contract between the underwriter and the broker. The broker acted unambiguously for the insured, while the underwriter accepted risks for a syndicate of Lloyd's members. They met directly within the Lloyd's underwriting room, where brokers were free to approach any of the many underwriters to seek a quote. This created a highly competitive market which attracted its business by offering low premium rates. The approach was retained when, from the 1870s, Lloyd's moved first into fire insurance and then pioneered many of the new policies that led to the explosion in accident insurance around 1900, thus entering into direct competition with the companies.[24]

Transaction costs were minimised at Lloyd's, because contracts were struck in a more favourable context for the underwriter than that of the company–agent relationship described above. A deal was assessed and confirmed in direct discussion between an underwriter and broker with the latter providing detailed information on the risk. The institution of Lloyd's supported the underwriter's decision through its culture, networks and structures. In the eighteenth and early nineteenth centuries, its strength lay largely in its informal sharing of expertise and information within a relatively small and defined community. This was buttressed by more formal arrangements voluntarily agreed by the members of Lloyd's. In the mid-nineteenth century, membership was first monitored, guaranteed, then supported by deposits. In 1908, leading underwriters led the membership to accept a stringent audit of their accounts. Vessels throughout the world were classified in the Lloyd's Register by marine surveyors. An expanding flow of accurate and up-to-date information on shipping movements was dispatched from Lloyd's telegraph stations to be published in Lloyd's List.

Within this framework, brokers negotiated with 'utmost good faith', not just because of the law and other formal requirements, but because they wished to protect their reputation in a vigorous community where gossip about transgressions would be widely reported.[25] Trust became a tangible business asset, almost a matter of 'branding' for both underwriters and brokers. Family, school and other social links between members created and sustained shared standards.[26] Risk sharing meant that initial acceptance by an underwriter of high repute or special expertise encouraged other underwriters to come in on the strength of that implicit guarantee. Thus Lloyd's underwriters were supported by a network that greatly reduced the potential transactions costs associated with underwriting otherwise uncertain risks. Conversely, information on the desirability of risks came to the broker directly. Unattractive risks would be quoted a penal rate or refused. If risks subsequently performed badly, a broker's capacity to place business might be permanently affected. Underwriters reacted with extreme severity to unexpectedly adverse experience.[27]

Information transparency between marketing and underwriting was not the only factor determining costs and competitiveness between Lloyd's and the companies. Lloyd's operated on the basis of an economically light administrative touch. The trust described above allowed brokers and underwriters to eliminate much of the clerical work from formal contracts. An underwriter's signature on a slip sufficed. This was initially because underwriters accepted too small an income to meet overhead costs of any size. Yet even after Marten demonstrated the competitive advantage of larger syndicates, Lloyd's continued to exploit its cost minimising traditional routines as an important competitive advantage.[28]

Light administration also allowed the more entrepreneurial members of the institution to move quickly into new markets without the inertia often implicit in large, hierarchical organisations.[29] C.E. Heath's career was marked by a continuing willingness to underwrite new risks promptly. Indeed, he saw the novelty of a risk as its chief advantage. It allowed him to gain a head start over competitors and this he did in fire, loss of profits, burglary, block, all risks, credit and many other new policies.[30] It was a service sector equivalent of the switching advantages of small firms in manufacturing. Lloyd's remarkable capacity for innovation, demonstrated so successfully in general insurance in the years around 1900, was as much a consequence of modest administrative arrangements as entrepreneurial quality. While the Committee of Lloyd's was apprehensive about the developments, they did not prevent innovation, as they could have done if they wished. Once shown the way by Heath, the routines of the institution proved naturally flexible and responsive to new opportunities.[31]

This was a striking transformation in the fortunes of the institution. In the eighteenth century it had dominated marine insurance and had undertaken some fire business. The fire duty had killed the latter, and the legislation that allowed far more companies to enter marine insurance market from 1824 allowed their greater acceptance capacity to give them a substantial competitive advantage. In the mid-nineteenth century Lloyd's became increasingly a marginal market organised in an apparently archaically individualistic way bound to wither away gradually as the organised company form expanded its hold on marine insurance.[32] Yet the market-based routines it had developed, based on trust and confidence that allowed transparent information flows, low administrative costs, and the possibility of rapid innovation, lay dormant, waiting for an environmental change that would prove more congenial to these capabilities. And the rise of the hierarchical company organisational structure effected just such a change that reinvigorated the Lloyd's approach to underwriting.

III

ORGANISATIONAL INTERMEDIATION

From the mid-nineteenth century, formal collusion organised by the Fire Offices Committee (FOC) was increasingly successful in controlling premium rate competition in fire insurance.[33] This encouraged non-price competition, especially the expansion in branch office organisations. Initially modest in scope, but with increasing effectiveness from the 1880s and 1890s, local inspectors motivated agents and brokers and dealt with large policyholders directly. From around 1900 branch offices encouraged the horizontal integration of fire and accident insurance to capture agents and brokers operating in both markets and reduce overhead costs. Branch office expansion continued apace through the inter-war years with the explosion in motor insurance.[34]

Alongside these marketing advantages, branch offices also allowed greater underwriting control through the monitoring of risk acceptances and claims settlements. Local inspectors and surveyors assessed large risks directly and could evaluate the quality of small agents' businesses. In principle, therefore, a form of vertical integration created a direct organisational line conveying information from the market to the underwriter, and back again, to direct marketing effectively, reducing the transaction costs when agency control had been less possible.

The scale on which companies operated enabled them to establish administrative procedures and organisational structures that allowed sufficient specialisation for economies of scale to be generated. Clerks specialised in particular aspects of work, and decisions requiring discretion could be referred up to more senior staff. Indeed, managing clerical procedures became one of the main organisational resources developed by insurance companies in the century following 1860, and these certainly offered scope for cost reduction in the handling of risks. This further encouraged horizontal integration, as similar procedures could be used in different markets. It is no accident that Kafka was an insurance official, for these companies provided the apotheosis of extreme bureaucracy, in which detailed administration was taken to its limit in a service sector version of the modernist industrial firm.[35]

The methodical nature of these procedures was encouraged by the tariff system through which the FOC controlled competition.[36] This specified the premium rate for each risk, identifying different rates for the components of more complex premises and indicating the policy terms that should apply. In motor insurance, vehicles were classified and rated by value and horsepower.[37] Within the companies, underwriters supplemented tariff regulations with additional underwriting guidelines. Proposal forms were scrutinised by armies of clerks, searching for discrepancies. These were referred to underwriting managers who might negotiate with branch managers or brokers. Risks covered insufficiently precisely by tariff regulations were passed up through company hierarchies, perhaps eventually being discussed at inter-company tariff meetings.[38] Tariff regulations for large fire risks required a surveyor to draw up a report with detailed plans. Branches would be expected to comment on the moral hazard associated with proprietors. Loss adjusters would assess the cause of a claim and ensure that the company only paid what was necessary. Claims clerks checked proposed settlements. This specialisation changed the character of underwriting by separating its various elements. Indeed, the creation of the hierarchical, administrative organisation was associated with the emergence of insurance as a 'profession'. Of course, there was something in this view. From the 1890s the Chartered Insurance Institute provided professional training that led to a more systematic approach to many technical aspects of the business. At Lloyd's, underwriting remained a matter of business. In the companies, it became a series of technical decisions which increased the difficulty of interpolating discretion or the integration of underwriting and marketing considerations.[39]

In principle, the new company organisation provided a unified vertical channel which facilitated this integration. In practice, however, companies internalised the tension between the two activities, institutionalising it as a conflict between branch offices and head office. In the best managed companies these tensions could be both accommodated and even creative, but they could lead to problems. Branch staff could see underwriting margins as beyond their control because of the random incidence of claims. They preferred the more tangible objective of expanding premium income, especially when inspectors were paid revenue commission. Fussiness about risks discouraged them. This encouraged an expansive culture and one in which all companies had an interest. Expanding premium incomes increased investment reserves and earnings and funded organisational expansion. By contrast, underwriters at head office were more concerned about the losses risks might involve. Daily routine concentrated on the minutiae of individual cases, which encouraged a pedantic culture. Underwriters' professional training and organisational methods encouraged a systematic rather than intuitive approach. By basing underwriting on administrative procedures, companies forced staff to take a narrow view in contrast with the swashbuckling inspectors out on the road, battling to secure risks against competition. The difficulty underwriters had in lifting their heads above the application of rules sometimes led them to see branches as subverting underwriting. In the branches, underwriters could become seen as the enemy to be circumvented. Negotiations were constrained by the administrative basis of operation, involving the costly time and effort of senior staff, enmeshed in the detail of tariff and company underwriting rules.[40]

Administrative procedures also locked companies into an approach to underwriting that was unresponsive to market changes. Adjustments in tariff regulations required prolonged negotiation between member companies with varying interests. As a result, there were few fundamental changes in the structure of the tariff rating of fire risks between the 1920s and the 1960s.[41] At the company level the reliance on administrative procedures meant that rules and regulations had to be committed to documentation for circulation to staff and agents. This involved cost and delay, so changes in underwriting policy were, in practice, rare. New policies always threatened to destabilise markets and were therefore unattractive to the tariff companies. They contributed none of the new accident insurance products that were introduced between 1890 and 1914, which nearly all came from Lloyd's, or from new companies initially working outside the tariff arrangements.[42] Inside fire insurance, they opposed important innovations such as loss of profits and burning cost policies, and saw the reduction in claims arising from sprinklers as a threat to premium income, rather than an opportunity to reduce premiums.[43] Indeed, their commitment to the heavy overhead costs implicit in an organisational structure created an obsession with revenue to cover costs, rather than profitability. It all reflected a deeply inflexible organisational structure that was principally concerned with resisting change.

The commitment to administrative routines and capabilities shaped the response to competitive threats. When the tariff companies faced rate discounting from Lloyd's and independent companies on individual risks with good claims experience, their response was to intensify their stance. From the 1890s the FOC began to agree reduced premium rates for individual risks threatened by competition. The procedure was rational in allowing concessions only where necessary. But the administrative cost was extraordinary in that it meant regular meetings of all the principal companies to agree on the rating of an escalating number of particular risks. The contrast with Lloyd's individualism could not be more pointed.[44]

Why was the hierarchical model of insurance organisation apparently so successful over the 100 years following 1890? At one level it seems an entirely rational system of scrutiny and selection. In this sense it is similar to the models of hierarchical organisation so lovingly described in the work of Chandler and his disciples, following the stereotype of the modern organisation with neat and rational structures. But the rise of this organisational form cannot be disassociated from the controlled competitive environment it created. And the same is true of the parallel growth of hierarchy and market control in British insurance, which can be briefly sketched.

The tariff organisation created to ensure stability in the weakly oligopolistic fire market, was extended to the accident insurance market in 1906 by the formation of the Accident Offices Association (AOA).[45] The branch office expansion, encouraged by formal collusion, increased the barriers to market entry, reinforcing the control established by restricting reinsurance and underwriting information to tariff members.[46] But because this carried the burden of competitive activity between tariff members, organisational costs climbed. In the inter-war years branch organisations escalated and the administrative costs of operating the tariff system rose.[47] If market control could be maintained, this did not matter, because the cost could be passed on to policyholders in premium rates. As risk improvement reduced claims through the twentieth century, premium rates moved little. Brokers were able to raise commission rates as they took firmer control of business. Thus, policyholders paid the cost of administrative control, branch organisations and commission rates.

The market power of the large companies, their branch offices, and the tariff system was sufficiently strong to resist competitive pressure for a very long time. At first it did no more than create an environment that revived Lloyd's, which re-entered fire insurance in the 1870s after the reconstruction of the tariff system in 1868. Its routines were ideally designed to handle large fire risks, often provided by the new provincial brokers, but it extended the scope of its British fire business by reinsuring independent companies who, because they were operating outside the tariff, were forbidden to reinsure with its members. In fact, many of these companies were effectively fronts for Lloyd's members.[48] The profitability of the tariff system, which the companies used to expand their organisations, allowed Lloyd's and its independent associates to reinvigorate the market approach to underwriting, utilising its flexibility and low costs. Then, in the period of rapid innovation around 1900, Lloyd's routines and capabilities proved far superior to the companies' in seizing new underwriting opportunities. In the inter-war years, Lloyd's brokers brought a growing business to the market from local high street brokers and from an early form of 'affinity' marketing through professional associations and trade unions. The companies followed where Lloyd's led, though their acceptance capacity and market power meant that they could always eventually substitute scale for sprightliness.

Through the twentieth century, Lloyd's expanded its share of general insurance business, especially in the motor insurance market.[49] Growth was constrained by Lloyd's capacity and because independent underwriters were prepared to allow the tariff companies to act as price leaders, never discounting sufficiently to destabilise the market, enabling them to share the profitability created by the tariff. Independent companies operated successfully with slimmer organisations, but, as competition intensified, the tariff companies actually reinforced their conventional routines. Branch organisations expanded particularly quickly to serve the motor insurance market in the inter-war years, and the tariff companies tried to resist the continued competitive pressures by further branch development in the post-war years.[50] But this failed. Competition from many sources, including

Lloyd's, flourished. The AOA abandoned the attempt to control the motor insurance market in 1968. The FOC, threatened by the Monopolies Commission began to dismantle tariff control of the fire insurance market in 1970, though the organisation remained until 1985.[51] As could be predicted, the end of tariff control was paralleled by some contraction in branch office organisations through the 1970s and 1980s, though implicit collusion and a continuing commitment to the now conventional routine of company insurance operation limited this process.[52]

Thus, the integrated, hierarchical model of insurance operation was in large measure the product of a collusive market and began to contract when opportunities for market control disappeared. Just as we often imagine with many of the Chandlerian managerial corporations, internal organisation was cushioned by the collusive market their scale created. Perhaps hierarchical management must be considered in the same way as we have been taught to view the innovative potential of monopoly. Paradoxically, the environment created by the rise and slow fall of the hierarchical form allowed the Lloyd's market-based approach to underwriting to flourish. The innovative and flexible approach to underwriting produced by Lloyd's internal procedures was ideally designed to challenge the company administrative method at its weakest point.[53]

IV
DIRECT MARKETING

From the late 1980s, the visible and invisible hands in insurance were challenged by 'direct' marketing. Direct Line, the pioneering company, was established as a subsidiary of the Royal Bank of Scotland in 1987 to market motor insurance directly by phone. The new method proved dramatically successful. By 1990 direct marketing was attracting 12 per cent of the UK private motor insurance market, by 1993 20 per cent and 1994 25 per cent.[54] Direct Line took the overwhelming proportion, for it had few initial emulators. The most important was Churchill, whose aggressively English name betrays, to the student of international business, its Swiss origins.[55] But before 1994 there was practically no direct marketing by existing British companies. By 1995 the company was diversifying from motor insurance into other personal lines and even life assurance, using the routines it had developed in motor insurance, just as Lloyd's had diversified into fire insurance from the 1870s, using market-based routines, and the conventional companies had diversified horizontally using administrative routines before 1914.[56]

Direct marketing was a product of information technology. Early computers in insurance in the 1960s had supported traditional administrative processes such as accounting. In the early 1980s computer networks connected head offices, branches, agents and brokers, supporting the traditional structure of underwriting and marketing. However, from the mid-1980s, new technology pioneered in the US allowed the relationship between policyholders and insurers to be transformed.

Direct marketing was based on massive advertising, using television and the press to persuade motorists to phone to obtain a competitive insurance quotation.[57] There was no cold calling. The innovation that facilitated this was the auto-call distribution unit which allowed any number of calls to be distributed to operators systematically.[58] Operators provided a friendly contact for policyholders, sometimes assisted by an appropriate regional accent.[59] The information they needed to handle calls was supplied on screens connected to interactive databases. These contained data that could immediately be linked to callers, supplemented by requested information. This helped in making the sale and in appraising the caller from the perspective of underwriting. The database then produced guidance to the operator on what to offer the caller. Access to potential policyholders was made possible by widespread phone ownership and payment by credit card. All the recording of information and assessment could be completed in one call. Paper documentation was supplied later, printed out directly from the data recorded during the call. In effect the new method was more than direct marketing – it was also direct underwriting and administration.

Direct marketing was successful for several reasons. A significant market segment found the new method more convenient. The elimination of agency commissions and branch expenses provided by the direct link saved between 20 and 30 per cent of premium income. However, during the early expansion of the business, the alternative cost of advertising was as high. National coverage involved a heavy overhead cost that could only be reduced by revenue growth.[60] Yet eventually the new cost and price base for underwriting supported major reductions in premium rates, which, given the high individual elasticity of demand for motor insurance, proved aggressively successful.

Other considerations consolidated the new method. In particular, it allowed insurers to integrate marketing and underwriting more successfully. In terms of the insurance contract, it largely eliminated the market and hierarchical interfaces that had previously inhibited the process. Underwriting and marketing now took place in one transaction under direct company control. The company was able to select risks by making direct enquiries about their characteristics and then processing these instantly through a database that instructed operators whether a risk should be accepted. Database management also allowed finer discrimination to be made between risks, in a way impossibly expensive with the paper-based systems of the past. Detailed postal codes could be used as a basis for refined geographical discrimination without creating major problems for marketing and administration by agency, branch and head office staff. This fed back into opportunities to use the database to establish more sophisticated rating structures derived from these finer discriminations. Furthermore, database management allowed premium rate adjustments to be made far more rapidly in response to changing experience than had been possible when these had been circulated in printed form. Reliance on the phone link allowed the company to take a closer control of claims settlement, dealing directly with the policyholder through 'help lines'.[61] This by-passed the agent, who had so often intervened in an informed and effective way to represent (or misrepresent) their clients' case. Some companies are now moving towards more direct control with claims settlements monitored from head office by video cameras in designated garages, so that claims can be assessed with even greater accuracy. Put briefly, direct marketing cut out most of the agency and transaction costs previously associated with the administration of underwriting.

Alongside this better control of underwriting, direct marketing allowed companies to take greater control of their market. Direct contact with the policyholder broke the power of the intermediary whose interest was always in protecting his own connection, rather than the company's. The traditional broker system had held policyholders within a network that provided them with alternative insurers whenever a company tried to raise its premium rates. Direct marketing avoided this link and one of its most striking characteristics was a far higher renewal rate at the end of each policy year.[62] This allowed revenue to grow more successfully and allowed insurers more control over the terms of sale. It also reduced administrative costs, which are higher on new policies than on existing ones, because of the initial exchange of documentation and risk assessment. Ending intermediary intervention also allowed insurers greater freedom in risk selection. They no longer had to satisfy agents' and brokers' requirements in accepting a mixed portfolio of risks. Each risk could be written on its merits. One of the striking consequences was that direct marketing focused on creaming off desirable risks in a way that agency and broker connections would rarely have allowed. Thus, direct marketing attacked the most profitable business of the conventional companies, leaving them with less attractive risks. They lost both premium income and margins. Conversely, the loss ratios obtained by direct marketing were better, allowing an appropriate combination of higher profitability or greater competitiveness in premium rating. Finally, integrated control over the underwriting–marketing process allowed insurers to manage product branding more successfully. This has always proved difficult in geographically diffused service sector businesses, where the character and quality of the product delivered to the purchaser is so much in the hands of branch organisations or intermediaries where detailed management control is difficult. With the whole transaction – and subsequent customer links – controlled by the insurer in a way that could be tightly managed through phone operators' screens, the character of the transaction could be specified to provide desired levels of service such as the speed of response to calls – Direct Line claimed in 1992 to answer 90 per cent of calls within ten seconds.[63] In short, direct marketing eliminated most of the transaction costs associated with the intermediary network.

The success of Direct Line in capturing such a large market share was largely due to the fact that there was for seven years or so practically no response from established insurance companies. The reasons lie in the internal organisation and marketing environment described earlier. The competitive advantage of the traditional insurance companies lay in their expertise in managing the hierarchical processes that attracted risks through the branch office system and then underwrote them on the systematic basis described above. Lloyd's also depended on brokers. While some rationalisation of company structures had occurred after the effective end of the formal cartels after 1968, the lack of any fundamentally different method of operation allowed implicit collusion to protect organisations that remained, in essence, bureaucratic.[64] Significantly, direct marketing in insurance was pioneered by a subsidiary of the Royal Bank of Scotland, untrammelled by any previous insurance commitment. Furthermore, the entrepreneurial individuals who created the new methods were not insurance professionals. Their background was in information technology and they allowed that to shape the new system. In ownership and control, the direct marketing of general insurance was developed quite separately from the conventional insurance business. In the late 1980s the conventional companies found it difficult to move into fundamentally different technologies, even when they saw these destroying their business. They did not have the resources to mount such a move – either technical or human – when the innovation would make redundant the work of most of their staff, especially the management cadre whose control function was eliminated by the new information technology. Their commitment to conventional bureaucratic routines locked them into an uncompetitive position.

Beyond this, they were faced with a critical marketing dilemma. On the one hand, there was the question as to how they could finance the major expenditure on advertising necessary to launch the new activity while continuing to carry the cost of a branch organisation. At the same time, their chief existing marketing resource was the goodwill they possessed with agency and broker networks, cultivated over decades by branch managers and inspectors in a multitude of accommodations and concessions. Agents and brokers were even more painfully aware than the companies of the threat direct marketing posed to their businesses. The moment an insurer entered the new mode, all the goodwill it possessed with these marketing connections could be destroyed. They would move to a company that appeared to be committed to the conventional modes of delivery.[65]

The decision to establish a direct marketing operation therefore threatened to destroy one of the conventional insurance companies' most valuable assets and one that was essential to the maintenance of what remained of their traditional business. Some fudged the decision by trying to set up direct marketing operations with quite different names that could be disowned.[66] But this was scarcely successful. In effect they were locked into the conventional mode of delivery that made them deeply uncompetitive, allowing Direct Line and other new companies entering the market for the first time, to expand without effective constraint. And by the time the older companies saw how much business they had lost, Direct Line had established a brand name which was for a time one of the most widely recognised in the United Kingdom.[67]

V

CONCLUSION

The 'contractual paradigm' has been used by historians to interpret institutional forms with great success, but its explanatory power is limited to the analysis of the given circumstances surrounding particular transactions or agency relations. This essay has shown that ideas drawn from evolutionary theory can enrich interpretation by explaining how institutions develop new capacities that shape subsequent institutional equilibria. The evolutionary approach also suggests that the study of the capabilities created within an institution is important in understanding its competitive strategy and success.

These ideas have been illustrated in the context of the emergence of administratively organised, integrated insurance companies in the nineteenth century which exemplify the advantages of hierarchy, specialisation and scale. However, Lloyd's, based on individualistic underwriting and fragmented organisation, managed to survive alongside the companies, and then gradually develop its special capabilities and routines in ways that allowed it to compete successfully with the companies. This development could be explained at each stage using transactions cost analysis and agency theory. The companies took closer control of marketing activity to reduce the transactions costs associated with local agents, and increase the flow of underwriting information reaching managers. At Lloyd's, transactions costs were minimised because they took place between two individuals whose reputation was well known and valuable to them over the long run and because the institution created facilities that improved information flows and reduced uncertainty in other ways.

However, evolutionary theory suggests that institutions will be limited in the ways they respond to competition or resolve difficulties and that these will take the form of developing existing routines and capabilities, rather than radical change. Thus, having set their hand to develop agency networks, the companies certainly focused on their motivation and control through local branch offices. At head office they concentrated on developing administrative routines that would generate economies of scale though specialisation and delegation. These routines were reinforced by the detailed administrative procedures of the tariff system of premium rate control which all the big offices were required to support to maintain market stability. When they faced competitive pressure between themselves or with independent insurers, including those from Lloyd's, the companies' response was to extend or intensify these routines. They expanded their branch office organisations or intensified the grip of the tariff system. This explains the degree to which organisational control was expanded – and thus the institutional framework observed within a 'contractual paradigm' approach. Similarly, the process whereby Lloyd's revived its activities was to reinforce the strengths of its networks and community. Larger syndicates were created to compete with the companies' financial strengths, without undermining the individual responsibility of the underwriter and the unlimited liability of his members. Changing requirements to enter the market, and more information about the financial affairs of individual underwriters, were two other ways in which the traditional Lloyd's system was recast to meet new challenges, creating greater protection for transactional relations.

This concentration on particular routines and capabilities meant that both institutions were best suited to particular market environments. The companies were able to use their financial scale to accept large risks, their branch organisations and collusive agreements to control the market and drive up margins, and their administrative systems to handle large numbers of risks expeditiously. They used this to control the bulk of the British domestic general insurance market for 100 years or more from 1870. The process of extension and intensification of their capabilities to cope with competitive pressures probably led to an over-expansion of organisational development whose focus became market control rather than social efficiency. The 'contractual paradigm' has always seemed to emphasise private costs and benefits, rather than welfare issues.

In any event, the direction and scale of the companies' development revived Lloyd's. The price of their scale, their market control and their administrative systems, was a lack of flexibility, of price competitiveness and of innovation. These were precisely the capabilities that Lloyd's routines provided, with a scale of operation that was still modest in scale, highly competitive and very innovative. Thus, in the late nineteenth century Lloyd's was transformed from what had seemed at mid-century a quaint eighteenth-century relic to a vigorous and expanding insurance market, which played an important role within the British market and attracted an enormous business from abroad.

The organisational and market-based routines dominated the operation of general insurance activity for most of the twentieth century. In the 1970s and 1980s the collapse of the tariff control of competition and the adoption of computer systems encouraged some contraction in organisations. But the real challenge came around 1990 with the introduction of direct marketing. This recent development marked a sharp break with the past because it eliminated most of the transaction and agency costs that had been implicit in both organisational and market-based routines. In this it sets the problems and institutional developments of the past in sharp and instructive contrast, illustrating the fact that contemporary change can help us to understand the past with greater clarity. Significantly, this radical change came from outside the insurance business and, as evolutionary theory would suggest, companies and Lloyd's have found it difficult to respond with equally fundamental revisions of their own methods. New and separate organisations are required. This emphasises the point that important strategic developments are rooted in internal capabilities and routines that are not, and cannot be, created overnight by management fiat. They are the product of institutional expertise and culture, shaped by the history of the organisation which possesses it, which must take its place at the centre of industrial theory and business history and draw the two more closely together.

NOTES

I am grateful to the editors, an anonymous referee and participants in the conference on 'Institutional and Evolutionary Theory and Business History' held at Lancaster University in May 1996 for comments on my initial draft. I also wish to acknowledge gratefully the support of the Leverhulme Trust for some of the research reported, which was carried out by Dr Sheila Oliver.

1. S. Douma and H. Schreuder, *Economic Approaches to Organizations* (Hemel Hempstead, 1992), p.169.
2. J. Oldham, *The Mansfield Manuscripts* (Chapel Hill, NY, 1992), Chapter 7. I am grateful to my colleague David Sugarman for this and other references on this legal topic.
3. H.A.L. Cockerell, *Insurance* (London, 1957), pp.15–16.
4. Oldham, *Mansfield*, p.478.

5. H.E. Raynes, *A History of British Insurance* (London, 1964), p.209.
6. R. Hasson, 'The Doctrine of Uberrima Fides in Insurance Law: A Critical Evaluation', *Modern Law Review*, Vol.32 (1969), pp.615–37.
7. Throughout this paper the term 'organisation' will be used to cover all forms of 'hierarchical' or 'planned' institutional activity.
8. Douma and Schreuder, *Economic Approaches to Organizations*, Chapters 6 and 7, provide an introduction to this field.
9. An introduction to this work can be found in A.D. Chandler, Jr, *The Visible Hand: The Managerial Revolution in American Business* (Cambridge, MA, 1977), pp.1–13 and O.E. Williamson, *Markets and Hierarchies: Analysis and Antitrust Implications* (New York, 1975).
10. A general survey of this process can be found in B. Supple, *Royal Exchange Assurance: A History of British Insurance, 1720–1970* (Cambridge, 1970), Chapter 12.
11. A good systematic account of the organisation of Lloyd's can be found in C.E. Golding and D. King-Page, *Lloyd's* (London, 1952); D.E.W. Gibb, *Lloyd's of London: A Study in Individualism* (London, 1957) remains the best history; while A. Raphael, *Ultimate Risk* (London, 1994) is an exciting and thorough account of its recent history.
12. Douma and Schreuder, *Economic Approaches to Organizations*, Chapter 9; J. Nightingale, 'Evolutionary Processes and Revolutionary Change in Firms and Markets: An Economist's Perspective', in P. Earl (ed.), *Management, Marketing, and the Competitive Process* (Cheltenham, 1996); and R.N. Langlois and P.L. Robertson, *Firms, Markets and Economic Change: A Dynamic Theory of Business Institutions* (London, 1995), Chapters 1 and 2, provide introductions to this literature.
13. Langlois and Robertson, *Firms, Markets and Economic Change*, pp.104–6.
14. The technicalities of insurance underwriting are deliberately not discussed here as the focus is intended to be the organisation of insurance operation. It does not examine such technicalities of underwriting as acceptance limits or reinsurance. An elementary introduction to underwriting can be found in Cockerell, *Insurance*, Chapter XIII.
15. One special case, not pursued here, is that of the mutual company where groups of insured co-operate to insure one another. In principle this can meet the requirements outlined in the previous paragraph ideally. Fellow businessmen are in a good position to assess technical risks and moral hazard and fraud will be quickly detected.
16. O.M. Westall, 'Marketing Strategy and the Competitive Structure of British General Insurance, 1720–1980', *Business History*, Vol.36 No.2 (1994), pp.22–3; D.T. Jenkins, 'The Practice of Insurance Against Fire, 1750–1840, and Historical Research', in O.M. Westall, (ed.), *The Historian and the Business of Insurance* (Manchester, 1984), pp.23–8.
17. Because profit commission could only be calculated after the event for a financial year and many companies preferred to work on the average of a run of years.
18. I am grateful for this point to an anonymous referee.
19. Jenkins, 'Practice of Insurance', p.29.
20. Ibid., p.30.
21. Westall, 'Marketing Strategy', p.25.
22. Ibid., pp.27–31.
23. O.M. Westall, *The Provincial Insurance Company, 1903–38: Family, Markets and Competitive Growth* (Manchester, 1992), p.204.
24. Liverpool Record Office, Liverpool & London & Globe, Secretary's Report Books, Vol.5, 1875–1880, 3 July 1877; O.M. Westall, "C.E. Heath', in D.J. Jeremy (ed.), *Dictionary of Business Biography*, Vol.III (London, 1984) p.136; D. Kynaston, T*he City of London, Vol.II The Golden Years 1890–1914* (London, 1995), pp.21–2.
25. Kynaston, *Golden Years*, p.29; Gibb, *Lloyd's*, p.359.
26. D. Kynaston, *The City of London, Vol.I: A World of its Own, 1815–1890* (London, 1994), p.294.
27. Gibb, *Lloyd's*, Chapter 8; Golding and King-Page, *Lloyd's*, Chapter 4; Kynaston, *Golden Years*, p.29 provides an evocative impression of the community of Lloyd's at work.
28. Gibb, *Lloyd's*, pp.177–80; A. Brown, *Cuthbert Heath: Maker of the Modern Lloyd's of London* (Newton Abbot, 1980), pp.61–2.

29. Westall, 'C.E. Heath', p.136.
30. Gibb, *Lloyd's*, pp.163–4.
31. Ibid., p.168.
32. Ibid., Chapter 5; S. Palmer, 'The Indemnity in the London Marine Insurance Market, 1824–50', in Westall (ed.), *The Business of Insurance*, pp.81–2.
33. O.M. Westall, 'David and Goliath: The Fire Offices Committee and Non-Tariff Competition, 1898–1907', in Westall (ed.), *The Business of Insurance*, pp.131–5.
34. Westall, 'Marketing Strategy', pp.32–4.
35. It is very difficult to support this statement from the published literature. Insurance historians have found it very difficult to find systematic evidence about the number of clerical staff or their work practices. Even when the former is available, its significance lacks clarity because it cannot be standardised against appropriate measures of work load such as policy counts. B. Supple, *REA*, p.376, reports that head office staff at the REA rose from 76 in 1890 to 149 in 1900 and 314 in 1913. R. Ryan, 'A History of the Norwich Union Fire and Life Insurance Societies from 1797 to 1914' (unpublished Ph.D. thesis, University of East Anglia, 1983), pp.426 and 433, suggests that the fire and life head office staff rose from about 50 in the 1850s to some 300 in 1914. P.G.M. Dickson, *The Sun Insurance Office, 1710–1960: The History of Two and a Half Centuries of British Insurance* (London, 1960), indicates, with qualifications, a growth in staff from 56 in 1866 to 150 in 1891, though the latter figure includes branch office staff. On the growth in branch offices see Westall, 'Marketing Strategy', p.30, Table 1.
36. Supple, *REA*, pp.127–30; Westall, *Provincial Insurance Company*, pp.28–31; Westall, 'Marketing Strategy', p.27.
37. O.M. Westall, 'The Invisible Hand Strikes Back: Motor Insurance and the Erosion of Organised Competition in General Insurance, 1920–38', *Business History*, Vol.XXX No.4 (Oct. 1988), p.436.
38. See Guildhall Library, Fire Offices Committee and Accident Offices Committee Minutes, passim, for discussions of particular cases. I am grateful to the Association of British Insurers for permission to study these records.
39. O.M. Westall, 'Entrepreneurship and Product Innovation in British General Insurance, 1840–1914', in J. Brown and M.B. Rose (eds.), *Entrepreneurship, Networks and Modern Business* (Manchester, 1993), pp.191–210.
40. Westall, *Provincial Insurance Company*, pp.271–9 discusses a case study of conflict between branches and head office; Supple, *REA*, pp.500–504 discusses similar problems and their resolution in a large company.
41. O.M. Westall, 'The Assumptions of Regulation in British General Insurance', in G. Jones and M. Kirby (eds.), *Competitiveness and the State: Government and Business in Twentieth Century Britain* (Manchester, 1991), p.153.
42. Westall, 'Entrepreneurship and Product Innovation', pp.200–204.
43. Westall, 'David and Goliath', p.144.
44. The earliest reference to this tactic the author has discovered can be found in Liverpool Record Office, London & Lancashire & Globe, Secretary's Reports, Vol.IV, 7 April 1874. For its implementation see Guildhall Library, Ms 29462/23 Fire Offices Committee Circulars 1895 for examples of notifications of special rates allowed for particular risks within tariffs. For example, in that year 21 premises were allowed special concessions within the Glasgow and Paisley tariff.
45. W.A. Dinsdale, *History of Accident Insurance in Great Britain* (London, 1954), pp.282–5.
46. Westall, 'David and Goliath', p.135.
47. Westall, 'Marketing Strategy', p.33.
48. The most obvious of these were Eagle Star, owned by the Mountain family, who were prominent Lloyd's members, and the Excess and the Fine Art and General, both of which were at one time owned by C.E. Heath. See Westall, 'C.E. Heath', and O.M. Westall, 'Sir Edward Mortimer Mountain' in D.J. Jeremy (ed.), *Dictionary of Business Biography*, Vol.IV, p.364.
49. Westall, *Provincial Insurance Company*, pp.191–2; Westall, 'Invisible Hand', pp.441–2.
50. Westall, 'Marketing Strategy', pp.35–6.

51. Westall, 'Assumptions of Regulation', pp.152–5.
52. Westall, 'Marketing Strategy', p.38.
53. Gibb, *Lloyd's*, pp.210–11 and 304–5 provide excellent comparisons between the operations of companies and Lloyd's.
54. Association of British Insurers, *Statistical Bulletin*, General Insurance Statistics Sources of Premium Income (London seriatim).
55. Winterthur Insurance, its Swiss parent company, invested £24 million in Churchill in 1992 and 1993. B. Ellis, 'Does it Pay to Go Direct?', *Accountancy*, Vol.112 No.1204 (Dec. 1993), pp.54–5.
56. A. Benady, 'Direct Line adds Home Extension', *Marketing*, 25 Aug. 1994, p.6; P. Whitaker, *Effective Distribution: The Key to Success and Survival in the Insurance Industry* (Henley-on-Thames, 1995), pp.178–82.
57. In 1993 Direct Line claimed to have spent £9.5 million on marketing, advertising, television commercials, direct mail and sponsorships. It was then predicted that £13.5 million would be spent in this way in 1994 on a turnover approaching £700 million. B. Susman, 'Get Marketing Right: Use Technology: Give Good Service', *Insurance Brokers' Monthly and Insurance Adviser*, Vol.44 No.4 (April 1994), pp.124–8; Whitaker, *Effective Distribution*, pp.194–5.
58. Whitaker, *Effective Distribution*, Chapter 14.
59. It is claimed that some direct marketing companies in financial services locate their call answering offices in order to be able to recruit operators with trustworthy regional accents in the north of England and Scotland and well away from the obviously dubious 'estuarine' accent of the London conurbation.
60. Whitaker, *Effective Distribution*, pp.194–6.
61. G. Holmes and A. Sugden, 'Direct Line Insurance: What Makes that Little Red Telephone Ring?', *Accountancy*, Vol.110 No.1191 (Nov. 1992), pp.32–4.
62. S. Rines, 'Never Mind the Glitz, Feel the Quality', *Marketing Week*, 25 March 1994, pp.33–4 claimed that Direct Line had achieved a year on year customer retention rate of 86 per cent, compared with an industry average of between 50 and 60 per cent. Whitaker, *Effective Distribution*, p.191 accepts this average figure for the industry and contrasts it with an estimated 80 per cent retention by brokers who can recommend policyholders to switch insurers without losing the business themselves. Whitaker confirms that other direct insurers obtain a similarly high retention rate and one firm claimed that 40 per cent of its new business was obtained through recommendations by existing customers.
63. Holmes and Sugden, 'What Makes that Little Red Telephone Ring?', p.34.
64. Westall, 'Marketing Strategy', pp.37–9.
65. Whitaker, *Effective Distribution*, p.180.
66. Ibid.
67. Anon, 'Direct Line Dials Hotline to Number Two', *Marketing*, 23 Feb. 1995, p.15.

Consultancies, Institutions and the Diffusion of Taylorism in Britain, Germany and France, 1920s to 1950s

MATTHIAS KIPPING

University of Reading

Neoclassical economic theory assumes that all transactions between buyers and sellers of goods and services take place in a 'market' and that purchasing decisions are determined by price, given that the goods and services have identical features (for example, regarding quality) or are at least interchangeable. While this model might help to explain the exchange of homogenous products, it is inadequate to understand the relationship between buyers and sellers of consultancy services, because of the very specific nature of this activity.

Consultancy is a business based on highly skilled human capital, which means that transactions are hard to separate from the individuals involved in their realisation. Contracts are concluded before the service has been delivered. In the absence of objective criteria regarding the value of outputs and in order to compensate for the uncertainty about quality, transactions will only take place if the client can meet the supplier personally and establish a relationship of co-operation and trust, often based on linguistic, cultural and social affinities. Once the transaction is agreed, the service itself is produced and consumed at the same time, a process often characterised as 'co-production'.[1]

Thus, only an explanatory framework which recognises forms of exchange other than pure market-based transactions can incorporate consultancy activities. The so-called new institutional economics, pioneered by Ronald Coase and developed more extensively by Oliver Williamson and others, provide such an alternative.[2] These authors have argued that, depending on the nature and the potential cost of the transaction, exchanges will take place in different economic institutions, within a single firm, on the marketplace or in the form of contracts which can be either explicit (that is, written) or relational (that is, largely based on trust).

The origins of consultancy activities remain relatively obscure. It seems that independent experts began to offer their advice to companies in the last quarter of the nineteenth century. They came from different backgrounds and included, for example, advertising agents, auditors and engineers.[3] On a larger scale, however, consultancy activities developed only with the emergence and diffusion of scientific management during the first decades of the twentieth century and especially after the First World War. Indeed, Frederick W. Taylor and his followers and competitors not only published or presented detailed descriptions of their respective systems at conferences, but also offered to install them for a fee. Subsequently, a growing number of 'efficiency engineers' contributed to the widespread application of the new methods in the United States and around the world.[4]

However, as will be shown, the evolution and the success of these consultants in the three major Western European economies differed quite considerably from one country to another. These differences were in part driven by the demand-side, that is, the need and the receptiveness of companies in each country for the Taylorist model of shop floor (and office) management.[5] However, in itself such an explanation remains insufficient, especially in the British case. On the one hand, British engineers and employers are widely believed to have been rather hostile towards Taylorism. On the other hand, the Bedaux Consultancy, which offered a popularised version of scientific management, was much more successful in Britain than in any other European country. This apparent paradox has fuelled an ongoing debate, with some authors suggesting a re-evaluation of the British attitude towards Taylorism and others downplaying the importance of Bedaux.[6]

While not intending to enter this debate directly, this article will consider an additional supply-side variable in order to understand the differences in the use of consultancies. It will look at the role of intermediary institutions, that is, institutions which are not involved directly in the transaction between consultants and their clients, but shape the exchange in a number of ways. Such a perspective is not incompatible with new institutional economics. In general terms, Mark Casson has recently proposed an extended model of the economy which incorporates what he calls 'market-makers', who influence the interaction between producers and consumers of goods and services.[7] With respect to consultancy activities, such intermediary institutions facilitate the establishment of the necessary trust-based relationship by providing so-called 'borrowed reputation'.

On the other hand, they also provide an alternative to consultancies when it comes to the transfer of management know-how and managerial fashions.[8] As a conduit, these institutions have two potential advantages compared to consultancies. First of all, they benefit from what could be called 'instant' trust, especially if they are established by the companies themselves. Secondly, unlike consultancies, which have to compete for business and therefore try to keep their proprietary approaches relatively secret, a single and strong institution ensures the adoption of uniform solutions throughout a country's industries. In this case, the development of consultancy activities is likely to be fairly limited.

It will be argued that institutions of the second type played a crucial role in Germany, while those of the first, intermediary, type were predominant in Britain, with France occupying a middling position. The analysis spans the period from the First World War until about 1960, when consultancies and institutions largely focused on work study. It is structured chronologically. The following section covers the inter-war years when the patterns outlined above emerged. In the period immediately before and during the Second World War, which is analysed in the third section, the necessary rationalisation efforts accelerated these developments. They continued unabated in the first post-war decade which is dealt with in the fourth section, followed by a brief summary.

II

Consulting engineers appeared in all three countries during the last quarter of the nineteenth century. They established specific associations before the First World War, the Verein beratender Ingenieure in 1903, the Chambre syndicale des ingénieurs-conseil de France in 1912 and the Association of Consulting Engineers in 1913. The British and German consulting engineers largely limited their activities to the technical field, while their French counterparts also offered business-related services.[9]

French engineers showed an early interest in Taylorism, mainly because of its 'scientific' character. Leading representatives of the profession, such as Henry Le Chatelier, helped to make the new approach widely known in France. Some of them started to work as independent consultants when attempts to implement the new methods in their companies failed.[10] The existing consulting engineers also saw scientific management as an opportunity to extend their activities. But most of the developments in the French consultancy market since the First World War were initiated by Americans. Already, in 1914, Harrington Emerson, a competitor of Taylor in the United States, had opened an office in Paris which introduced his organisation methods to a number of French metal-working and automobile factories. Shortly after the war, C. Bertrand Thomson, a professor at the Harvard Business School, established a consultancy in France, followed by Wallace Clark in 1927. The first French consultancies emerged in the late 1920s and during the 1930s when most of the foreign engineers left as a result of the economic and social crisis in France. Quite often, their founders had originally worked with one of the US consultancies. This is, for example, the case with Paul Planus, who joined Thomson in 1918, but started his own business in 1929.[11]

While consultancy activities in France developed early and expanded significantly during the inter-war period, institutional channels got off to a slower start and remained rather weak. Taylor's followers had founded an association, but they competed with the supporters of the French engineer Henri Fayol. His doctrine focused on the planning, co-ordinating and controlling role of management rather than on the scientific organisation of the work process.[12] Both associations merged in 1926 to form the Comité National de l'Organisation Française or CNOF. A few months later, however, leading French employers, including Louis Renault and André Citroën, created a competing organisation for the promotion of scientific management, the Commission Générale de l'Organisation Scientifique du Travail, or CGOST. It received the support of the French government and the peak employers' association.[13]

As a result of this split, the contribution of both institutions to the diffusion of Taylorism in France was limited. Their major activities involved the promotion of an exchange of experiences among those interested in the new methods. To this end, the CGOST formed working parties on different subjects, including, for example, the determination of production costs, which were attended by managers, technicians and researchers. The CNOF, on the other hand, published an information bulletin at more or less regular intervals. It took more far-reaching initiatives, aiming at the training of work study engineers, and the standardisation of time measurement came only very belatedly, with the creation of the Ecole d'Organisation Scientifique du Travail in 1934 and the Bureau des Temps Elementaires in 1938, respectively.

The extent to which such institutions could have influenced the diffusion of scientific management can be gauged from a comparison with the German example.[14] In Germany, the number of consulting engineers continued to grow after the First World War and reached more than 100 by the mid-1920s. In addition, another group of consultants focusing on organisational questions also developed and, in 1926, created their own association, the Verein beratender Organisatoren. But, despite these developments and the emergence of a few larger consultancies, such as Koch & Kienzle and Eduard Michel, the dissemination of the new methods was clearly dominated by institutional channels.[15]

Some of them had been established during the First World War, including, for example, the Ausschuß für wirtschaftliche Fertigung, or AWF, which aimed at improving the efficiency of the production process.[16] The most important step in the development of the institutional framework, however, was taken in 1921 with the creation of the National Efficiency Board (Reichskuratorium für Wirtschaftlichkeit, or RKW).[17] While receiving most of its funding from the German government, the RKW was controlled and administered by industry representatives, with Siemens playing a particularly important role. It was not directly involved in the implementation of scientific management in Germany, but acted as an umbrella for other organisations in the rationalisation movement. From 1927 it published a monthly newsletter which reached a circulation of 12,000 in 1932 and served as a forum for the exchange of information. From 1929 onwards it also carried out industry surveys in different branches of the German economy. By compiling averages for a number of key indicators and describing best practices they provided companies with benchmarks for their own performance and suggestions for improvement.[18]

Concerning work study, the most important institution among the RKW affiliates was the National Committee for Work Time Determination (Reichsausschuß für Arbeitszeitermittlung, or REFA), established in 1924 by the employers in the metal-working industries.[19] In 1928, the REFA published a handbook which provided detailed guidance for the calculation of standard piecework times as a basis for 'fair' remuneration.[20] More importantly, by 1933 it had trained more than 10,000 engineers in the new methods, the vast majority of whom worked in specific firms rather than as independent consultants. The predominant role of the REFA in the diffusion of scientific management in Germany had clear advantages, especially concerning the uniformity of approach and terminology.

Britain, on the other hand, lacked a comparable institutional framework. The various institutions of the engineering professions grew significantly during the inter-war period, but served at best as a forum for the exchange of experiences and were in general rather sceptical of Taylorism. The National Institute of Industrial Psychology, created in 1921 with the support of leading industrialists, conducted a number of studies into the effect of scientific management methods. However, in line with the interests of an influential group of British employers such as Seebohm Rowntree, it shifted its attention more and more towards human relations and motivations.[21] Rowntree was also instrumental in the creation of the so-called Management Research Groups or MRG, the first of which he founded in 1926 together with Lyndall Urwick. An Oxford graduate, Urwick had joined the Rowntree Company in the early 1920s and was to become one of the most influential British and European management thinkers of the twentieth century. Following a US example, the MRG were intended to provide a forum where member companies could confidentially discuss a wide range of management problems. They subsequently established a number of regional groups, but their overall appeal and their membership remained rather limited.

Unlike their German counterparts, none of the organisations mentioned above was involved in the training of work study engineers or the standardisation of approaches. For the introduction of scientific management, therefore, many British employers turned towards consultants, especially after the late 1920s, when the Great Depression created a need to control and reduce production costs. The main beneficiary of these developments appears to have been the consultancy which the French immigrant Charles Bedaux had established in the United States in 1916.[22] The Bedaux system was based on his own version of scientific management, which would not have gained the approval of Taylor or his followers.[23] But it was a considerable commercial success and his consultancy developed rapidly in North America and, from the mid-1920s, also expanded internationally, often based on work for the subsidiaries of his US clients.

Bedaux was neither the first nor the only consultant to introduce scientific management methods into British companies. Between 1910 and 1924, for example, the motion study pioneer Frank B. Gilbreth and his wife Lillian had already consulted a number of firms in Britain.[24] Some of the above-mentioned institutions apparently facilitated the penetration of consultancies in Britain. The MRG's Labour Section, which had been set up in 1929, examined different work study and payment-by-results schemes, including Bedaux.[25] And Rowntree himself invited American businessmen and consultants, such as Wallace Clark, to visit his factory or to give talks at conferences.[26]

However, none of these could match the expansion of Bedaux's British subsidiary, which was established in 1926. The number of its assignments grew steadily from only two in the first year to 40 in 1933, with the cumulative total reaching 170.[27] Much of this success has been attributed to the salesmanship of Bedaux himself.[28] However, credit also needs to be given to the specific features of his system, which to a certain extent emulated the German REFA organisation.[29] It measured and standardised *all* human efforts according to a single unit of measurement, the so-called 'B', which made comparisons across any range of activities possible and thus facilitated the calculation of payments to workers and simplified monitoring. In addition, and more importantly, Bedaux claimed that the measurements to calculate the various standards were derived from the combined experience of all his engineers. As a result, the time considered 'normal' for each task lost most of its potentially arbitrary character.[30]

The success of Bedaux in Britain becomes even more apparent when compared to his performance in Germany and France, where he had also established offices in 1927 and 1929 respectively. In early 1932, only five German companies had installed the Bedaux System compared to 30 in Britain and 16 in France.[31] Since Bedaux was the only consultant active in all three countries, these numbers provide a good indication of the differences in the respective development of consultancy activities. As shown above, these differences were to a large extent driven by the availability and the role of institutional channels in the diffusion of scientific management. They increased further in the subsequent period, and especially during the Second World War.

III

In Germany, the Nazi regime initially adopted a rather critical attitude towards the rationalisation movement, because it was seen as one of the reasons for the high unemployment in the country. The German Labour Front (Deutsche Arbeitsfront, or DAF) which replaced the dissolved trade unions appeared particularly hostile. It was upon its initiative that the Bedaux Consultancy was outlawed in 1933 and its property seized.[32] However, the new government soon re-evaluated its position when it became apparent that a major improvement in productive efficiency was needed to carry out the rearmament programme and prepare the country for war. In 1935, the DAF itself established a research institute to investigate all aspects of German working people and labour.[33] Subsequently, it examined different work study systems, including REFA and Bedaux, and attempted to define the essence of 'true' rationalisation.

Consultants were among those benefiting from this change. The number of consulting engineers increased rapidly, especially during the war, from about 100 in the mid-1920s to 320 in 1942 and almost 700 in 1944.[34] In 1937, Bedaux was authorised to re-establish a consultancy together with German partners under the name Gesellschaft für Wirtschaftsberatung. In doing so, he apparently benefited from high-level protection, possibly in conjunction with the visit of the Duke of Windsor to Germany, which he helped to organise.[35] Two years later, however, Bedaux was forced to withdraw from this consultancy, which continued to operate during the war under German control. This was the result of a confidential report on the Bedaux System written by the DAF research institute. It criticised the foreign control of the consultancy rather than the technical value or usefulness of its approach.[36] Another author who compared the REFA and Bedaux systems in detail also came to a rather positive evaluation of the latter, characterising it as especially appropriate for industries with a high content of manual rather than machine labour.[37] Not surprisingly, representatives of REFA therefore did not insist on the superiority of their own system when criticising Bedaux, but on the need for a single, standardised approach in Germany as the basis for inter-firm comparisons.[38]

Both REFA and RKW played a crucial role in the intensified German rationalisation efforts before and during the Second World War. They were now controlled by the Nazi authorities which had already appointed supervisory commissioners in 1933. REFA expanded the scope of its activities, reflected in a change of name to National Committee for Work Studies (Reichsausschuß für Arbeitsstudien) in 1936. Between 1933 and 1945, it trained an additional 30,000 engineers. The RKW vastly increased the number of industry surveys started in 1929 with the declared intention to improve economic efficiency. By 1940, about 900 companies had participated in these surveys, covering over 100 branches of the economy.[39] It also carried out a number of special rationalisation studies, some of them of a rather sinister nature, concerning, for example, the 'optimum economic use' of the Jewish ghetto in Warsaw.[40]

Thus, once again, the common institutions, now under the control of the Nazi authorities rather than industry, carried the brunt of the rationalisation effort in Germany. In Britain, by contrast, much of the increase in productive efficiency during the same period was accomplished by private management consultancies. In the 1930s, the British Bedaux Consultancy continued to expand in terms of new clients and assignments, but more or less stagnated in terms of annual turnover, which reached a peak of £165,000 in 1934 and then declined slightly until the outset of the war.[41] This development might have been influenced by a few highly publicised strikes against the installation of the Bedaux system at the beginning of the decade.[42] But the consultancy also fell victim to its own success, which prompted a number of spin-offs. Thus, in 1934, Leslie Orr, a Sales Manager at Bedaux, formed a consultancy partnership with Lyndall Urwick, who had been Director of the International Management Institute in Geneva from 1928 until its closure in 1933. In the same year, Maurice Lubbock, who had experienced the Bedaux system as a client, established Production Engineering, for which he hired the Bedaux consultant Robert Bryson as Managing Director.[43]

Probably even more important was the increasing unpopularity of Bedaux himself, due to his association with the Duke of Windsor and the Nazis. In 1936, under pressure from his directors, Bedaux agreed to relinquish the majority financial control, and British Bedaux Ltd became the first and, for a long time, only consultancy to be quoted on the London Stock Exchange. Two years later, an operating company was formed, called Associated Industrial Consultants or AIC.[44] AIC's fortunes turned with the beginning of the war, together with the prospects of the consultancy industry as a whole. From £134,000 in 1939/40 annual turnover soared to £342,000 in 1944/45, and the cumulative number of assignments increased from 375 at the end of 1939 to 659 by the end of 1945. The government, and especially Sir Stafford Cripps, the Minister in charge of Aircraft Production, encouraged the use of consultancies.[45] But with the exception of his Ministry and the Royal Ordnance Filling Factories, all of AIC's clients during the war were private firms. The government thus acted as an intermediary and helped to overcome potential reluctance of the users, similar to the role played by the MRG in the previous decade. Comparatively little is known about the French consultancy market during the same period. A number of new consultancies were established in the 1930s, including, for example, the Bureau des Ingénieurs-conseil en Rationalisation, or BICRA, which pioneered human relations approaches in France, but disappeared with the death of its founder Jean Coutrot in 1941.[46] The French Bedaux subsidiary expanded significantly and by 1939 employed about 80 consultants and had installed his system in 350 companies.[47] It continued to operate during the war, introducing his system in several factories of the French aluminium producer Pechiney.[48]

Thus, at the end of the Second World War, the British and the French consultancy markets were well developed. In both countries, but especially in Britain, institutions appear to have played a rather minor role in the wartime rationalisation efforts. In Germany by contrast, the RKW and its affiliates, especially REFA, continued to be the major channels for the improvement of efficiency.

IV

The first post-war decade saw a remarkable degree of continuity. In Britain, consultancies continued to expand considerably. The same was true for France where the government also began to play an important role in the efforts to improve productivity. In Germany, after a short period of uncertainty, the old institutions re-emerged and, once again, occupied centre-stage. The respective involvement of consultants, private sector institutions and governments in the so-called productivity drive is particularly instructive in this respect, and highlights the differences between the three countries very well. The technical assistance programme was launched as part of the Marshall Plan in 1948, and included productivity missions of representatives from industry, labour and government to the United States as well as road shows, training programmes and factory visits by American specialists in Europe. Participating countries established their own productivity centres and, in 1953, a European Productivity Agency, or EPA, was created to co-ordinate their work.[49]

In Britain, consultants were closely associated with the efforts to increase productivity. Norman Pleming, the Managing Director of AIC, was seconded to the Anglo-American Council on Productivity (AACP) as 'Honorary Consultant'. Together with his US counterpart, he drafted a comprehensive report on the Council's activities which later served as a basis for Graham Hutton's book, *We Too Can Prosper.*[50] In addition, the Labour government supported a number of showcase consultancy interventions, especially in the textile industry. For example, in 1946 Production Engineering was asked by the Cotton Board to improve the efficiency of the cardroom in the Musgrave Spinning Company Mill in Bolton, Lancashire. The consultancy recommended a number of measures, including the introduction of an incentive wage scheme, which were approved by the management, the workers and the local union. Their implementation resulted in increased earnings of 30 per cent for the operatives, while reducing total labour costs by ten per cent.[51]

Consultants also became involved in the British Institute of Management, or BIM, where business and labour representatives could discuss ways to improve management methods. Its creation in 1947/48 was actively promoted by Sir Stafford Cripps, then President of the Board of Trade, and, from 1947, Chancellor of the Exchequer.[52] Lyndall Urwick and three other consultants were invited to become members of the BIM Council. Most importantly, in 1952 the BIM established a register of 'approved' consultants, intended to address the quality control problem. Consultancies wanting to be included had to provide details about the qualifications of their staff and submit names of clients who were contacted and asked to assess the quality of the services received. Panel members also had to subscribe to a code of conduct.[53]

The British consultancy market grew at an unprecedented pace, both in terms of fee income and staff. It was dominated by four large service providers, the so-called 'Big Four': AIC, Urwick, Orr & Partners, Production Engineering and Personnel Administration, which had been established by the former AIC Director Ernest Butten in 1943. The Big Four founded the Management Consultancies Association (MCA) in 1956. In its annual report for 1961, the MCA estimated that the revenue of its member firms had increased by more than ten per cent per annum since 1952, 'after allowing for any increase in fees to offset the rising costs of high grade staff over the period'. By 1962, the Big Four together employed 1,100 consultants in the British Isles, making it the most developed market in Europe.[54]

In Germany, the number of those involved in different types of consultancy activities apparently doubled between 1950 and 1960. However, compared to Britain, the German consultancy market remained rather underdeveloped. In 1954, 25 individual consultants established the Bund Deutscher Unternehmensberater, or BDU, as a sort of 'club'. Until the 1960s, no large service providers emerged, with the exception of the consultancy founded by the engineer Gerhard Kienbaum in Gummersbach immediately after the war. Focusing initially on technical services, he gradually expanded into other areas, such as management consulting and executive search. By the mid-1960s, he employed more than 100 consultants in several offices.[55]

Once again, the availability and strength of institutional channels has to be seen as a major reason for these developments. Both the RKW and the REFA re-emerged shortly after the war, initially at a regional level. They were officially re-established in 1950, with a number of important changes, mainly concerning the participation of union representatives in their governing bodies and the decentralisation of activities. The importance of the RKW, now Rationalisierungs-Kuratorium der Deutschen Wirtschaft, can be seen in the fact that it became the German productivity centre.[56]

Among those who went on a productivity mission to the United States in the spring of 1952 was a group of German REFA engineers. They met leading proponents of time and motion study, visited a number of companies and spoke to management and labour representatives. Overall, they were not impressed, and pinpointed especially the lack of uniformity in the development, teaching and application of work study. In contrast, they highlighted the advantages of the German system, where the REFA created standardised terminology and principles in collaboration with representatives of the trade unions and the employers' associations.[57]

German engineers showed some interest in other systems, such as Methods Time Measurement (MTM). The Bedaux system was also back on the agenda, at least judging from the number of publications about it in the early 1950s.[58] However, the REFA continued to dominate the implementation of work study in Germany. Its monopoly-like position was confirmed by a representative survey, conducted on its behalf among industrial firms in March 1956.[59] An overwhelming majority of companies (71 per cent) considered work study to be indispensable, and 78 per cent had their own internal work study department. Asked which system they used, 80 per cent of respondents named REFA, three per cent Bedaux and five per cent others.[60]

In France, the comparable institutions were further weakened after the war as a result of the growing public influence on the one hand and the activities of private consultancies on the other. Unlike the RKW, the CNOF was not chosen as the French productivity centre. This task fell to a specially created Commissariat which was government-controlled despite participation from employer and – initially – labour representatives. The CNOF subsequently tried to get more involved in further management education, but initially with little success.[61] The CGOST, renamed the Commission Générale d'Organisation Scientifique (CEGOS) in 1936, gradually developed into a consultancy with a focus on training and human resources. Overall, the French consultancy market developed considerably during the immediate post-war period, with the expansion of the existing service providers like Paul Planus and the emergence of a 'second generation', including André Vidal, Pierre Michel and Yves Bossard. Almost all of them were firmly anchored in the Taylorist tradition. This is clearly reflected in the name of their association, Association Française des Conseils en Organisation Scientifique, or AFCOS, which was established at the end of the 1940s.[62]

The change of its name to Association Française des Conseillers en Direction, or AFCOD, in the early 1960s was one indicator of the major changes which occurred in the European consultancy markets from the late 1950s. They gradually became more similar, both in terms of the service providers and the types of services, but without the differences described above being completely eradicated.[63]

V

The preceding sections have demonstrated that these differences in the use of consultancies can be explained to a large extent by the availability and the strength of institutions providing an alternative channel for the diffusion of Taylorism. Germany is the best example of the effect of these institutions on the evolution of consultancy activities. The REFA all but monopolised the diffusion of work study in German industry. It developed standardised approaches which were widely disseminated through the training of engineers. The RKW provided an umbrella for the rationalisation movement as a whole and, based on this unique position, managed to compile industry-wide data which served as a useful benchmark for inter-firm comparisons. In such a framework, where information was shared relatively freely among companies, there was little need for consultancies.

Britain occupied the opposite end of the spectrum. Here, institutions and, at certain times, the government acted as intermediaries between the consultancies and their users. Their actual role ranged from the promotion of an exchange of experiences to an active encouragement of consultancy use. It probably reached its most developed stage in the establishment of the BIM consultancy register, which provided potential users with important information about the quality of possible service providers. These institutions thus contributed to the significant development of the British consultancy market since the 1930s.

France was situated somewhere between the other two. A number of institutions emerged which had similar ambitions to their German counterparts. However, they never achieved the same level of unity and, as a consequence, largely failed to provide an alternative channel for the diffusion of Taylorism. Most of them focused on the exchange of information and experiences, which left enough room for the development of consultancies, many of them of American origin. Unlike their British equivalents, the French institutions do not seem to have facilitated the penetration of these consultancies.

These patterns emerged in the inter-war period. They changed little until the late 1950s. The Second World War played an important role, because the need to improve productive efficiency accelerated developments and thus accentuated the existing differences. This is particularly obvious in the case of Germany, where the Nazi regime, after some initial hesitation, relied extensively on the existing institutions for the rationalisation of industry in preparation for war. With the exception of France, where the government assumed a more important role, the developments after 1945 show a significant degree of continuity, highlighted by the different involvement of consultancies and institutions in the productivity drive.

NOTES

The author would like to thank Mary Rose, Mark Casson, Patrick Fridenson as well as two anonymous referees for valuable comments on an earlier draft. The usual disclaimer applies. He is also indebted to Nick Tiratsoo for providing him with a number of useful references and the Nuffield Foundation for sponsoring his research on the Bedaux Consultancy.

1. See V.-W. Mitchell, 'Problems and Risks in the Purchasing of Consultancy Services', *The Service Industries Journal*, Vol.14 No.3 (July 1994), pp.315–39; C. Sauviat, 'Le conseil: un marché-réseau singulier', in J. de Bandt and J. Gadrey (eds.), *Relations de service, marchés de service* (Paris, 1994), pp.241–62; and T. Clark, *Managing Consultants: Consultancy as the Management of Impressions* (Buckingham, 1995).
2. R.H. Coase, 'The Nature of the Firm', *Economica*, new series, Vol.4 (Nov. 1937), pp.386–405; and O. Williamson, *The Economic Institutions of Capitalism: Firms, Markets, Relational Contracting* (New York, 1985).
3. More details and additional references can be found in M. Kipping, 'Management Consultancies in Germany, Britain and France, 1900–60', University of Reading, Discussion Papers in Economics and Management, Series A, Vol.IX (1996/97), No.350.
4. See, for the diffusion of Taylorism in general, J.A. Merkle, *Management and Ideology: The Legacy of the International Scientific Management Movement* (Berkeley, CA, 1980) and D. Nelson (ed.), *A Mental Revolution: Scientific Management since Taylor* (Columbus, OH, 1992). This article will use the terms scientific management and Taylorism interchangeably.
5. For an overview, B. Kogut and D. Parkinson, 'The Diffusion of American Organizing Principles to Europe', in B. Kogut (ed.), *Country Competitiveness: Technology and the Organizing of Work* (Oxford, 1993), pp.179–202, and M.F. Guillén, *Models of Management. Work, Authority, and Organization in a Comparative Perspective* (Chicago, IL, 1994); for the evolution of British, German and French companies during the twentieth century the contributions of Jones, Wengenroth and Fridenson in A.D. Chandler *et al.* (eds.), *Big Business and the Wealth of Nations* (New York, 1997).
6. For the former, S. Kreis, 'The Diffusion of an Idea: A History of Scientific Management in Britain, 1890–1945' (unpublished Ph.D. dissertation, University of Missouri-Columbia, 1990); for the latter, K. Whitston, 'Scientific Management and Production Management Practice in Britain between the Wars', *Historical Studies in Industrial Relations*, No.1

(March 1996), pp.47–75. Earlier, Craig Littler had suggested yet another explanation, according to which Bedaux was important, but the actual implementation of his system hampered by widespread resistance from the shop floor: C.R. Littler, *The Development of the Labor Process in Capitalist Societies: A Comparative Study of the Transformation of Work Organization in Britain, Japan and the USA* (London, 1982).

7. M. Casson, *Information and Organization: A New Perspective on the Theory of the Firm* (Oxford, 1997).

8. There are other conduits for the transfer of management know-how, such as graduates, management literature or multinationals; see, for an overview, P. Fridenson, 'La circulation internationale des modes manageriales', in J.-P. Bouilloud and B.-P. Lecuyer (eds.), *L'invention de la gestion: Histoire et pratiques* (Paris, 1994), pp.81–9. These are, however, not directly comparable with consultancies or intermediary institutions, since they do not require the establishment of a trust-based relationship.

9. See, for Britain and Germany, J. Hammerschmidt, 'Die unabhängige Wirtschaftsberatung in Deutschland. Stand und Ausbaumöglichkeiten unter Berücksichtigung ausländischer Erfahrungen' (doctoral dissertation, University of Erlangen-Nürnberg, 1964), pp.49–50, 64 and 87; for France, P. Fridenson, 'Un tournant taylorien de la société française (1904–1918)', *Annales ESC*, No.5 (Sept.–Oct. 1987), pp.1031–60, here p.1040.

10. For this and the following in detail ibid. and A. Moutet, 'Les origines du système de Taylor en France. Le point de vue patronal (1907–1914)', *Le mouvement social*, No.93 (Oct.–Dec. 1975), pp.15–49.

11. For the developments during the inter-war period, see A. Moutet, *Les logiques de l'entreprise. L'effort de rationalisation dans l'industrie française de l'entre-deux-guerres* (Paris, 1997).

12. Merkle, *Management and Ideology*, pp.158–66, and D. Reid, 'Fayol: excès d'honneur ou excès d'indignité?', *Revue française de gestion*, No.70 (Sept.–Oct. 1988), pp.151–9.

13. See for details on these institutions R.R. Locke, *The End of the Practical Man: Entrepreneurship and Higher Education in Germany, France and Great Britain, 1880–1940* (London, 1984); O. Henry, 'Le conseil, un espace professionel autonome?', *Entreprises et Histoire*, No.7 (Dec. 1994), pp.37–58, here pp.41–4; and Moutet, *La logique de l'entreprise*.

14. See, for the diffusion of scientific management in Germany, among others H. Homburg, 'Le taylorisme et la rationalisation de l'organisation du travail en Allemagne (1918–1939)', in M. de Montmollin and O. Pastré (eds.), *Le taylorisme* (Paris, 1984), pp.99–113; Guillén, *Models of Management*, pp.100–121; and M. Nolan, *Visions of Modernity: American Business and the Modernisation of Germany* (New York, 1994).

15. W. von Schütz, 'Das Treuhandprinzip steht im Vordergrund. Über die Entwicklung der freiberuflichen Wirtschaftsberatung in Deutschland', *Junge Wirtschaft*, Vol.6 No.7 (July 1958), pp.293–4; M. Ricke, 'Die freiberufliche Unternehmensberatung 1900 bis 1960: Entstehung und Entwicklung eines Berufs im deutschen Sprachgebiet' (unpublished MA dissertation, University of Munich, 1989), pp.22–4; and Hammerschmidt, 'Die unabhängige Wirtschaftsberatung', pp.50–51.

16. *50 Jahre AWF 1918–1968* (Freiburg/Br., 1968). In 1923, the AWF became affiliated with the RKW (see below) and after 1950 co-operated closely with the REFA.

17. For the history of the RKW, in addition to the references in note 14 above, see Locke, *The End of the Practical Man*, pp.273–84; H.W. Büttner, *Das Rationalisierungs-Kuratorium der Deutschen Wirtschaft* (Düsseldorf, 1973); and M. Pohl, 'Die Geschichte der Rationalisierung. Das RKW 1921–1996', in *Rationalisierung sichert Zukunft. 75 Jahre RKW* (Eschborn, 1996), pp.85–115.

18. See the RKW's annual reports for 1929 and 1931, pp.16–18 and 44–65 respectively, RKW Library, Eschborn.

19. For the early history of REFA, see H. Böhrs *et al.*, *Grundlagen und Praxis des Arbeits- und Zeitstudiums* (Munich, 1948), Vol.I, pp.19–28; and '30 Jahre REFA', *Refa-Nachrichten*, Vol.7 No.4 (Dec. 1954); for later developments and the current structure see REFA, *Methodenlehre des Arbeitsstudiums*, Teil 1: *Grundlagen* (München, 1984), pp.28–33.

20. *Refa-Buch. Einführung in die Arbeitszeitermittlung* (Berlin, 1928). A second, revised and extended version was published in 1933.

21. See Guillén, *Models of Management*, pp.205–53; and Whitston, 'Scientific Management', pp.52–60. For the life and influence of Rowntree, see A. Briggs, *Social Thought and Social Action: A Study of the Work of Seebohm Rowntree, 1871–1954* (London, 1961).

22. J. Christy, *The Price of Power: A Biography of Charles Eugène Bedaux* (Toronto, 1984), which has to be read with caution since it contains a number of inaccuracies; for the development and expansion of his consultancy, see M. Kipping and C. Sauviat, 'Global Management Consultancies: Their Evolution and Structure', University of Reading, Discussion Papers in International Investment & Business Studies, Series B, Vol IX (1996/97), No.221; and S. Kreis, 'The Diffusion of Scientific Management: The Bedaux Company in America and Britain, 1926–1945', in Nelson (ed.), *A Mental Revolution*, pp.156–74.

23. According to Kreis, they would have considered him 'little more than a quack or charlatan', ibid., p.168.

24. P. Tisdall, *Agents of Change: The Development and Practice of Management Consultancy* (London, 1982), pp.16–20. For the early experiments of British companies with Taylorism see also Kreis, 'The Diffusion of an Idea'.

25. Meeting reports of 5 Sept. 1929, 8 May 1930 and 21 April 1932 in the MRG papers at the Archives of the British Library of Political & Economic Science in London, Box 12, Slip 474 (W/8/29-34/12).

26. Briggs, *Social Thought*, pp.182–3.

27. Some of these assignments were for the same companies, but in different factories or workshops, see Client/Assignment List, 1924–1947, from the private archives of John E. Pleming, who joined the consultancy in 1948 [hereafter: Pleming Papers]. I am very grateful to Mr Pleming for letting me use this material.

28. For example, by Kreis, 'The Diffusion of Scientific Management'.

29. For each task, the 'normal' time of activity and of rest were established and translated into a standard hour which consisted invariably of 60 B. For example, if a specific task required two minutes of activity and one minute of rest, 60 B corresponded to a normal worker carrying out this task 20 times; see in detail P. Laloux, *Le système Bedaux de calcul des salaires* (Paris, 1950); for a summary, see Littler, *The Development of the Labor Process*, pp.108–12, and Kreis, 'The Diffusion of Scientific Management', pp.161–5.

30. For more details, see Kipping, 'Management Consultancies'.

31. According to information provided by the British Bedaux Consultancy to the Trade Union Congress. See 'The TUC Examines the Bedaux System of Payment by Results', TUC General Council, 1933, p.7, Modern Records Centre, Warwick University, MSS.292/112/2.

32. Christy, *The Price of Power*, p.93.

33. See for this and the following the Institute's first annual report, *Jahrbuch 1936*. Hrsg. vom Arbeitswissenschaftlichen Institut der Deutschen Arbeitsfront (Berlin, n.d.), REFA Archives, Darmstadt.

34. Ricke, 'Die freiberufliche Unternehmensberatung', p.27.

35. For details of this visit and Bedaux's association with the former Edward VIII, see Christy, *The Price of Power*, chapters 11 to 13.

36. *Das Bedaux-System* (Berlin, [1938]). It can be found in the Staatsbibliothek München.

37. E. Rochau, *Das Bedaux-System, seine praktische Anwendung und kritischer Vergleich zwischen Refa- und Bedaux-System* (Würzburg, 2nd edn. 1939).

38. See F. Schlund, 'Das Bedaux-System', in *Refa und Leistungssteigerung. Vorträge der Refa-Jahrestagung Gotha 1939* (Berlin, 1940), pp.46–67. He characterised the simultaneous use of both systems in Germany as 'unhealthy'.

39. RKW, *Größere Wirtschaftlichkeit durch geordnetes Rechnungswesen und Betriebsuntersuchungen* (Leipzig, 2nd edn. 1942), pp.63–97, especially the table on p.94. This book also covered accounting, another area where the Nazi regime aimed for and achieved more standardisation.

40. Pohl, 'Die Geschichte der Rationalisierung', pp.92–3.

41. To £134,000 in 1939/40; AIC Ltd (and predecessors), Annual Turnover, Pleming Papers.

42. For the strikes against Bedaux, see especially Littler, *The Development of the Labor Process*, chapter 9; for the only known case where attempts to install the system were completely

82 INSTITUTIONS AND THE EVOLUTION OF MODERN BUSINESS

abolished, see L.L. Downs, 'Industrial Decline, Rationalisation and Equal Pay: The Bedaux
Strike at Rover Automobile Company', *Social History*, Vol.15 No.1 (Jan. 1990), pp.45–73.
43. Tisdall, *Agents of Change*, pp.28–35, 55–9.
44. For this and the following, see M. Brownlow, 'A History of Inbucon', unpublished
manuscript, chapters 4 and 5, Pleming Papers. In 1943, the holding company was renamed
Inbucon.
45. Tisdall, *Agents of Change*, pp.35–41. For the important role of Cripps in general, see N.
Tiratsoo and J. Tomlinson, *Industrial Efficiency and State Intervention: Labour 1939–51*
(London, 1993).
46. For more details, see Henry, 'Le conseil', pp.44–6; for Coutrot's role see also L. Boltanski,
The Making of a Class: Cadres in French Society (Cambridge, 1987), pp.121–2.
47. Laloux, *Le système Bedaux*, p.10.
48. From ongoing research of the author, who would like to thank Ludovic Cailluet for his help
in identifying some of the relevant sources in the Pechiney Archives at the Institut pour
l'histoire de l'aluminium in Paris.
49. For details, see A.B. Carew, *Labour Under the Marshall Plan: The Politics of Productivity
and the Marketing of Management Science* (Manchester, 1987); R.F. Kuisel, 'The Marshall
Plan in Action: Politics, Labor, Industry and the Program of Technical Assistance', in M.
Lévy-Leboyer and R. Girault (eds.), *Le plan Marshall et le relèvement économique de
l'Europe* (Paris, 1993), pp.335–58; and J. McGlade, 'The Illusion of Consensus: American
Business, Cold War Aid and the Reconstruction of Western Europe 1948–1958'
(unpublished Ph.D. dissertation, George Washington University, 1995).
50. Pleming was the first British national who joined the Bedaux Consultancy in 1926. He
became Managing Director of AIC in 1939 when the two American Directors, Frank Mead
and Colwell Carney, went back to the United States; for his career and his role in the AACP,
see Brownlow, 'A History of Inbucon', Pleming Papers.
51. *Report on Labour Redeployment in the Musgrave Mill Cardroom, Bolton*, published by the
Labour Department of the Cotton Board, March 1948. Many thanks to Mary Rose for
providing me with a copy of this report. See also J. Singleton, *Lancashire on the Scrapheap:
The Cotton Industry, 1945–1970* (Oxford, 1991), chapter 4.
52. See note 45 above.
53. 'Role of the Business Consultant', *The Statist*, 28 June 1952, pp.932–3. This register, initially
reserved to BIM members, was later made available to the general public as Management
Consultancy Services Information Bureau. It was closed in 1980 for budgetary reasons; see
Tisdall, *Agents of Change*, pp.93–4, 107–8.
54. The above is based on information in the MCA Archives in London, boxes 6 and 22; see also
Tisdall, *Agents of Change*, pp.9 and 41.
55. Ricke, 'Die freiberufliche Unternehmensberatung', pp.30–37, and *Kienbaum und Partner:
Geschichte einer Unternehmensberatung 1945–1995* (Gummersbach, 1995).
56. See the RKW's annual report for 1951/52, especially pp.21–32, and for the German
participation in the productivity missions see *Internationaler Erfahrungsaustausch.
Zusammenstellung der Studienreisen und deren Teilnehmer im Bereich der gewerblichen
Wirtschaft* (Berlin, 1957), both available in the RKW Library.
57. *Das Arbeitsstudium in den USA. Bericht einer deutschen Studiengruppe* (München, 1955).
58. For example, B. Fischer, 'Grundzüge des Bedaux-Systems', *Zeitschrift für
Betriebswirtschaft*, Vol.20 No.10 (Oct. 1950), pp.637–46, and 'Methode der analytischen
Arbeitsbewertung zur Bestimmung der Grundlohnskala nach Bedaux', ibid., Vol.21 No.1
(Jan. 1951), pp.35–43. In 1952, a third edition of Rochau's comparison between REFA and
Bedaux systems (see note 37 above) was published.
59. Summarised in *Refa-Nachrichten*, Vol.9 No.3 (Sept. 1956), pp.91–4.
60. Twelve per cent named no specific system and 13 per cent did not reply. It should be noted
that Bedaux obtained its share mainly in the rubber industry where it almost equalled the
importance of REFA (46 versus 53 per cent). This is no surprise, since the largest producer,
Continental, had adopted the system in 1926, becoming Bedaux's first German client. In line
with its origins, the REFA was strongest in the producer goods sector (92 per cent).
61. M. Kipping and J.-P. Nioche, 'Much Ado about Nothing? Productivity Drive and

Management Training in France (1945–1960)', in T. Gourvish and N. Tiratsoo (eds.), *Missionaries and Managers* (Manchester, 1998).
62. Henry, 'Le conseil', pp.48–52.
63. For these developments, see M. Kipping, 'The U.S. Influence on the Evolution of Management Consultancies in Britain, France, and Germany Since 1945', *Business and Economic History*, Vol.25 No.1 (Fall 1996), pp.112–23.

Financial Reconstruction and Industrial Reorganisation in Different Financial Systems: A Comparative View of British and Swedish Institutions during the Inter-War Period

HANS SJÖGREN

University of Linköping

Studies of financial distress have recently enlivened the institutional economics literature. While the main focus has been on the role of banks in the transformation of industry, other economic historians and economists have concentrated on the relationship between financial reconstructions and capital structure. Some have tried to answer the somewhat speculative question of whether banks have failed industry or not, whilst others have explored the role of commercial banks' in inter-war Europe.[1] The tools of institutional economics allow for a reinterpretation of the traditional view of financial reconstructions, or at the very least provide new insights into these phenomena. Similarly, theoretical models are enhanced by being placed in an historical context. Although economic history demonstrates that countries' financial systems differ institutionally depending on the timing of industrialisation,[2] few comparative studies have been carried out on the micro- as opposed to the macro-level. This empirical study combines a survey approach with a comparative historical methodology and has the objective of discovering the inner logic and structure of financial reconstructions in the UK and Sweden during the inter-war period. This essay will identify and explain the differences in experience.

II

When empirical analyses are related to the institutional economics literature, they show that the composition of financial contracts and the affiliation of contracts by various investors have a substantial impact on the process of reconstruction.[3] The capital structure determines the direction of future capital flows and the influence this will have on strategic decision making within the firm. In a reconstruction situation, these functions are very often renegotiated, since either the firm cannot meet its obligations or it simply does not want to. Another strand of this expanding literature is the bargaining which occurs between the external providers of capital; shareholders (trustees), holders of debentures/bonds, and the banks. Studies have, for example, analysed how variations in bankruptcy laws affect bargaining.[4] A fundamental issue is the impact which the possibility of renegotiating in the future has on the initial design of the contract, and whether the contracting parties, through the design and the distribution of financial contracts, are able to influence such renegotiations. This indicates an information problem in the interaction between financial and non-financial organisations in which investors as outsiders lack full knowledge of the circumstances of the borrower. It has been argued, however, that the existence of certificates of indebtedness strengthens the bargaining power of the shareholders in future negotiations between management and shareholders.[5] Similarly, another study has shown how a capital structure, where many investors specialise in short- and long-term claims, can lead to lower costs for capital compared to a structure with only one investor.[6]

A starting point in the theoretical literature is the difficulty which external investors have in distinguishing between firms that are able to pay and companies that cannot, even though they have enough liquidity. According to the theory of incomplete contracts it is nearly impossible to stipulate and write down exact criteria for each situation. In a case where a firm claims that it is unable to pay, although it is in fact capable, the investor might have to force a liquidation of assets. Here the company refuses to meet the obligations stipulated in the contract, despite the fact that substantial firm-specific values are being spoiled. To a certain extent, the capital structure is determined by an adjustment between the demand for pushing the management to pay when it is capable *and* immediate liquidation when it is incapable of paying. Thus, the costs of financial crisis are determined by endogenous factors. When there is an obvious risk that the management of the firm is incorrectly arguing that it is unable to pay, the external financial costs for continuing the commitment have to increase. A possible prediction is that larger and more complex firms, with relatively better possibilities to withhold resources, will have a compound capital structure aiming to take measures against renegotiation. This prediction corresponds with data from the US.

There are significant international differences in the financial arrangements and governance structure of firms which influence the behaviour of both lenders and borrowers during periods of crisis and reconstruction. At the one extreme are countries such as Japan and Germany, where close ties between industrial firms and banks, within financial groupings, lead to an increase in investment during crises. In such circumstances the interests of the group exceed those of the individual investor, a situation which reduces the likelihood of liquidation if a firm becomes financially distressed.[7] At the other end of the spectrum is the United States, where the interests of the creditor are distinct from those of the borrowing firm, a situation which increases the likelihood of liquidations during periods of financial stringency. Set against these two extremes, the Swedish system is generally assumed to be reminiscent of the Japanese and German system, whereas British arrangements are more like the American system.

Arm's length financial arrangements, such as those in Britain and the United States, explicitly aim to deter firms from claiming an inability to meet debts during a crisis when they are capable or just capable of paying. On the other hand, in control-oriented countries such as Japan, Germany and Sweden, financial arrangements stress the importance of reducing potential liquidation costs when a firm is distressed. Viewed in this way, it would seem that the costs of arm's length arrangements appear to be due to liquidations of firms which were suffering from short-term crises but were profitable in the long term. On the other hand, under the control-oriented system, costs stem from firms which are unprofitable over a long period. It is questionable which system is preferable, since arm's length arrangements may be better when a liquidity crisis is a sign of long-term difficulties of profitability. On the other hand, the control-oriented system may be better when a liquidity shortage is less informative, for example, during a general economic downturn.

In Sweden, more than 50 per cent of the industrial workers during the 1980s were linked to one of the two main financial groups. In addition, the Swedish financial groups have traditionally, at least during downturns, provided rescue packages and had extensive ties to the large firm sector. During liquidity crises in the inter-war years, the banks were influential on both the debt and the equity side, and thus increased their already strong positions. Reconstructions, in relation to the Deflationary Crisis of 1920–22, revealed a certain pattern where firms belonging to a financial group got more help from the house bank to stay in business than firms outside.[8] In one-bank relationships the investor kept all the main financial contracts in the firm (credit, deposit, bond, even shares). The bank was playing the role of unofficial receiver, and, in case of renegotiations of debt contracts, or when the firm was likely to go bankrupt, the main banks sometimes presented the other investors with an ultimatum to carry all the responsibility for the reconstruction of the firm.

In Britain, on the other hand, without the close ties of a financial grouping, the investor's position is strengthened during renegotiations through the sharp distinction between the interests of the firm and those of the creditor. Such arrangements inevitably deter firms from arguing they are incapable of paying when they are in fact able. In the context of the financial reconstructions of large firms in Britain, a number of studies have discussed the role of clearing banks, merchant banks and the state.[9] In Britain's staple industries, such as steel and textiles, the government and the Central Bank played a key role in the industrial reorganisation which followed the financial problems in both branches. However, the plans drawn up by the Bank of England, institutionalised and implemented through two sub-organisations, the Securities Management Trust (SMT) and Bankers Industrial Development (BID), were not successful in the long run. To some extent, the behaviour of the Central Bank preserved the old industrial structure by rescuing firms which had long been unprofitable. These examples suggest, therefore, that whilst there are similarities with the American model and parallels with the Swedish system, instead of maintaining an arm's length relationship with clients, the Bank of England imposed certain institutional arrangements on the industry. Many British banks developed long-term commitments to firms, giving them a control-orientation more akin to that in Germany, Japan and Sweden.

The objective of this article is to provide a reinterpretation of the process of financial reconstruction and industrial reorganisation in inter-war Britain and Sweden through a comparison of the two systems. Special attention is paid to the behaviour of private banks in the two countries during a period of financial distress, when bargaining power was likely to have been transferred from the firm to any external investors.[10] The essay will demonstrate that traditional views of bank–industry relations can be misleading. Instead of banks in Britain pursuing arm's length arrangements and those in Sweden being more control-oriented, financial institutions in the two countries pursued similar policies. Thus, whilst in Britain banks became involved in industrial transformation, in Sweden there were elements of a more distant relationship between banks and industry.

The behaviour of the investors might differ depending on the business cycle, so it is important to remember that the central hypothesis of this essay only holds when firms are financially distressed. It therefore focuses on the effects of financial distress on debt and equity and the consequences for production, management and employment. In theoretical studies of industrial finance, the role of the state and the Central Bank has been left out.[11] Since these institutions were deeply involved in the transformation of industry during the inter-war period, it seems natural to incorporate them in this analysis. Secondly, studies of financial reconstructions do not consider the social network of interlocking directorships which were used as an instrument for information transmission and control over the distressed firm.[12] A principal reason for studying the behaviour of intermediaries during a period of industrial downturn is that their intentions, with regard to their commitments, become even more evident under stress. The situation calls for intervention whilst the statements from the various parties concerned are also relatively more frequent. In addition, during a financial crisis measures may be taken that go beyond the conditions stipulated in the formal contract. As a result it becomes possible to focus on how new sets of rules are introduced and institutionalised.

III

In this comparative analysis, two samples of firms from the UK and Sweden have been chosen, each consisting of 12 firms, although there is no particular reason for this sample size. It would, of course, have been statistically possible and desirable to use a larger sample, and perhaps to concentrate on just one branch over a more limited period of time, instead of focusing on various branches during the whole inter-war period. The argument for keeping the numbers down is to enable the use of case studies at a later stage in the research (not included in this discussion), which would not be feasible with a large number of companies. It will, however, be difficult to form clear conclusions concerning a branch or a whole industry on the basis of these two samples. Nevertheless, use of the secondary literature allows for generalisation concerning the pattern of financial reconstruction in large-scale mature firms for the inter-war period.

To allow for comparability, only non-financial companies from the industrial sector have been chosen. The firms have been collected through a stratified random sample of companies that have had losses over a minimum of two years. A sub-criterion is a minimum share capital, to ensure they are all large-scale firms. In the case of the UK, the minimum is £3.5 million, which corresponds to SEK2 million in the Swedish case. The third criterion is that firms must have made losses during the inter-war period. If the firms had had losses more than once during this time, only the first phase of the financial problems have been taken into account in the analysis.[13] Other criteria, such as region or any other type of corporate status, have not been used in the selection of firms. (For data on share capital and bank relationships of individual firms, see the appendix.)

The selected firms are spread among a number of branches with variation partly a reflection of differences in the country-specific industrial structure and the concentration of capital intensity. British firms are mainly in iron, steel and mines, with eight out of 12 firms belonging to that branch (see Table 1). The remaining companies are in the field of shipbuilding/armaments, engineering and textiles. The Swedish sample is more diversified, although this should not be taken to indicate a generally wider

TABLE 1
SELECTED COMPANIES AND THEIR MAIN BRANCHES

Firms	Ship-building, Armaments	Iron & Steel, Mines	Engineering	Chemicals	Paper, Pulp, Sawmills	Textiles	Furniture, Carpets
Armstrong	X		X				
Austin			X				
Baldwin's		X					
Beardmore	X	X	X				
Bolckow		X					
Colville		X					
Consett		X					
Dorman Long		X					
Harland & Wolff	X						
Lancashire Cotton Corporation						X	
Richard Thomas		X					
United Steel		X					
Atlas Diesel			X				
Baltic			X				
Claes Johansson						X	
Fagersta		X	X				
Larsbo-Norns		X	X				
Lineoleumab Forshaga							X
Ljusnan					X		
Munktell			X				
Reymersholm				X			
Svenska Tändsticksab				X			
Ytterstfors-Munksund					X		
Åtvidabergs Industrier							X

Sources: Stock Exchange Official Intelligence; Stock Exchange Yearbook; Svenska aktiebolag och banker.

business structure, and the majority belong to staple industries. Thus, both samples are biased towards mature industries, since these were the ones that mainly made losses during the period. Following the prime criterion, the firms chosen, as well as the subsequent results, are only representative for large firms and branches that were financially distressed during the inter-war period. Given these characteristics, it is likely that the treatment of the firms by both banks and the Central Bank was firmer than would have been the case with younger and smaller firms.

In the analysis, certain concepts will be used to highlight particular stages in the development of the firm. 'Financial distress' characterises a stage when a company is suffering from two or more years of losses. The term 'financial reconstruction' is used as a general concept for various operations taking place in the firm due to the losses, for example, write-downs and write-offs of share capital and loan capital, building up of a reserve fund, and so on. These measures, which are presented in Tables 2 and 3 below, are the practical results of negotiations between the firm and investors. They all have one thing in common, namely the effect which they have on the capital structure. This distinguishes them from the next concept, 'industrial reorganisation', which is used in relation to changes of production. A new line of production, a reduced workforce, or managerial changes are all examples of consequences that initially strike non-financial parts of the firm.

IV

Among British financial intermediaries, the clearing banks had large commitments in the industrial sector. In relation to the total portfolio of commitments, nearly a third of the credits were granted to industry,[14] with the two most indebted branches being iron and steel, and textiles. As an example, the National Provincial Bank was heavily involved in the steel industry during the inter-war years. Of the 36 largest companies, nearly one-third had their account with National Provincial,[15] which also provided ten per cent of their overdrafts. In the case of Midland Bank and Lloyds Bank, the proportions were 7.75 and 3.4 per cent respectively. If we concentrate on the firms in our sample, most firms had so-called multi-bank relationships (see Appendix, Table 7).[16] Beside credits in one or two of the 'Big Five', it was also common to have credits with regionally based banks. Just one firm, Austin, had a one-bank relationship, with the Midland Bank. The rest had at least two credit relationships, but none had more than four. The Midland Bank had commitments in five of the firms, whilst Lloyds Bank and the National Provincial Bank were involved in four each.

During the period studied, all British firms were financially reconstructed. In addition, nearly all of them also had their industrial activity reorganised. In the majority of the cases, the financial reconstructions took the form of write-downs or write-offs of the share capital (see Appendix, Table 5). A general reduction took place in the second half of the 1920s, when half of the firms made write-downs.[17] Three other firms were forced to do the same in the 1930s. More than half of the firms had the same or less share capital in 1935 than they had had 15 years before. Thus, in real terms, the total share capital decreased during the period.

Comparing the equity and debt structure, the financial reconstructions affected the share capital to a higher degree. Although there were write-downs of loan capital, changes of creditors and loans converted to shares, these events were less frequent. Nevertheless, the evidence demonstrates that banks played an active role in reconstructions. In six cases, either the Bank of England or the banks or issuing houses became either majority or minority shareholders in the firm. The state of financial distress also had substantial non-financial implications, because in the majority of the cases

TABLE 2

OPERATIONS AND YEARS FOR BRITISH RECONSTRUCTIONS

No name given	Ar 29	Au 19-24	Ba 28	Be 28-29	Bo 29	Cl 29-30	Cn 22-25	Do 34	Ha 37	LC 35-37	Ri 28	Un 28	Freq. (n)
Type of change													
Financial reconstruction	X	X	X	X	X	X	X	X	X	X	X	X	12
Industrial reorganisation	X	X	X	X	X	X	X	X	X	X	0	X	11
Liquidation	0	0	X*	X*	X	0	0	0	0	0	0	0	3
Effects on capital structure													
Loan capital written down	0	n/a	X	X	0	0	0	0	0	0	X**	X	4
Share capital/debenture stock written down	X	X	X	X	X	0	0	X	X	X	0	X	9
Issuing of new ord. shares	X	X	X	0	0	0	0	0	X	X	0	0	6
Issuing of new pref. shares	X	X	0	X	0	X	0	X	X	X	0	0	7
Issuing of new bonds/debenture	X	X	X	X	0	X	X	X	0	X	0	X	9
Change of creditors	X	0	0	X	X	0	0	X	0	0	0	X***	5
Central Bank or banks becoming large shareholders	X	0	0	X	X	0	0	X	X	X	0	0	6
Short-term loan converted to shares	X	0	0	0	n/a	0	0	X	X	0	0	0	3
Non-financial effects													
New top management	X	X	X	X	X	X	0	X	X	0	0	X	9
Change on the board (new chairman = C)	XC	X	X	XC	XC	X	0	XC	X	X	0	XC	10
Changes of production	X	X	X	X	X	X	X	0	0	X	0	X	9
Effects on the number of employees	X	X	X	X	X	n/a	n/a	n/a	X	0	n/a	n/a	6

Notes: X   means that the operation took place whilst 0 is no operation.
        *   Some subsidiaries were liquidated.
      **   In fact an agreement on extended amortisation.
    ***   In 1924, according to the first signals of financial distress, i.e. before the actual reconstruction.

Sources: Stock Exchange Official Intelligence; Stock Exchange Yearbook; various biographies.

it led to managerial and board level changes. In five of the firms, for example, a new chairman was appointed. In addition, firms were rationalised, with changes in the extent of production and with a narrower product range being manufactured by a smaller workforce.

V

As far as the linkages between Swedish banks and industry are concerned, the commercial banks made a large part of their advances to mines, iron and steel, and manufacturing, which, in 1929, accounted for 39 per cent of the total.[18] Substantial parts of their commitments were also in sectors in the retail and commercial sectors, in finance and to private individuals. The indebted firms in the Swedish sample show a similar pattern to that in Britain. The majority of companies had multi-bank relationships, very often including one of the three major banks.[19] At this time, the 'Big Three' were Svenska Handelsbanken, Skandinaviska Kreditaktiebolaget and Stockholms Enskilda Bank (see Appendix, Table 8). The first two banks each provided short-term credits to seven of the 12 firms, whilst Stockholms Enskilda Bank had commitments in five companies. The geographical position of the firm's activities attracted various smaller and regionally based banks to provide short-term credit. In contrast to the large banks, these commitments were limited to one or two types of short-term loans, and the average length of the relationships was shorter. Often the firm increased the number of creditors at the time of the financial distress – taking rescue credits – in order to survive.[20] However, the majority of these commitments were temporary, and disappeared when the danger of bankruptcy had receded. The relationship with house banks continued as before, and, besides the rescue credits, distressed firms also got help from these banks to raise further capital on the bond and share markets.

All the Swedish firms were financially reconstructed, and most of them also had their industrial production reorganised. Six firms had to be liquidated, which was more than in the British case. Most financial reconstructions included sharp write-downs of both the loan and the share capital, and in half of the firms the share capital was reduced by more than 50 per cent between 1920 and 1925 (see Appendix, Table 6). These write-downs corresponded to reductions on the asset side in the form of devalued stocks, useless plant, overestimated portfolios of various types of certificates, and cancelled claims. Changes of capital structure were more frequent among the Swedish companies than the British. An exception to this is the turnover of creditors, which might indicate a higher degree of endurance on the side of the Swedish banks. To a large extent, new credit structures also meant new claimholders and more prominent positions for

TABLE 3
SWEDISH RECONSTRUCTIONS

Type of change	At 23-25	Ba 20-21	Cl 25-30	Fa 21-24	La 21	Lin 31-33	Lju 21-25	Mu 22-23	Re 22-24	Sv 32-35	Yt 21-26	Åt 22	Total (n)
Financial reconstruction	X	X	X	X	X	X	X	X	X	X	X	X	12
Industrial reorganisation	X	X	X	X	X	X	X	X	0	X	X	X	11
Liquidation/bankruptcy	0	X	X	0	X	0	0	X	0	0	X	X	6
Effects on capital structure													
Loan capital written down	0	X	X	X	X	0	0	X	X	0	X	X	8
Share capital written down	X	X	X	X	X	X	0	X	X	X	X	X	11
Issuing of ord. shares	0	X	0	0	X	0	0	X	X	0	0	X	5
Issuing of pref. shares	X	X	0	0	0	0	X	0	X	0	0	0	4
Issuing of bonds	0	0	X	0	0	n/a	0	0	0	0	0	0	1
Change of creditors	0	X	0	0	0	n/a	0	0	X	X	0	0	3
Central Bank or banks becoming large shareholders	X	X	n/a	X	X	n/a	X	X	X	X	X	X	10
Short-term loan converted to shares	n/a	X	X	X	X	n/a	n/a	n/a	X	0	X	0	6
Non-financial effects													
New top management	n/a	0	n/a	n/a	X	0	X	X	0	X	0	X	5
Changes on the board (new chairman = C)	0	XC	X	XC	X	XC	X	XC	0	XC	XC	0	9
Changes of production	0	X	0	0	0	0	0	0	0	0	X	X	3
Effects on the numbers of employees	X	X	X	X	n/a	0	0	X	0	X	X	X	8

Note: X means that the operation took place, whilst 0 is no operation.

Source: Svenska aktiebolag och banker, Annual reports.

the external debtholders. As in the British case, it was common that, through the process of financial reconstruction, both the Central Bank and individual commercial banks became shareholders in the distressed firms, following either the issue of new preference shares or the conversion of loans into shares.

With regard to the non-financial effects of financial distress, a similarity between the Swedish and the British firms is evident. Changes on the board, including a new chairman in six of the firms, were accompanied by new top management in at least five firms. Similarly, in most cases the workforce contracted during and after the reconstruction process.

VI

The figures above indicate, at least statistically, a similar pattern for the British and Swedish reconstructions and reorganisations during the inter-war period, and a similar institutional setting in the two countries. This makes the traditional view, with its emphasis on dissimilarities between the two countries, questionable.

In both Sweden and Britain, shareholders and debtholders began to control and govern firms at the time of their individual crises. However, there were basic structural variations between the two cases. Since many Swedish banks, through their investment companies, also had indirect ties of ownership in the large firm sector, their commitments were through both equity and debt. This implied a stronger bargaining power during the reconstructions as compared to the situation in the UK. Secondly, the British merchant banks and the issuing houses were more active in relation to the clearing banks. This was in contrast to the corresponding organisations in Sweden, where most issuing houses were controlled by the commercial banks. Regardless of which actors were involved, however, the original involvement of banks in industry was involuntary.

In Sweden, the situation after the deflationary crisis led to a discussion on how new and strong linkages between banks and industry should be avoided in the future. A state committee began to work in the 1920s, which resulted in the sale of shareholdings by banks from the mid-1930s. In contrast to the UK, the Swedish Central Bank played no active role in industrial transformation. When the Central Bank intervened, it acted as a temporary lender of last resort, as in the case of Fagersta in the first half of the 1920s and in the process following the debacle of the Kreuger Group (including Swedish Match) in the early 1930s.

When the Swedish state decided to reconstruct Wermlands Enskilda Bank in 1923, it also undertook to clear the bad debts of the clients, for example Fagersta. The state took over the liability of payment from the acceptance credit and became the major owner of the company.[21] A representative from the public lender of last resort (Earl G. von Rosen) was appointed to the board, as well as a representative from the prime creditor, Wermlandsbanken (Mr A. Eriksson). But state ownership was only temporary, and by 1926 the public share had been transferred to Svenska Handelsbanken.

The debacle of the Kreuger group and the reconstruction of Swedish Match (Svenska Tändsticksab) in the first half of 1930s illustrates to what extent the financial reconstruction was predetermined by the initial capital structure.[22] Regarding the debt structure, loans from banks totalled SEK361 million, of which 249 million was from the Swedish banks and the rest was linked to foreign creditors. Among the Swedish lenders, Skandinaviska Banken had the largest single commitment, consisting of more than SEK200 million. Representatives from both Swedish and foreign banks gave evidence to the Reconstruction Committee set up in August 1932. From the Skandinaviska Banken's point of view, the presence of Björn Prytz, who was also a member of the central board of the bank, guaranteed that the bank had a certain influence over the negotiations. Together with Jacob Wallenberg, with his international reputation, the Committee was able to produce a long-term solution to the comprehensive problems in the firm. In the aftermath of the debacle, two emerging financial groups, the Wallenberg Group and the Handelsbank Sphere, continued to control the firm from the mid-1930s, and guaranteed enough goodwill for the international business to survive.

Given that the Kreuger Group's business activity was immense and unique in Sweden, commercial banks, the Central Bank and the government became involved at an early stage. The policy of the Swedish Central Bank, however, was to leave long-term structural problems – the reorganistion of branches and individual firms – to the market and the actors themselves. After a temporary stage of cleaning up in the distressed firms and banks, the government transferred its interests to either the banking sector or the firm itself. It might be argued that the interventions from the Central Bank paved the way for industrial transformation. However, the Central Bank and the government never took the initiative or actively participated in any industrial reorganisation on a long-term basis in the way the Bank of England did under Governor Montagu Norman. Whether the British involvement was on an *ad hoc* basis or was part of a wider strategy has been discussed by several economic historians.[23] The most common line in the literature is that the Bank's participation tended to be partial and defensive, and that SMT and BID generally only became involved when the industrial and financial parties could not be persuaded to work together by any other means. Since bankruptcy did not seem to be in anyone's interest, and the lender of last resort function was less relevant, the situation with distressed areas and branches called for a new nationwide institutional arrangement, although it proved insufficient in practice.

With regard to the British clearing banks, they did not wish to be involved in British industrial transformation, and wanted to avoid active participation in reconstructions. The result, however, was similar to that in Sweden, since the clearing banks were as trapped as their Swedish counterparts. In Britain, there are many examples of the way in which the clearing banks initiated reconstruction plans, such as the transformation of Baldwin's, Beardmore, Bolckow, Colville, Dorman Long and Richard Thomas.[24] Although it is not analysed in this paper, the Midland Bank's commitment to the Royal Mail Group gives further proof of deep commitment.[25] During periods of financial distress, control of these firms was transferred to the creditors. The British creditors took part in the reconstructions by extending the overdraft limit and by providing special loans, bank guarantees and extremely short-term advances. To help the company with working capital, casual overdrafts were common in the majority of the British firms, as was the case in Sweden. These far-reaching commitments gave the banks a key role in case of prolonged distress. An important characteristic of the Swedish case was that decisive steps concerning the future of the firm appeared earlier in firms without a clear house bank relationship than occurred in Britain. In contrast, when there was a main bank involved that provided rescue credits through prolonged overdraft, the firm had a much better chance of survival. Often this delay meant that firms belonging to a financial group either overcame the difficulties when the business cycle improved or the firms merged with other firms belonging to the same financial group. However, the numerous liquidations in Sweden do not contradict the theory that reduced liquidation costs occur in a control-oriented system. The Swedish financial groups seemed to have pushed the distressed firms towards liquidation to a higher degree than expected. In addition, some of these liquidations led to mergers, initated by the banks.

Since investor-led mergers also occurred in the British case, there was a discrepancy between the official attitude from the UK banks towards distressed firms and the actual measures taken in the financial and industrial restructuring. This ambiguity could be illustrated on the micro-level. At Colville, the main creditor, the National Bank of Scotland, informally supported a regionally based merger by increasing the overdraft. This, combined with the merger with Dunlop, suggests that the bank was control-oriented, as this quotation illustrates:

(i) Massive *increase* in security ... (ii) no repayment to private cash lenders without Bank's consent. (iii) No further security to that arranged in the course of the formation of Colvilles Ltd. to be granted to the cash lenders. (iv) D.C. & S. not borrow money from any source whatsoever other than the Bank without Bank's consent. (v) Increase in interest payable.[26]

The risk had obviously increased, and, consequently, the costs of the commitment had to be adjusted, so the bank pushed the firm to make a debenture issue to clear off cash loans and overdrafts. In Dorman Long, the main creditor, Barclays Bank, used its power, which came from an unsecured overdraft of £2 million, to sell a part of the collateral, consisting of the share capital of Redpath, to a competitor. When Harland & Wolff began to make losses in 1936, the major creditor, the Midland Bank, reacted immediately and began to co-ordinate the interest of the holders of securities in case of liquidation.[27] Despite pressure from the Midland Bank for changes in the management, the chairman, Frederick Rebbeck, referred to the worldwide depression and was at first rather reluctant to agree to any kind of reconstruction. After having waited in vain for a reply from Rebbeck, the Midland proposed a 'drastic reconstruction of the capital and also the appointment of voting trustees for the Company, with wide powers to sell surplus assets and to investigate its affairs'.[28] The authorised share capital was reduced from £12.1 million to about £1.8 million, including depreciations of both ordinary and preference shares. In 1937, the general reserve, the reserve against losses on contracts and the reserve for interest, a total of £771,284 were released.[29]

Efforts by banks to carry the financially distressed firms through their periods of crisis were not confined to the mature staple industries. For example, in relation to Rover's problems during the inter-war period, it has been pointed out that 'banks and large suppliers of intermediate goods played a significant part in the shaping of industrial structure at least in the motor industry'.[30] The motive for continuing the commitment was purely a fear of losing even more capital in case of bankruptcy. A similar role was played by the bank in the case of the sugar giant Tate & Lyle, when the firm got into financial difficulties in the late 1920s.[31]

VII

In the 1950s, it was argued that 'the activities of the banks in the financial reorganisation of Baldwins and Ebbw Vale will serve to dispose of a popular illusion and show that banks are more heavily involved in industrial affairs than they are generally supposed to be'.[32] Recent studies have also stressed that the clearing banks certainly did not play a passive role in the industrial transformation.[33] One of Governor Norman's chief advisers claimed that there was no substantial difference between the *modus operandi* of a British clearing bank and a German one with respect to the combination of ownership and credit in the same firm. British banks were often 'just as much implicated in the conduct of industry as were their German counterparts. They differed only in never having systematically faced the responsibilities of the position into which they had slipped, the position of controlling partners in industry, and using their powers to compel a reorganisation of industry.'[34] The same attitude was given in the plans for the British–Italian Corporation. The chairman of Lloyds Bank 'believed the Corporation to be the natural channel through which competing manufacturers would be brought into touch with one another, unnecessary wasteful competition avoided. The Corporation could collaborate to achieve the three essential factors necessary to rival the German commercial strength, i.e. industrial, commercial and financial'.[35] This belief in the capacity of industrial capitalism (cartelisation, trusts, and so on) was definitely shared by the Swedish Wallenberg Group as well as other financial groups surrounding the Swedish commercial banks. However, as in both the UK and Germany, large Swedish firms also went bankrupt despite the control of the universal banks.[36]

The reason Swedish financial actors succeeded in reorganising more substantial parts of industry than was the case in Britain was the networks of contact surrounding nearly every bank. Through these networks the Swedish banks were able to dominate the Central Bank and others. To say that only banks in countries with market-oriented financial systems will protect their own interests and those of their depositors is misleading, for their strategies may differ.[37] Secondly, if banks do not play an active role in industrial transformation, as in the market-oriented system, the focus has to shift to the shareholders. From the Swedish case, it is clear that it was the combination of credit function and ownership that made the story successful. Since many British economic historians, however, are only occupied with the operation of banks rather than their wider relationships, they are likely to neglect this issue. Thirdly, to suggest that the British financial system was entirely market-oriented is misleading, since merchant banks were deeply inolved in the intermediation of capital. Moreover credit markets in countries such as Sweden and Germany were both sophisticated and efficient. Therefore, it is more appropriate to focus on the issue of control, and whether they are tight or on an arm's length basis.

There are many examples from both the British and the Swedish samples of how the initial capital structure influenced the reconstruction process, and led to bank control (*bankenmacht*). Bank control will be further extended if the legislation allows bank representatives to take a place on the board, especially the executive board of directors.[38] Such personal links enable the gathering of information, which in turn allows the bank both to initiate and to respond better to changes in the firm. It is likely that, by making out the documents of debt with a claim on current payments, investors could ensure that the control of the firm was transferred to the creditors in case of financial distress, or if there was a need for a reorganisation of the business. Another interpretation would be that the capital structure implicitly specified that the largest creditor would have the responsibility if the need for a reconstruction arose. The bank could demand share certificates as collateral against its claims and could be an accessory to new shares in the introductory phase of the reconstruction. Thus, the contracts of the bank were, partly automatically, to be converted into share certificates, as well as providing the power of ownership and influence as in both Japan and Germany.[39] In addition, the reconstruction processes above show similarities to corresponding situations in those countries. A reconstruction with a large investor with unprivileged instruments of debts that were converted into share certificates was also similar to the proposal for 'optimal' bankruptcy proceedings that has been outlined.[40]

This essay has shown that the UK case was more control-oriented than traditional interpretations have suggested, whilst the Swedish case sometimes reveals a reluctance from central actors to deal directly with industry, that is, a preference for an arm's length relationship with industry. Analysis of the frequency with which lenders directed reconstructions shows that both private banks and equity-holders were equally active in Sweden and the UK, and that they played a major role throughout the reconstruction process (see Table 4). Among the other actors, both management and consultants, outside the group of investors, were more active in the UK, although the small number of firms makes it difficult to generalise.

Economic historians have generally concluded that the UK financial system was not control-oriented in the inter-war years, whilst the Swedish system was. The cases presented here, however, contradict this generalisation. For example, the relatively large number of liquidations in the Swedish case indicates a significant willingness on the investors' side to protect their claims, a key feature which so far has only been observed in the United States. It is likely that Swedish banks may have sought to enforce financial contracts by threatening liquidation rather than accepting capital write-offs where these were believed to be unnecessary. The extent to which these threats were credible depended on the capital structure of the firm. Since the Swedish banks were the dominant investors, their bargaining power was strong enough to give them influence over production and the commercial decision-making process in the firms. It is plausible that the

TABLE 4
FREQUENCY OF ACTORS DIRECTING FINANCIAL RECONSTRUCTIONS AND
INDUSTRIAL REORGANISATIONS

Actors	Number of British firms	Number of Swedish firms	Total
Shareholders/trustees	7 + (1)	6	13
Management	7	4	11
Government/Treasury/Central Bank	3	2	5
Clearing banks	9 + (1)	10	19
Merchant banks/issuing houses/syndicates	1	1	2
Other consultants*	2	0	2

Note: * engineers, accounting houses, 'company doctors' etc., hired by the firms or the trustee.
In some firms it has been impossible to decide whether the initiative was taken by one,
two or three actors. Thus, the total number of actors above exceeds the number of firms.
Source: See above, Tables 2 and 3.

rapid and drastic measures used by some Swedish banks represented a conscious strategy to ensure payment in the long run. The British financial institutions, on the other hand, showed an unwillingness to pursue companies to liquidation, which might reflect the lack of government involvement in restructuring and the failure of the Bank of England's measures to win wide approbation. Since the banks exercised their responsibilities in a way that does not fit into the theory, the relation between incentive structure, bargaining power and capital structure seems to be more complex than suggested.

The behaviour of the banks, firms and the Central Bank was embedded in institutions that allowed the actors only to operate within the legal framework of their financial contracts. The exercise of these formal rights, mainly through credit committees, did not differ substantially between the two countries, although the set of instruments varied as well as official attitudes. On the other hand, the actors continuously developed informal rights, which also gave them freedom to participate actively in the transformation of industry on a longer term basis.

Since all firms in the study had liquidity problems, it could certainly be argued that this status automatically led to a more control-orientated and investor-led situation. Firmer conclusions regarding the similarities and differences in bank–industry relations in Britain and Sweden will require the analysis of a much larger proportion of firms. Further research, therefore, should explore the experience of small and medium-sized firms in a wider range of economic sectors and should include firms which were not financially distressed. In addition, in order to understand the impact of capital structure on long-term corporate control it will be necessary to explore the experience of firms after reconstruction.

APPENDIX

TABLE 5
SHARE CAPITAL FOR SELECTED COMPANIES,
1920, 1925, 1930, 1935 AND 1937 (£M*)

Company	1920	1925	1930	1935	1937
Armstrong	11.0	11.0	1.5/11.0**	11.0	11.0
Austin	5.0	5.0	3.8/5.0**	5.0	5.0
Baldwins	7.0	8.0	4.2/8.0**	8.0	8.0
Beardmore	3.0	8.0	5.1/8.0**	8.0	8.0
Bolckow	5.0	6.0	n/a	n/a	n/a
Colville***	1.5	5.0	5.0/4.5	4.5	6.0
Consett	3.5	3.5	3.5	3.5	3.5
Dorman & Long	4.5	8.0	11.2	2.0/11.2**	11.2
Harland & Wolff	8.1	12.1	12.1	12.1	1.8/12.1**
Lancashire CC	–	–	4.4	5.2	0.6/5.2**
Richard Thomas	9.0	9.0	9.0	9.0	11.0
United Steel	9.3	9.3	9.3	6.6	10.0

Notes: *   authorised share capital (not paid-up capital).
        **   first the share capital was partly written off, than it was immediately increased to
            the former amount by issue of new shares.
     ***   the company was renewed in 1930.

Sources: Guildhall Library, City of London; *Stock Exchanged Yearbook*; *Stock Exchange Official Intelligence.*

TABLE 6
SHARE CAPITAL FOR SELECTED COMPANIES,
1920, 1925, 1930, 1935 AND 1935 (SEK MILLION*)

Company	1920	1925	1930	1935
Atlas Diesel	20.0	8.0	8.0	6.8
Baltic	32.6	7.0	7.0	1.0
Claes Johansson	5.5	5.5	2.0	2.0
Fagersta Bruk	14.0	7.5	7.5	7.5
Larsbo-Norns	4.2	5.0	5.0	5.0
Linoleum ab Forshaga	2.0	4.0	8.0	4.0
Ljusnan	3.2	4.2	4.2	4.2
Munktell	7.5	2.5	2.5	5.0
Reymersholm	32.9	11.1	11.1	4.0
Svenska Tändsticksab	45.0	180.0	270.0	90.0
Ytterstfors-Munksund	32.5	16.2	1.0	5.0
Åtvidabergs Industrier	5.0	2.0	2.0	2.0

Note: *authorised share capital (not paid-up capital).

Source: Svenska aktiebolag och banker.

TABLE 7
BRITISH COMPANIES AND THEIR MAIN CLEARING BANKS

Company	B	BoE	GM	L	Ma	Mi	NBS	NP	RBS	W	WD
Armstrong	X				X						
Austin						X					
Baldwins				X							
Beardmore				X			X		X		
Bolckow						X		X			X
Colville						X					
Consett		X	X	X							
Dorman & Long	X						X	X			X
Harland & Wolff						X	X	X	X		
Lancashire CC		X			X	X					X
Richard Thomas				X	X						
United Steel								X		X	
Total	2	2	1	4	3	5	3	4	2	1	3

Key: B=Barclays Bank; BoE=Bank of England; GM=Glyn Mills Bank; L=Lloyds Bank; Ma=Martins Bank; Mi=Midland Bank; NBS=National Bank of Scotland; NP=National Provincial Bank; RBS=Royal Bank of Scotland; W=Westminster Bank; WD=Williams Deacon's Bank.

Sources: Stock Exchange Official Intelligence; S. Tolliday, Business, Banking and Politics: The Case of British Steel, 1918–1939 (Cambridge, MA, 1988) pp.180–81.

TABLE 8
SWEDISH COMPANIES AND THEIR MAIN COMMERCIAL BANKS

Company	GöB	MäB	NHB	SHB	SkaK	SkEB	SmEB	StEB	SydK	WEB
Atlas Diesel								X*		
Baltic					X*			X		
Claes Johansson	X				X*	X				
Fagersta				X*		X				X
Larsbo-Norns	X			X				X*		
Linoleumab				X						
Forshaga										
Ljusnan					X					
Munktell	X	X*		X				X		
Reymersholm			X	X*	X		X			
Svenska				X	X*	X	X	X		
Tändsticksab										
Ytterstfors-Munksund				X*	X					
Åvidabergs Industrier					X				X*	
Total	3	1	1	7	7	3	2	5	1	1

Key: GöB=Götabanken, MäB=Mälarebanken/Mälarprovinsemas Bank, NHB=Nordiska Handelsbanken, SHB=Svenska Handelsbanken, Skak=Skandinaviska Kreditaktiebolaget, SkEB, Skaraborgs Enskilda Bank, SmEB=Smålands Enskilda Bank, StEB=Stockholms Enskilda Bank, Sydk=Sydsvenska kreditaktiebolaget, WEB=Wermlands Enskilda Bank.

Note: *means that this bank was the principal bank in the total financial relationships. The figure measure only the bank relationships at the time before (0–3 years), during and after (0–3 years) the reconstruction.

Sources: Bank Inspectorate, Register of Engagement, Bank Investigation Reports, Swedish Bond Yearbook.

NOTES

I am grateful for comments and ideas from Erik Berglöf, Håkan Lindgren, the two editors of this volume and two anonymous referees. Geoffrey Jones and Mikael Lönnborg-Andersson also helped to find relevant materials. This research was financed by HSFR, the Wallenberg fund, Stockholm University and EHF, Stockholm School of Economics.

1. See, for example, F. Capie and M. Collins, *Have the Banks Failed British Industry?* (London, 1992); M. Collins, *Banks and Industrial Finance in Britain 1800–1939* (London, 1991); H. James, H. Lindgren and A. Teichova (eds.), *The Role of Banks in the Interwar Economy* (Cambridge, 1991); P.L. Cottrell, H. Lindgren and A. Teichova (eds.), *European Industry and Banking 1920–39: A Review of Bank–Industry Relations* (Leicester, 1992); A. Teichova, T. Gourvish and Á. Pogany (eds.), *Universal Banking in the Twentieth Century* (Aldershot, 1994).

2. A. Gerschenkron, *Economic Backwardness in Historical Perspective* (New York, 1965); R. Cameron, *Banking and Economic Development: Some Lessons of History* (London, 1972).

3. For the American case, see S. Gilson, K. John and J. Lang, 'Troubled Debt Restructuring: An Empirical Study of Private Organization of Firms in Default', *Journal of Financial Economics* (Sept. 1990), pp.315–31; P. Asquith, R. Gertner and D. Scharfstein, 'Anatomy of Financial Distress: An Examination of Junk Bond Issues', *Quarterly Journal of Economics* (Aug. 1994), pp.625–58. For the Japanese case, see T. Hoshi, A. Kashyap and D. Scharfstein, 'Corporate Structure, Liquidity and Investment: Evidence from Japanese Industrial Groups', *Quarterly Journal of Economics* (Feb. 1991).

4. J. Franks and K. Nyborg, 'Workouts versus Formal Bankruptcy: Incentives and Inefficiences under Different Bankruptcy Codes' (mimeo, London School of Economics, 1992).

5. R. Wells, 'Strategic Debt' (mimeo, University of Southampton, 1992).

6. E. Berglöf and E.L. von Thadden, 'Short-Term versus Long-Term Interests: A Model of Capital Structure with Multiple Investors', *Quarterly Journal of Economics*, Vol.CIX No.4 (Nov. 1994). Also see P. Bolton and D. Scharfstein, 'Optimal Debt Structure and the Number of Creditors', *Journal of Political Economy* (Feb. 1996), pp.1–25, the choice between one or many short-term investors is also analysed.

7. Hoshi, 'Corporate Structure'; T. Hoshi, A Kashyap and D. Scharfstein, 'The Role of Banks in Reducing the Costs of Financial Distress in Japan', *Journal of Financial Economics* (Sept. 1990), pp.67–88.

8. See K.-G. Hildebrand, *I omvandlingens tjänst. Svenska Handelsbanken 1871–1955* (Stockholm, 1971); idem, *Expansion, Crisis, Reconstruction, 1917–1939: The Swedish Match Company, 1917–1939* (Stockholm, 1985); H. Lindgren, *Bank, investmentbolag, bankirfirma. Stockholms Enskilda Bank 1924–1945* (Stockholm, 1987); H. Lindgren, 'Long Term Contracts in Financial Markets: Bank–Industry Connections in Sweden, illustrated by the Operations of the Stockholms Enskilda Bank 1900–70', in M. Aoki, B. Gustafsson and O.E. Williamson, *The Firm as a Nexus of Treaties* (London, 1990); H. Sjögren, *Bank och Näringsliv* (Stockholm, 1991).

9. See J.H. Bamberg, 'The Government, the Banks and the Lancashire Cotton Industry' (unpublished Ph.D. thesis, University of Cambridge, 1984); S. Tolliday, *Business, Banking and Politics: The Case of British Steel, 1918–1939* (Cambridge, MA, 1987).

10. Control orientation has sometimes been called bank orientation, as opposed to market orientation, since the debt/equity ratio has been higher, the credit and the ownership structures more stable and more concentrated, and the relationships longer term and including large positions from the commerical banks.

11. One exception is J. Zysman, *Governments, Markets and Growth: Financial Systems and the Politics of Industrial Change* (London, 1983).

12. For an insight into the role of the social factor, see J. Ottosson, 'Stability and Change in Personal Networks. Interlocking Directorates in Banks and Industry 1903–1939' (Ph.D. thesis, Uppsala University, 1993); M. Dritsas, P. Eigner and J. Ottosson, '"Big Business" Networks in Three Inter-War Economies: Austria, Greece and Sweden', *Financial History Review*, Vol.3 Part 2 (Oct. 1996).

104   INSTITUTIONS AND THE EVOLUTION OF MODERN BUSINESS

13. There is always a chance that certain criteria have an implicit impact on the sample. For example, the type of industry in which a firm is engaged might be correlated with capital structure. As an example, fixed capital/gestation periods will presumably influence the risk attached to different types of liability.
14. Archives of Lloyds Bank, Head Office, Ad/Ana.1, Book No.1593.
15. Tolliday, *Business*, p.179.
16. *Stock Exchange Official Intelligence*; Tolliday, *Business*, pp.180–81.
17. Records of every company are taken from the *Stock Exchange Yearbook*; *Stock Exchange Official Intelligence*.
18. Sjögren, *Bank*, pp.22–3.
19. Archives of Bank Inspectorate, Register of Engagement, Bank Investigation Reports; *Swedish Bond Yearbook*.
20. See Sjögren, *Bank*.
21. For a thorough description of the Fagersta case, see Hildebrand, *Omvandlingens*, pp.249–67.
22. The financial development and the importance of the Kreuger Group was studied in a special project during the late 1970s and early 1980s: 'The Kreuger Group on the Swedish and International Capital Market'. See B. Gäfvert, *Kreuger, Riksbanken och Regeringen* (Stockholm, 1979); J. Glete, *Kreugerkoncernen och krisen på svensk aktiemarknad* (Stockholm, 1981). In another project working at the same time, the Swedish Match's internationalisation was analysed. See L. Hassbring, *The Industrial Development of the Swedish Match Company, 1917–1924* (Stockholm 1979); H. Lindgren, *Corporate Growth: The Swedish Match Industry in Global Setting* (Stockholm, 1979); H. Modig, *Swedish Match Interests in British India during the Interwar Years* (Stockholm 1979); U. Wikander, *Kreuger's Match Monopolies, 1925–1930. Case Studies in Market Control through Public Monopolies* (Stockholm, 1979). For the reconstruction, see Hildebrand, *Expansion*, pp.243–5 and 365–98.
23. See C.E. Heim, 'Limits to Intervention: The Bank of England and Industrial Diversification in the Depressed Areas', *Economic History Review*, Vol.XXXVII No.4 (1984); S. Bowden and M. Collins, 'The Bank of England, Industrial Regeneration, and Hire Purchase between the Wars', *Economic History Review*, Vol.XLV No.1 (1992); W.R. Garside and J.I. Greaves, 'The Bank of England and Industrial Intervention in Interwar Britain', *Financial History Review*, Vol.3 Part 1 (1996).
24. J.P. Addis, 'The Heavy Iron and Steel Industry in South Wales 1870–1950' (unpublished Ph.D. thesis, University College of Wales, 1957); J.R. Hume and M.S. Moss, *Beardmore: The History of a Scottish Industrial Giant* (London, 1979); P.L. Payne, *Colvilles and the Scottish Steel Industry* (Oxford, 1979); J.S. Boswell, *Business Policies in the Making: Three Steel Companies Compared* (London, 1983): Tolliday, 'Business'.
25. See E. Green and M.S. Moss, *A Business of National Importance: The Royal Shipping Group 1930–37* (London, 1982).
26. Payne, *Colvilles*, p.186.
27. M. Moss and J.R. Hume, *Shipbuilders to the World: 125 years of Harland and Wolff, Belfast 1861–1986* (Belfast, 1986), pp.314–15. See also Green and Moss, *A Business of National Importance*, pp.191–3.
28. Moss and Hume, *Shipbuilders*, p.314.
29. Ibid., pp.290–91.
30. J. Foreman-Peck, 'Exit, Voice and Loyalty as Responses to Decline: The Rover Company in the Inter-War Years', *Business History*, Vol.XXIII No.2 (1981), p.204.
31. P. Chalmin, *The Making of a Sugar Giant: Tate and Lyle, 1859–1989* (London, 1990).
32. J.P. Addis, 'The Heavy Iron and Steel Industry in South Wales, 1870–1950' (unpublished Ph.D. thesis, University College of Wales, 1957), p.237.
33. D.M. Ross, 'The Clearing Banks and the Finance of British Industry, 1930–1959' (unpublished Ph.D. thesis, London School of Economics, 1989), pp.52–70.
34. Tolliday, *Business*, pp.178–9. The analysis by Tolliday also includes contrasting opinions.
35. Lloyds Bank Archives, Lloyds Bank Monthly Report, Vol.1, 1917–18, p.120; HO/T/Gen.5, file 3371: Later on, Lloyds Bank made huge losses on this affair, see J.R. Winton, *Lloyds Bank 1918–1939* (Oxford, 1982), pp.57–9. The debacle of the British–Italian Corporation

thus illustrates the problem with expansive industrial capitalism.

36. See, for example, Hildebrand, *Omvandlingen*; Sågvall-Ullenhag, *AB Åtvidabergs förenade industrier och dess föregångare* (Uppsala, 1970); L.-E. Thunholm, *Oscar Rydbeck och hans tid* (Stockholm, 1991).

37. D.M. Ross, 'Commercial Banking in a Market-Oriented Financial System: Britain Between the Wars', *Economic History Review*, Vol.XLIX No.2 (1996), p.328. This article explores the use of market- and bank-dominated financial systems. Earlier contributions by Lindgren and Berglöf in Aoki, *Firm as a Nexus*; H. Sjögren, 'Long-term Contracts in the Swedish Bank-Oriented Financial System during the Inter-War Period', *Business History*, Vol.33 No.3 (1991); H. Sjögren, 'Long-Term Financial Contracts in the Bank-Oriented Financial System', *Scandinavian Journal of Management*, Vol.10 No.3 (1995); S.Knutsen, 'Norwegian Banks and the Legacy of the Interwar Years', in Teichova, Gourvish and Pogany (eds.), *Universal Banking*.

38. See H. Wixforth and D. Ziegler, 'Bankenmacht: Universal Banking and German Industry in Historical Perspective', in Y. Cassis, G. Feldman and U. Olsson (eds.), *The Evolution of Financial Institutions and Markets in Twentieth-Century Europe* (London, 1995); Ottosson, 'Stability'.

39. See Hoshi, 'Corporate Structure'.

40. P. Aghion, O.D. Hart and J. Moore, 'The Economics of Bankruptcy Reform', *Journal of Law, Economics and Organisation* (Oct. 1992), pp.523–46.

Post-War Strategic Capitalism in Norway: A Theoretical and Analytical Framework

SVERRE KNUTSEN

Norwegian School of Management

This essay explores the efforts of the Norwegian state to influence industrial development during the period 1950 to 1980. To do this it is necessary to clarify the meaning of 'industrial policy': it is defined as a purposeful set of measures used by governments to influence investment decisions, and the direction of development and performance of individual businesses. It is important, therefore, to emphasise the planned supply and distribution of financial resources for investment purposes as an integral part of industrial policy. In every national economy, the financial markets and institutions are among the most important factors constraining the ways government and business can interact. For this reason, it is essential to get a deeper understanding of the important function the financial system has in the moulding of industrial policy, as well as in its accomplishment. This essay therefore focuses on state efforts in the field of industrial credit allocation and regulation of capital markets.[1] It will discuss the way in which government policy and arrangements for industrial finance influenced the governance structure and investment strategies pursued by Norwegian firms. In addition, it will explore the extent to which government action to promote growth affected inter-firm relations and sectoral development. It is divided into five parts. In the first, there will be a discussion of the theoretical and methodological tools which have been used, and this is followed by a brief outline of post-war strategic capitalism in Norway to test the argument. Thirdly, the cultural and institutional basis for the Norwegian financial system is explored, whilst in the fourth section there is a brief discussion of industrial performance and growth during the period under consideration. Conclusions are drawn in a final section.

II

The analysis of the shaping of national policies requires a discussion of the international economic and institutional environment. For example, Norway's approval of the Marshall Plan and OEEC membership in 1948 promoted the liberalisation of the country's trade relations. The conclusion of the GATT in 1947 and the building up of an international free trade regime also stimulated liberalisation of trade in the international economic system. Clearly, such developments, as well as other economic and institutional factors at the international level, have had an impact on domestic institutions in different countries. It should be emphasised, however, that this was not a one-way process. On the contrary, in the present era of 'international interdependence', strategies of foreign economic policy depend on the interplay of domestic and international forces. In this context, Peter Katzenstein has argued that 'a selective emphasis overlooks the fact that the main purpose of all strategies of foreign economic policy is to make domestic politics compatible with the international political economy'.[2] The *way* this happens, however, depends on the configuration of domestic institutions and organisations.

In order to explore the interaction between the government, finance and industry this essay uses an institutional approach, drawing mainly on historical institutionalism within political economy and the institutional economics of Douglass C. North.[3] In line with North's approach, institutions are defined as 'the rules of the game' and there is a conceptual division between institutions and organisations.[4] Institutions have been broadly defined as ranging from organisations and networks of organisations to professions and cultures. According to Sjöstrand, 'institutions are embedded in concrete, empirical organizations as well as in the ideas and concepts which human beings use to sort out – construct – their views of reality'.[5] Since the 'rules of the game' that shape the legal environment of business firms are particularly linked to the state, the interaction between state and business is central to this study. In addition, ideology and culture influence the evolution of institutions. This means that the analysis explores the cultural and ideological elements underpinning key institutions.

From comparative historical studies, it is clear that industrial policy has varied considerably across nations.[6] This is also true with respect to the structure of the state and the type of financial system. These institutional characteristics were developed in connection with the shaping of modern national states, and were also closely linked to *how* and *when* different nations industrialised. Thus, this process must be studied historically and empirically if we are to be able to obtain adequate insights into the continuities such social institutions have developed, as well as the changes they have undergone at critical junctures.

This essay is principally concerned with the way in which Norwegian business is financed. It is necessary, therefore to discuss the characteristics of financial systems, though not on consumer financing, rather the financing of industry. The financial system of capitalist countries has usually been divided into two main types, namely *market-based* systems and *credit-based* (or *bank-oriented*) systems.[7] The credit-based system can also be subdivided into bank-oriented and state-led categories.

The different characteristics used to construct a taxonomy are largely tied to factors such as the role of government in financing industry, the relative importance of capital markets in corporate finance, the role of banks and bank lending, the mechanisms through which interest rates are fixed and the way influence is exercised. All these factors affect important relations between the financial sector and business. The taxonomy is based on three groups of combinations, each making up a distinctive system. There are, of course, possibilities for other combinations, or other configurations. But this is irrelevant in the context of this discussion, since empirical analysis with the three ideal types depicted in Table 1 has a socioeconomic and political relevance. All three systems have different kinds of intermediaries, banks as well as non-bank financial institutions, securities markets and so forth. The main point, however, is the relative importance of these different institutions, especially the relative importance of two types of financial markets: capital markets and loan markets.

Table 1 presents the key criteria used to classify financial systems. A capital market system is characterised by the central role of capital markets in industrial financing. In such markets, resources are allocated by prices established in competitive markets. Bank lending is typically and traditionally short-term. In contrast, the main source for corporate finance in a credit-based system is loans or credits. As distinct from a market-based system, long-term loans are typical in a credit-based system. The allocation of credit for investment purposes is predominantly discretionary, either by universal banks or by governments, which make choices about whom to lend to and under what terms.

The importance of borrowing in credit-based systems is also reflected in the balance sheets of the firms, which show higher debt ratios than in a market-based system, as is illustrated in Table 2. Credit-based systems can, as has already been discussed, be classified as bank-oriented and state-led. The German financial system, with its formative phase during the last quarter of the nineteenth century, and with large universal banks, has been characterised as the archetype of a bank-oriented system. In contrast, Japan and France have been depicted as typical credit-based and 'price administered' systems, as Zysman describes them, or state-led as they are described here. The latter have also been designated 'credit based systems influenced by government'.[9]

Some scholars have claimed that the basic feature of a bank-oriented system is that the major source for financing investments is either retained earnings or funds collected and provided by banks. Banks monitor and

TABLE 1
NATIONAL FINANCIAL SYSTEMS: CRITERION OF CLASSIFICATION

	Market-Based	Credit-Based	
		Bank-Oriented	State-Led
The Relative Importance of Capital Markets	High	Low	Low
The Relative Weight of Loans in Industrial Finance	Low	High	High
The Relative Weight of Bank Lending on the Credit Market	Low	High	Low
The Relative Importance of Public Credit Institutions	Low	Low	High
The Prevalent Mechanisms in Pricing of Capital	Free	Oligopolistic	Admin. Fixing
Internal Financing Ratio	High	High	Low
Debt Ratio	Low	High	High
Short-Term vs. Long-Term Lending	Short-Term	Long-Term	Long-Term
Mode of Influence	Exit	Voice	Voice
Characteristics of Allocation	Arm's Length	Discretionary	Discretionary
Archetype	USA UK	Germany Sweden	France Norway

TABLE 2
DEBT IN MANUFACTURING ENTERPRISES AS PERCENTAGE OF TOTAL ASSETS (1975)

	Debt Ratio (%)
Japan	85
Norway	81
Germany *	76
France	70
Sweden (1977)	69
UK	54
USA	37

Note: * Provisions for pension funds, classified by OECD as 'borrowed funds', is classified here as debt.

Source: OECD, Financial Statistics 1984.

control 'the performance of users to whom they channeled savings they had collected. Such savings tend to be channeled almost entirely in the form of loans'.[9] Universal banks also frequently hold equity in client firms. Bank-oriented systems are thus characterised by strong relations between banks and business firms, often during long periods of time, as Sjögren and others have pointed out.[10] Hence, network banking is an outstanding feature of a bank-oriented system.

The literature is ambiguous concerning the criteria of internal financing, and the importance of this factor in a bank-oriented system. Berglöf emphasises a low degree of internal financing as typical for bank-oriented systems, while Rybczynski claims that the opposite is true.[11] Empirical comparative studies of Germany, Britain and the USA reveal relatively small differences in the degree of internal financing in manufacturing firms. The picture is quite different, however, when we compare these countries with, for example, France, Japan or Norway. Consequently, I have chosen to use a low degree of internal financing as one of the criteria of a credit-based, state-led financial system.

In a state-led and credit-based system, institutions and lending have a dominant position in the financing of industry. But interest rates are typically administratively fixed in a credit-based system influenced by government. Consequently, credit rationing is a typical feature of such systems, and there is a strong element of discretion in the allocative process. In addition, the government often uses the bond market as a means of raising money for its own projects as well as an instrument for directing capital flows to targeted industries. Hence, the bond market usually is not easily accessible to private companies, unless they are prioritised by the government.

TABLE 3

MARKET VALUE OF LISTED EQUITIES AS PERCENTAGE OF GDP, SELECTED COUNTRIES, 1975

Country	Stocks / GDP
USA	45 %
UK	41 %
Japan	29 %
Germany	13 %
France	11 %
Norway	6 %

Source: J. Zysman, *Governments, Markets and Growth: Financial Systems and the Politics of Industrial Change* (London, 1983), p.124; Norwegian Official Statistics (NOS A 969); Jacobsen og Lundhagen, 'Aksjer og inflasjon i Norge 1915–1990' (unpublished Masters thesis, Norwegian School of Management,1991), p.49.

The Stock Exchange has traditionally played a more significant role in the long-term financing of industrial firms in a market-based than in a credit-based system. Table 3 reveals significant differences in this respect and shows that the importance of the market in equities is much larger in a market-based system than in a credit-based one. Consequently, specialised investment banking is also significantly more common in market-based systems.

Table 1 gave a stylised outline of financial systems, although empirical evidence reveals a more blurred picture. Some scholars have argued that in the German case aggregate figures for external finance falsify the 'conventional wisdom' of bank dominance, and emphasise that large firms are primarily internally financed.[12] Examination of the German financial system during the post-war period demonstrates that 'universal banks' together with a broad range of other types of bank institutions, not just the 'Big Three', are important in credit allocation. In addition, recent research demonstrates that there is still a close involvement of banks in business development.[13] The concept of differing financial systems discussed above is still the most promising and comprehensive approach to historical and comparative analysis.

In this analysis of industrial policy, the independent variables are the financial system and the structure of the state, whilst the dependent variables are industrial policy, the corporate adjustment process and so forth. From this analytical framework it is possible to develop the hypothesis that, in every national economy, the financial markets are one of the critical factors which constrain the ways government and business can interact. For this reason, it is essential to get a deeper empirical understanding of the important function of the financial system in the moulding and accomplishment of industrial policy. To study the change in these factors over time, the Norwegian case will be used to trace financial flows in the economy during the post-war period.

III

In October 1945 the Norwegian Labour Party won the parliamentary elections, and a new Labour government came to power. This regime endured for a considerable time, and between 1945 and 1980 the Labour Party was in power for 28 of 35 years. A comprehensive modernisation of the economy through purposeful and planned industrialisation was regarded a major vehicle for the achievement of economic growth. When, during its exile in London, the leadership of the party drew up a party programme for the period 1945–49 it stated that 'a highly developed manufacturing industry is ... decisive for our people's standard of living'. As a consequence, the Labour Party became the driving force behind industrial policy.

Planning and active economic policy management, eventually combined with the use of the market mechanism, formed the basis of a large-scale industrialisation drive. In the 1930s, however, the party had rejected what was considered a dogmatic, orthodox socialism. Among other things, it believed that welfare policy and redistribution depended on increased production. The party chairman and Prime Minister, Einar Gerhardsen, gave expression to this policy at the national convention of the Norwegian Federation of Trade Unions (LO) in 1949: 'The policy of re-distribution has reached its peak. If we want a better standard of living, we have to increase production in order to have *more* to distribute.'[14]

A more *imperative* type of planning was implemented during the reconstruction period of the immediate post-war years, based on an interventionist policy of price control, subsidies, rationing and extensive import–export controls. The government tried to curb private consumption through rationing. At the same time, it attempted to control investments by keeping them low in certain sectors, and thus ensuring that resources were invested in targeted projects, enterprises and sectors. This kind of planning gave the government capacity to allocate limited resources according to political priorities.

During the period 1949–52, however, this regime of direct controls and regulations was gradually dismantled. Although the *dirigiste* version of planning and direct regulations was abandoned, the Labour Party did not abandon economic planning. Modernisation and growth through planned industrialisation was still the main, overall strategy of the party. For several reasons, however, it became necessary to re-establish economic planning and management on a new basis. Hence, the social democratic party and government started to seek new instruments for economic policy making in general, and industrial policy in particular. In a relatively short time a seemingly extreme *dirigiste* version of planning was changed to an indicative type, which also gave more scope for use of the market mechanism.[15]

Economic, institutional and political factors were the underlying causes for this reorientation. As far as economic factors are concerned, these particularly involved price and currency problems, which contributed to change. After some initial hesitation, the Labour government found it necessary to accept Marshall Aid in order to achieve exchange rate stabilisation. This decision, at the same time, required a gradual liberalisation of foreign trade. As a consequence of the Norwegian acceptance of Marshall Aid and the membership of OEEC, trade was gradually liberalised. When the rationing of consumer goods was removed, a rise in prices occurred. Subsidies increased substantially, as did the demand for foreign currency. This development undermined the efficiency of the price stabilisation policy based on extensive price and import controls. As regards institutional factors, the Labour Party tried to have the *dirigiste* planning system firmly rooted in a comprehensive corporatist structure. The government established 'Councils' with corporatist representation on the national level, at the sectoral level and even on the enterprise level, in order to co-ordinate economic policy, rationalise sectors and increase productivity. But this attempt to base planning within a state-initiated, formal corporatist framework failed, and was actually given up during the early 1950s. The owners and managers did not want to co-operate, because they regarded these 'councils' as a government controlled 'one way channel'. The trade unions were also very reluctant to accept this project, mainly because they did not want to contibute to planned rationalisation of their own jobs. Finally, conflicts were intensified among the political parties in the late 1940s.[16]

All these factors led to a growing pressure for change in the macroeconomic policy regime, as well as in the system for microeconomic planning. But the leading politicians of the Labour Party had been deeply rooted in pragmatism since the 1930s. The main issue for them was not nationalisation or state ownership, but industrialisation and growth. The ability to control investments was considered a key to achieve these goals. What really mattered was the allocative capacity of the system, and not whether capital and credit flows were managed by direct or indirect means.

The Labour Party established a new system for planning and economic policy making in the early 1950s. The governance mechanisms, as well as the regulatory regime which underpinned this system, were to last for more than 30 years without significant systemic changes. One basic element was an industrial policy characterised by active government intervention for the purposes of industrial development so that Keynesianism was an important part of Norwegian policy making. The proper use of the techniques provided by macroeconomic planning, to maintain economic stability, was regarded a key task for the government. But the Norwegian government did not confine itself to assume stability by managing fiscal and monetary aggregates at arm's length. A strong element of neo-mercantilism was just as important as Keynesian fine-tuning in Norwegian economic policy.

A key element of the change in the financial system was a new emphasis on credit policy measures.The government White Paper of winter 1952 outlined the principal goals of the new credit policy.[17] These were to maintain stable prices, to prevent increases in interest rates, to secure state bank funding, to govern the supply of liquidity to the private banks and to secure financial arrangements which could allow targeting of particular schemes.

Interest rate pegging to keep a low interest rate by administrative measures had already been introduced during the immediate post-war reconstruction period. But this policy was not limited to this period. At the outset, the legal basis for administratively fixed interest rates was a temporary Act, passed in December 1947. New temporary legislation on interest rates was enacted in 1953 and confirmed the government's right to control interest rates on loans. This act even contained new regulations on bond market entry. According to this legislation, everybody who wished to issue bonds was obliged to apply to the authorities for permission. The interest rate, and all other conditions connected with the floating of bonds, had to be examined and approved by the authorities. Even the purpose of borrowing and the actual investment plans of the borrower had to be approved. This policy and legislation introduced a protracted system of credit rationing in Norway, as discretion substituted for the price mechanism in lending decisions. Credit rationing was considered to be a precondition to ensure low-cost credit to targeted industries.

The government chose a corporatist solution, based on voluntary co-operation between the banks and the authorities in order to carry out these new monetary and credit policies. Co-operation took part within the framework of the so-called Co-operation Committee, which was established in 1951. This committee was composed of representatives from the Bank of Norway, the Ministry of Finance, the Bank Inspectorate and the commercial and savings banks. In 1955 they were joined by representatives from the life insurance industry.[18]

As a consequense of strategic credit allocation, the financial system was very segmented. In addition to banks, there were a lot of institutions with specialised lending, including several state-owned banks with specialised purposes. A separate bank for long-term industrial credit, partly owned by the state (51 per cent) and partly by private banks (49 per cent), was in operation. The state banks increased their loans substantially after the war, and two new public banks were established to finance housing and education. During 1951 the financing of the state banks met with great obstacles, because it became impossible to sell state bank bonds at the low interest rate level fixed by the authorities. The government then had to transfer funds from the Treasury to the state banks. In order to drain capital from the private financial institutions, it became very important for the government to get the banks, as well as the life insurance companies, to buy more government securities. This was the government's principal motive for including representatives of the life insurance companies within the Co-operation Committee. The Norwegian Life Insurance Companies' Association was very reluctant to become a member, mainly to avoid any increased pressure to buy low interest rate bonds. After a while, however, they were forced to take part in the Co-operation Committee, since the Ministry of Finance and the Bank of Norway expressed the view that 'the life-insurance companies have a substantial impact on the development of the monetary and credit market'.[19]

During the first four years of its existence, the Co-operation Committee passed resolutions laying down general guidelines for the lending and investment policies of the banks. In principle the banks were free to follow these instructions. From 1955, however, a system with one-year binding agreements was adopted. These annual agreements laid down the rules for the lending policies the banks were obliged to carry through the following year, the amount of government securities which the financial institutions were obliged to buy, and so on. Hence, the financial institutions and markets were actually subject to a new regulatory regime during the early 1950s. The main reason why the commercial banks, as well as the other financial institutions, accepted this development was because, in return for the voluntary co-operation of the banks and the other financial institutions, the government did not introduce new, extensive regulatory legislation.

In 1965, however, an extensively reformed Law on Money and Credit was introduced. The main purpose was to centralise credit policy decisions in the Ministry of Finance and to control the volume of credit supplied by the banks by managing their liquidity. But the policy to keep the level of interest rates low, the control of the floating of loans in the bond market, and so forth, continued.

According to the 1953 legislation, the Bank of Norway decided who should be permitted to float loans in the bond market. In 1955, this authority was centralised in the Ministry of Finance. However, a committee under the Bank of Norway was established to administer all the applications for issuing bearer bonds on behalf of the Ministry. This committee was composed of representatives of the Bank of Norway, the Ministry of Finance, the Ministry of Industry, the Ministry of Trade and the two state banks in charge of financing industry and the construction of hydro-electrical power plants. The committee continued to operate until 1980, when the bond market was deregulated.

The currency regulations, based on legislation passed in 1950, laid down that all short-term foreign capital transactions were dependent on a licence from the Bank of Norway. The floating of bonds and long-term borrowing on foreign capital markets had to be licensed by the Ministry of Trade. To co-ordinate these activities and to prepare decisions concerning permissions for long-term borrowing abroad, a so-called 'Currency Regulations Council' had been established. This council was composed along the same lines as the one for the domestic bond market. Several committees and agencies were set up by the authorities during the 1950s to promote and provide industrial finance. Some of them had a corporatist character, but most of them had not. Among these agencies, a separate Agency for Industrial Finance, headed by Trygve Lie, was set up in 1959 to attract foreign investment to Norwegian projects.[20] This agency played an important role in finding the investors and credit sources necessary to finance the huge expansion and modernisation of the Norwegian aluminum industry which took place in the 1960s.

The system for industrial finance which thus emerged in the 1950s can be described as the 'quadrature for industrial finance', consisting of a network of public and quasi-public organisations, which operated within a framework bounded by the Bank of Norway, the Ministry of Finance, the Ministry of Industry and the Ministry of Trade. Around 1960 the state's efforts at industrial credit allocation were further bolstered by the establishment of new state agencies to strengthen public industrial finance by direct means. These new agencies were the Regional Development Fund (DUF) and the Development Fund. The purpose of the latter was to finance new projects in so-called 'growth industries' such as electronics. New semi-public institutions for the financing of shipbuilding, based on state-guaranteed loans, were established and the state bank for the long-term financing of manufacturing industry – 'Industribanken' – was strengthened. New institutions and arrangements were introduced and some were also reorganised during the 1960s and 1970s.

The industries prioritised within the framework of Norwegian industrial policy were primarily export industries. These industries, as well as the large Norwegian shipping industry, were dependent on entry to foreign markets. As has already been pointed out, trade was liberalised around 1950. Membership of the OEEC and the system of 'freelists' had opened competition between Norwegian and foreign merchandise. In 1959, the Labour government pushed for Norway to enter EFTA, and for the removal of tariff barriers. Strategic allocation and capital market regulations were thus combined with the exposure of Norwegian product markets to competition.

However, the economic policy regime was extremely stable. In 1965, when 20 years of continuous Social Democratic rule was interrupted, a coalition of the liberal, conservative and agrarian parties came to power for six years. In spite of this change in policy regime, no significant shift in economic and industrial policy took place until the end of the 1970s, when major changes occurred in Norwegian economic policy. These changes were characterised by more market-oriented solutions and extensive re-regulation of financial markets.[21]

At the outset, the Labour Party leadership based industrial policy on what they saw as the comparative advantage of Norwegian industry: a huge capacity to produce cheap hydro-electrical power, as well as electro-chemical and -metallurgical production based on this capacity. From around 1960, this policy was reinforced as substantial resources and industrial finance were directed to the aluminium sector, while the shipbuilding industry was also given high priority. Already in 1947, these sectors were picked out and given high priority. During the second half of the 1960s, electronics was also included in the prioritised sectors.

These strategic aims were institutionalised in the network of state agencies, briefly sketched above. With the aid of this network, and by the shaping of the credit system, the government attempted to accomplish its industrial policy goals by strategic resource allocation, which became one of the Norwegian state's most crucial levers for effecting strategic industrial transformation. Table 4 illustrates the impact of this policy and reveals two important developments. Firstly, the importance of commercial banks in financing industry was drastically reduced during the period under consideration. Secondly, industrial finance provided by the allocative institutions and agencies directly controlled by the government (3+7+8), increased substantially from 38 to 58 per cent. In addition, the government heavily influenced the lending policies of banks and life insurance companies.

TABLE 4
OUTSTANDING LOANS TO MANUFACTURING INDUSTRY ON THE REGULAR,
DOMESTIC CREDIT MARKET (%)

	1955	1960	1965	1970	1975	1977	1980
1. Commercial banks	43.7	40.8	33.5	32.6	29.1	25.9	22.5
2. Savings Banks	11.1	11.3	8.1	7.9	7.5	6.3	6.6
3. State Banks	6.6	5.8	7.1	7.1	9.6	11.6	18.5
4. Financing Companies	0.0	0.0	3.4	3.7	3.4	2.5	2.9
5. Non-Life Insurance	0.9	1.2	1.2	1.9	3.3	3.0	2.6
6. Life Insurance	6.4	11.4	10.9	9.5	9.9	9.0	7.8
7. Mortgage Banks	6.8	7.6	13.9	19.7	23.4	29.9	28.1
8. Bond Market, directly	24.8	21.9	21.9	17.5	13.8	11.9	11.1
Total	100	100	100	100	100	100	100

Note: All figures from the end of the year. Category (7), mortgage banks, includes credit unions.

Source: S.Knutsen, 'Finanssystem, Næringspolitikk og Industriell Utvikling 1950–1990. Forstudie og Forskningsdesign' (Working paper No.21, Norwegian School of Management, 1994).

Furthermore, the table indicates a considerable growth of the mortgage banks and credit unions after 1965. At the same time we see that the issue of bonds by individual firms directly on the bond market decreases in importance as a source for long-term industrial finance. The main reason for this was a policy shift in the early 1960s, when the government strengthened its focus on industrial sectors even further. Thus the authorities gave priority to the allocation of quotas to specialised mortgage banks, which provided loans to firms operating in targeted industries rather than licensing individual borrowers.

In addition, when the distribution of lending by sector is scrutinised, a distinctive pattern is revealed. Both in the bond market directly, as well as the institutions' lending, the following sectors were prioritised: hydro-electrical power plants, shipbuilding and electro-metallurgical industries. If we add the distribution of loans provided by the development fund for new industrial projects, which started its operation in 1965, the prioritised sectors in this institution's lending were shipbuilding, electronic industry and machine production.[22] From a strategic point of view, the importance of these sectors even increased, because of the building up of the offshore industry from the early 1970s.

As has already been pointed out, one of the major objectives of post-war industrial policy was the funding of specific industries with competitive advantage. The intersectoral profile of Norwegian government credit, channelled through the bond market, as well as the intersectoral profile of direct government credit, clearly demonstrates that the results were consistent with the objectives of industrial policy. To what extent this policy was optimal in terms of economic performance will be discussed in section V. First, however, a brief outline of the development of the Norwegian banking system is provided. This will clarify the opportunity which the government had after the Second World War, when it wanted to shape the financial system as a tool for industrial policy.

IV

This essay has demonstrated that the evolution of the financial system provides the key to the understanding of both the development in political economy and industrial change in post-war Norway. It is also necessary to examine more closely the institutional and cultural basis for regulation and configuration of the Norwegian financial system.

The structure of the Norwegian economy has traditionally been very decentralised, consisting of a large number of small firms with strong, local ties. This is an entrenched feature of the Norwegian economy, and, as has already been demonstrated, small and medium-sized firms still characterise the industrial structure. Although the impact of the largest companies in the Norwegian economy has increased substantially during the post-war period, the largest Norwegian enterprises still have less impact on the economy than is the case in, for example, Sweden or Finland. Industrial production as well as employment is spread over more units in Norway than in the two neighbouring countries. Actually, a typical dualistic structure developed in Norwegian manufacturing industry after the turn of the century. On the one hand, a large-scale, energy-intensive industry developed, producing chemical and metallurgical products for export, whilst on the other there was the large sector of small enterprises in more traditional industries. Even Norwegian shipping, operating one of the largest merchant fleets in the world, was usually organised in fairly small units.

Moreover, the decentralised Norwegian business system, characterised by locally based small enterprises, has traditionally operated within the framework of a decentralised banking system. In 1939 a German bank analyst outlined in a book what he regarded as the distinguishing Norwegian socioeconomic features: 'Das von jeher in Norwegen stark entwickelte Selbständigkeits-gefühl der Fylker und Gemeinden führte dazu, das man den kredit im kleinsten Wirtschaftskreis organisierte' ('The strong and old-established sense of local independence which has developed in counties and municipalities in Norway has confined the organisation of banking and provision of loans to business to a local level').[23]

Norway developed a so-called 'unit bank' system consisting of local, small, independent banks. This distinctive character of a decentralised banking structure is even more prominent when we take into account the strikingly large number of local savings banks that mushroomed in Norway, reaching a peak of 623 in 1929. The ideological and legal basis of this system was integrated in Norwegian banking legislation. Thus the state guaranteed the decentralised structure by means of a legislation which, among other things, underpinned a system of concession. In parliament, it was decided that the basic principle for this system was to prevent the establishment of local branches and obstruct branch banking on a national level.

In a decentralised economic structure like this, local patriotism simmered beneath the surface, and competition was very often influenced by local rivalries. However, local co-operative networks also developed as an important governance mechanism in this environment. But consensus did develop in one major area: a major task of the state was to secure the maintenance of the locally based, decentralised organisation of economy, as well as a widespread distribution of power. The arrangement and balancing of interests, securing this goal, gained general support.

From this perspective, a basic and culturally generated 'accepted' pattern of interaction can be distinguished: the Norwegian democratic egalitarian localism. This notion expresses a kind of collective 'meaning', or culturally shaped rules or norms of behaviour. Such informal institutions, which give 'meaning' to collective action, very often underpin formal institutions as well as organisations. It was such 'accepted' patterns which became the basis of the Norwegian system of 'unit banking' as well as the underpinning principles of banking legislation in Norway. This pattern was an important impediment to the emergence of 'financial dynasties' in Norway. Egalitarianism is linked to a dispersed type of ownership and a broad participation in local economic life, relatively small differences in income, and so on. The democratic aspect is linked to communalism and the very strong tradition for municipal self-determination in economic matters. The close ties between savings banks and municipalities illustrate this relationship. These factors have been important in moulding the typical features and forms of organisations of the financial system, as well as in moulding national industrial strategies.

Altogether, the development of the particular traits of the Norwegian financial system should be understood as politically and socially established in connection with the nineteenth-century industrialisation process. As already indicated, the relationship between the state and the local communities in Norway can be valuably studied in a centre–periphery perspective. The peripheral influence on the centre has traditionally been very strong in Norway. For instance, there has always been an over-representation of MPs from small towns and rural districts in the Norwegian parliament. This was formally institutionalised in the electoral legislation during the nineteenth century and continues today. In order to be able to govern, the state had to give concessions to a strong periphery. In the nineteenth century, the state had to contribute by providing financial resources to the periphery. The National Bank (the Bank of Norway) was strongly engaged in the supply of credit to local business through a widespread web of local branches during the first decades after the division from Denmark in 1814. From the middle of the century, a wide range of state banks was established to carry out this task, while the evolving local savings banks and commercial banks guarded their independence. Financial assets were not allowed to be 'drained out' from the local communities. The savings banks had very strong support in the parliament (Stortinget) and experienced extensive growth. Even the government's attempt to establish a nationwide postal savings bank was impeded during the late 1880s by the Storting, where the spokesmen of the savings banks were in majority. The main reason for this action was that a postal bank would drain resources away from the periphery. Political support for the savings banks, and strong and successful local action against the development of branch banking, meant that commercial banks were crowded out.

Universal banking of the continental type, which combined deposit banking and short-term lending with long-term industrial financing and ownership of client firms, was inherently unstable. Initially, such banks were dependent on a 'lender of last resort'. The Norwegian national bank did not develop 'lender of last resort' functions until the turn of the century, and its role in this respect remained ambiguous for a long time after that. The main reasons for the late development of 'lender of last resort' functions was political. The major target of the bank during the nineteenth century was to establish and maintain a stable currency. This was very important for the senior civil servants who dominated government. The purchasing power of their salaries was very easily undermined by inflation. At the same time, at least until the 1860s, a large part of the national bank's resources was tied up in direct long-term lending. Thus, the basis for development of universal banking was very weak in Norway.

The national bank was privately owned, but actually it was under the tight control of the parliament (Storting). The government was also heavily engaged in the provision of credit to local businesses as well as agriculture. Different types of state banks, with special purposes, were established to accomplish this task. Since then, government influence has remained an important factor within the Norwegian financial system. The capacity to organise public or semi-public arrangements for selective lending has traditionally been fairly strong.

As has already been outlined, the Labour Party leadership pursued a strategy in the early 1950s with a large-scale industrialisation scheme which was based on the selective allocation of credit, made possible by the credit-based and price-administered financial system. This type of financial system was an institutional arrangement built upon elements which had specific historical origins. Here, the stable pattern of 'democratic egalitarian localism', rooted in the nineteenth-century industrialisation process, was important. Other elements can be traced back to the upheavals and the crises of the inter-war years and still others can also be traced to purposeful, politically motivated changes in the financial regulatory regime, which were carried through around 1950.

The shaping of the financial system through this historical process produced trajectories, both for the Norwegian state's steering capacity and, especially, its capacity for strategic action. On the one hand, the Norwegian state had traditionally pursued development. Further, the Norwegian national state had been rooted in an ethnically homogenous population. These are factors that have strengthened the strategic capacity of the state. The strong impact of democratic egalitarian localism has both facilitated and constrained the government's capacity to accomplish industrial strategies. When the goals have been in line with the logic of this pattern, it has strengthened the capacity for intervention in economy. When, on the other hand, political action has conflicted with this pattern, it has met with strong resistance.

In analysing institutional change it is clear that a change in the 'identity' of an institution is rare. Changes usually occur during crises, and are then usually followed by long periods of stability. The political scientist J.P. Olsen asserts that 'this reveals a picture showing that certain historical events open up for large changes'.[24] The socioeconomic crisis in the 1930s, followed by war and occupation, can be regarded as just such a train of events, which created a new set of opportunities for change during the immediate post-war years. Another important mechanism for change can be described as 'dramatic crisis', including revolutions, wars, depressions, while mismatches between capacities and tasks can be singled out as another basic mechanism of change.[25] In 1945, the Labour Party leadership believed that the private financial institutions had neither the ability nor the capacity to carry through the growth objectives of the government. As a result, during the autumn of 1948, the party leadership rejected all proposals to nationalise banks. But at the same time it was emphasised in a report that 'as suppliers of credit, the commercial banks have decisive impact on the business sector'.[26] The report also stated that the aim of the banks was to maximise profit for its owners. Consequently, the report concluded, this could easily 'come in conflict with the monetary and credit policies that the government wanted to carry through based on society's point of view'.

Against this background, the party leadership wanted to bring the banking sector under control. The reason for rejecting nationalisation was the desire to avoid the fierce conflicts which would result from a step like this. Such a step would certainly not be in accordance with democratic egalitarian localism. The policy that the leadership decided to adopt was to carry through continuous efforts to 'build up the position of society in the banking sector by developing the state banks as well as to build up the ability of government to control and affect the policies of private banks'. To carry through this policy, the government chose to make the banks serve as its credit policy allies, on terms negotiated between the government and finance. This took place within the framework of a corporate solution, which has been described above. The transformation of the financial system, based on a policy like this, had a better chance of succeeding than the nationalisation option, because it did not come into conflict with the basic norms and rules of society.

It is clear that three major features of the Norwegian financial system can be distinguished to explain why the government could successfully utilise the financial system for strategic resource allocation. Firstly, there was a historical tradition for a developmental type of state. Secondly, when the state acted in a way that did not conflict with the prevalent decentralised socioeconomic structure, its capacity to govern the economy was fairly strong. Thirdly, the decentralised and segmented financial system was characterised by relatively weak actors. This provided the state with considerable capacity to intervene in the industrial economy and allocate credit strategically, which became one of the Norwegian state's most crucial levers for effecting industrial promotion and transformation.

V

To analyse economic development and performance of a small and open economy like Norway's, it is crucial to take the external environment of business decisions, especially government–business relations, into account. It has been shown that a very active industrial policy has been a distinguishing feature of Norwegian government policy during the post-war era. The main objectives of such a policy were full employment, redistribution and social security, accomplished by a systematic and comprehensive construction of the welfare state. Sustained economic growth was seen as vital to the achievement of these ambitions. To a varying degree, Norway shared most of these objectives with other countries in the industrial West. But historical analysis demonstrates differences between these countries, with regard to how these goals were to be accomplished, and even reveals variations in performance.

As shown in Table 5, Norway's economic growth was relatively high in the period 1950–73, in spite of rather sluggish growth rates during the 1950s. During the 1960s, however, the table reveals that Norwegian growth rates were among the highest, reaching the top rank amongst the selected

TABLE 5
ECONOMIC GROWTH IN SELECTED OECD COUNTRIES
(AVERAGE ANNUAL RATES OF GROWTH IN REAL GDP, 1960–80)

	1950–73	1974–80	1960–80
Japan	9.3	3.7	7.7
France	5.0	2.8	4.6
Norway	4.1	4.7	4.4
Germany	5.9	2.3	3.7
USA	3.6	2.3	3.5
Sweden	4.0	1.8	3.3
Switzerland	4.5	0.3	3.0
UK	3.2	0.9	2.3

Source: OECD, *Historical Statistics, Economic Outlook* (No. 32, 1982); A. Maddison, *Dynamic Forces in Capitalist Development* (Oxford and New York, 1991).

OECD countries after 1973. According to Leslie Hannah, Britain had the most effective industrial policy in post-war Europe, but at the same time the most inefficient one.[27] This may have been the case for Britain. But, in countries like Japan, France, Norway and several others, an active industrial policy produced relatively high growth rates, both in industrial output and GDP. The study of the Norwegian case indicates that the configuration of the financial system is one of the critical factors explaining this difference.

As already has been pointed out, firm–market relations, as well as the institutional context in which they are embedded, vary considerably among different national economies. Hence, even the efficiency of industrial policy has to be contextualised. The fact that apparently similar industrial policies were carried through with success in some countries, while ending in failure in others, illustrates this point. The economic outcome of economic policy in each country 'depends in part on the capacity of governments to conduct development policies and in part on purposes they pursue'.[28] Thus, the efficacy of industrial policy has to be judged in a specific national, institutional and historical context. In addition, investments in capital, labour, innovative activities and ability to adapt to new possibilities are critical determinants of economic performance. The political system interacts with the institutional framework, whilst the institutions provide the incentive structures for firms and influences the critical determinants of economic performance. The outcome – either growth or stagnation – then has an impact on the political system.[29]

The provision of funds to specific industries with competitive and comparative advantage promoted growth in Norway. The long-term relationship between the state network of industrial planning and industrial finance, the financial institutions and industrial firms, helped to reduce uncertainty, and thus informational and transaction costs. This made it possible for relatively small Norwegian firms to undertake large investment projects in capital-intensive industries. The Norwegian system for industrial finance also mobilised substantial foreign capital, both loans and direct investments, to prioritised sectors, even in a period when international credit markets almost dried up during the 1950s and 60s. Involvement by the government network provided funds for small Norwegian firms on international capital markets, which otherwise would have been very difficult for them to obtain because of poor information flows.

Because of the configuration of the financial system and popular support, the government had considerable room for manoeuvre. The reason for this was that the enterprises in the targeted sectors were mainly localised in different parts of the country. Thus upgrading and investments in these sectors did not conflict with the deep-rooted culture of democratic egalitarian localism. Concentration and rationalisation was accomplished over time in a balanced way rather than rapidly within this geographical structure. This secured a stable social situation, which also promoted growth. Thus deeply rooted egalitarian patterns did not conflict with flexibility. On the contrary. OECD data, in the form of gini-coefficients covering the 1980s, show that the Scandinavian countries have the smallest wage differentials among the OECD countries.[30] Among the Scandinavian countries, Norway scores lowest of them all on this index, having stability over time. The evidence shows large differences among the OECD countries, in spite of the fact that these countries experienced very similar technological and demographic developments during this period. A possible explanation lies in the cultural differences across these countries and the institutionalisation of this differences. These may also have affected other factors, including the organisation of the economy. Egalitarian motives have characterised some important institutions in Norway. The emphasis on equal opportunity has enhanced social mobility and small wage differentials have promoted job mobility since workers have little to lose from changing from one sector to another.

It has been claimed that the growth rate indicated in Table 5 for the period after 1980 has been caused by the oil sector, and thus is a result of pure luck. Clearly, oil has been very important to the Norwegian economy since the middle of the 1970s. However, history has demonstrated that substantial and rapid increases in income may be damaging. But this has not been the case for Norway, since it has been possible to maintain macro-economic conditions, and an institutional environment for business, which has promoted growth. The combination of state capacity and an effective institutional framework made it possible to readjust the large shipbuilding sector to offshore business. In turn this opened up the possibilities for exploring promising new technologies. Together with a similar development in maritime-based industries, this has created the foundation for a new hi-tech industry, exporting goods valued at nearly NOK10 billion in 1995. But the Norwegian system for industrial finance did have a negative impact on certain industries. For example, the paper and pulp industry experienced great difficulties during the 1960s. A readjustment to larger and more effective units was necessary to regain productivity and competitiveness. But this sector was not among the targeted sectors and with regulated capital markets there was no market for corporate control. This put the industry in a lock-in situation characterised by an ineffective production structure and obsolete technology.

VI

In conclusion, this article has demonstrated that the credit-based, state-led system that developed in Norway became the institutional basis for the government to accomplish its industrial policy. At the same time, the government gradually built up a network of agencies, organisations and *ad hoc* committees within the framework of an indicative system of planning, which utilised the financial system to reach major targets in industrial policy. The article supports the hypothesis that in the Norwegian case the specific configuration of national systems for industrial finance contribute to the differing capacities of governments to intervene in the industrial economy. The specific historical features of the Norwegian banking system moulded the system of industrial finance after the Second World War, which allowed the government to accomplish strategic resource allocation. This became one of the Norwegian state's most crucial levers for accomplishing strategic industrial promotion and transformation.

NOTES

The research underlying this paper has been funded by the Norwegian Research Council (the Naerings-LOS Program).

1. Since investment strategies comprise investments in people, technology and physical plant, this definition even covers the relationship between industrial policy and technological change.
2. P. Katzenstein, 'Introduction', in P. Katzenstein (ed.), *Between Power and Plenty: Foreign Economic Policies of Advanced Industrial States* (Madison, 1984), p.4.
3. D.C. North, *Institutions, Institutional Change and Economic Performance* (Cambridge, MA, 1990).
4. Ibid., p.3 *et seq.* North introduces the notion of an 'institutional framework', which comprises 'legal rules, organizational forms, enforcement, and norms of behavior'.
5. S. Sjöstrand, 'Towards a Theory of Institutional Change', in S. Sjöstrand *et al.* (eds.), *On Economic Institutions* (Aldershot, 1995), p.23.
6. See, for example, J. Zysman, *Governments, Markets and Growth: Financial Systems and the Politics of Industrial Change* (London, 1983); P. Hall, *Governing the Economy* (New York, 1986); P. Gourevitch, *Politics in Hard Times: Comparative Responses to International Economic Crises* (Ithaca and New York, 1986)
7. See Zysman, *Governments, Markets and Growth*; T. Rybczynski, 'Industrial Finance System in Europe, U.S. and Japan', *Journal of Economic Behavior and Organization*, Vol.5 (1984); G. Dosi, 'Finance, Innovation and Industrial Change', *Journal of Economic Behavior and Organization*, Vol.10 (1990).
8. J.L. Christensen, 'The Role of Finance in National Systems of Innovation', in B.-Aa. Lundvall (ed.), *National Systems of Innovation* (London, 1992).
9. T. Rybczynski, 'Innovative Activity and Venture Financing: Acess to Markets and Opportunities in Japan, the U.S. and Europe', in R.H. Day *et al.* (eds.), *The Market for Innovation, Ownership and Control* (Amsterdam, 1993).
10. See, for example, H. Sjögren, *Bank och Näringsliv* (Uppsala, 1991).
11. E. Berglöf, 'Corporate Control and Capital Structure-Essays on Property Rights and Financial Contracts' (Ph.D. thesis, Stockholm School of Economics, 1990); Rybczynski, *Innovative Activity and Venture Financing*.
12. J. Edwards and K. Fischer, *Bank, Finance and Investment in Germany* (Cambridge, 1994). Although a valuable contribution, the framework of Edwards and Fischer is neo-classic and largely static. A more long-term and dynamic, historical approach thus gives a broader empirical basis to discuss comparative, financial systems. Furthermore, the authors do not

really discuss the concept of differing financial systems in a more coherent and comprehensive way. Finally, the interpretation of data is also a question of definition. For instance, they classify provisions for pension funds as 'equity'. However, if a bankruptcy occurs it is quite clear that the funds are the specific property of retirement pensioners. This type of debt can hardly be classified as 'equity', See Table 2 in this paper.

13. J.L. Christensen, *The Role of Finance*, p.160 *et seq.*; J. Franks and C. Mayer, 'Capital Markets and Corporate Control: A Study of France, Germany and UK', *Economic Policy*, No.10 (1990).
14. Quoted from E. Bull, *Norsk Fagbevegelse* (Oslo, 1968), p.172 .
15. S. Knutsen, *Finanssystem, Næringspolitikk og Industriell Utvikling 1950–1990. Forstudie og forskningsdesign* (Working Paper No.21, Norwegian School of Management, 1994) and S. Knutsen, 'Norwegian Banks and the Legacy of the Interwar Years', in A. Teichova *et al.* (eds.), *Universal Banking in the Twentieth Century: Finance, Industry and the State in North and Central Europe* (1994), pp.75–96.
16. There had been a political consensus on the system of direct and extensive regulation during the reconstruction period with the aim of establishing a fast recovery of the economy after the occupation. But already in 1946–47 this consensus began to crack, especially when the Conservative Party started an ideological critique against planning and state intervention.
17. White Paper No.75 (1951–52).
18. The organisational forms of the financial regulatory regime is elaborated in more detail in S. Knutsen, 'Phases in the Development of the Norwegian Banking System, 1880–1980', in Y. Cassis, G. Feldman and U. Olsson (eds.), *The Evolution of Financial Institutions and Markets in Twentieth-Century Europe* (London, 1995).
19. Archive of the Bank of Norway, Box 42, Correspondence of the Cooperation Committee: Letter from Governor E. Brofoss to the Norwegian Life Insurance Companies' Association, 28 Sept. 1955.
20. Trygve Lie was a member of the Labour government from 1935, Minister of Foreign Affairs in the Norwegian exile government in Britain during World War II and the UN's first Secretary-General. Later, he was also appointed Minister of Industry in 1963 and Minister of Trade in 1964.
21. Even in this process, the Labour Party was the motive force.
22. S. Knutsen, *Etterkrigstidens Strategiske Kapitalisme og Styringen av Kapitalmarkedet som Industripolitisk Virkemiddel 1950–1975* (Working Paper No.50, Norwegian School of Management, 1995).
23. Dietrich Stünkel, 'Die Arbeitsteilung der Banken in Norwegen', here quoted from H. Kofoed, *Den Norske Bankforening 1915–1940. Trekk av norsk bankhistorie* (Oslo, 1940), p.14.
24. J.P. Olsen, *Statsstyre og Institusjonsutforming* (Oslo, 1988).
25. J. Zysman, 'How Institutions Create Historically Rooted Trajectories of Growth', *Industrial and Corporate Change*, Vol.3 No.1 (1994), pp.243–83.
26. Report to the Executive Board of the Norwegian Labour Party (DNA) (Oslo, 1948), p.9.
27. L. Hannah, 'Technological, Managerial and Market Explanations of Differential Rates of European Business Convergence on American Productivity Levels, 1945–1973', in *Proceedings of the Conference on Business History, Rotterdam October 24 and 25, 1994* (Rotterdam, 1995).
28. Zysman, *Governments, Markets and Growth*, p.16.
29. This heuristic model is partially inspired by J. Myhrman, *Hur Sverige blev rikt* (Stockholm, 1994), pp.13–52.
30. See, for example, S. Hargreaves Heap, 'Rational Action and Institutional Change', in S. Sjöstrand *et al.*, *On Economic Institutions* (Aldershot, 1995).

The Politics of Protection: An Institutional Approach to Government–Industry Relations in the British and United States Cotton Industries, 1945–73

MARY B. ROSE

Lancaster University

Against a background of progressing, if often hesitant, world trade liberalisation since 1945, the cotton textile industries of the developed world have generally been cushioned against foreign imports, as Table 1 demonstrates. Between 1945 and 1973 lower than average tariff reductions, quota arrangements and international agreements, none of which could be justified on economic grounds, protected most Western cotton industries from the worst ravages of low labour cost competition. Ironically, more than any other Western government the United States, the post-war guardian of international trade liberalisation, was especially sympathetic to the demands of its cotton industry.[1] This was in particularly sharp contrast to the position in Britain. There, despite sustained pressure, successive governments were at best half hearted in any concessions they granted on low labour cost competition. At worst, they were positively obstructive. Whereas in the United States, from 1955, the cotton interests gained a range of concessions from administrations intent on general trade liberalisation, in Britain successive governments remained deaf to appeals for duties against Commonwealth imports and for other protective measures.[2] This suggests either that the economic case for protection was stronger in the United States than in Britain, or that British cotton industry pressure groups exerted less effective power over government than their counterparts across the Atlantic.

As mature industries in advanced economies, protection of cotton manufacturing could not be justified on the grounds of 'learning by doing' in either country. Similarly, product cycle theory predicts a relative decline in older economies of simple industries in favour of more sophisticated sectors, as comparative advantage shifts to later developers. Clearly neither country had a demonstrably superior economic case for protection. It is, therefore, the purpose of this essay to explore why the cotton industry in the United States became a more potent political force than was the case in Britain.

TABLE 1

TARIFFS ON COTTON TEXTILES IN INDUSTRIALISED COUNTRIES IN 1966 (%)

	EEC	United Kingdom	United States	Japan
Cotton yarn	8	7.5	5–29	5, 7.5
Woven fabrics	14–16 19	17.5	7.75–33	10–25
Ribbons	16–21	17.5–20	5–42.5	10–25
Tulle, lace, embroidery	14–22	25	19–60	15–30

Source: GATT, A Study in Cotton Textiles (Geneva, 1966), p.80.

For Britain, growing attention has been given by both economists and business historians to the emergence of a protectionist lobby in the cotton industry as it declined. Although there has been debate on the desirability of protection, there has been a general consensus that any efforts were largely ineffective because of the fragmentation of interests in a vertically specialised industry.[3] This essay will demonstrate that to understand why British groups were less successful in their quest for protection than their American counterparts, it is necessary to look beyond industrial structure to explore the relationship between government–industry negotiations and the wider institutional and policy environment.

The essay is divided into three substantive sections, the first of which briefly surveys economic pressures stimulating calls for protection. The second section examines the reasons for the differing performance of pressure groups in Britain and the United States. It evaluates, in particular, the economic and cultural factors which influenced the effectiveness of pressure groups on either side of the Atlantic as an introduction to the impact of institutional differences. The following section demonstrates that contrasts in the British and United States political systems had a profound impact upon the ability of the representatives of the cotton industry to gain concessions. However, it also shows the importance of placing campaigns against the background of wider macroeconomic policy objectives and in the context of the international environment. In a concluding section the implications of these differences are considered.

II

The collapse of the post-war sellers' market in 1952 witnessed a rise in imports of cotton piece goods in both the United States and Britain, as Table

2 demonstrates. In Britain, these grew especially from 1955 onwards and followed a period when export markets in Latin America, the Commonwealth and the colonies had been eroded by a combination of import substitution, domestic government subsidies and foreign competition, especially from Japan in colonial and Commonwealth markets. At the same time, rising tariffs in both the Indian and Pakistani markets curtailed exports to these destinations.[4] As Table 3 shows, imports came first predominantly from Japan but increasingly and more significantly from the Commonwealth. Similarly, in the United States imports came largely from the low labour cost economies of the Far East. Cotton industry jobs were dwindling on both sides of the Atlantic from the early 1950s. In Britain, therefore, between 1951 and 1960 105,000 jobs were lost in the British cotton industry with employment in spinning and weaving each falling by around 40 per cent. In the United States, on the other hand, a total of 87,000 cotton industry jobs were lost between 1947 and 1958.[5] In reality, import penetration was only part of the explanation of the job losses, but it was a sufficiently emotive issue to become central to campaigns by cotton interests on both sides of the Atlantic.

TABLE 2
VOLUME OF UK AND US COTTON PIECE IMPORTS 1950–72 (M SQ. YDS) AND EXTENT OF IMPORT PENETRATION

Date	UK	(% Import penetration)	US	(% Import penetration)
1950	287	16.93	51	0.48
1951	377	20.69	48	0.45
1952	180	14.41	36	0.37
1953	99	7.50	65	0.61
1954	268	15.57	74	0.72
1955	244	16.60	141	1.31
1956	306	21.19	197	1.97
1957	416	26.20	127	1.40
1958	387	27.03	146	1.62
1959	537	35.17	250	2.67
1960	728	42.95	464	4.96
1961	731	43.56	266	3.00
1962	575	39.96	465	5.00
1963	636	43.00	455	5.19
1964	767	46.68	396	4.42
1965	589	39.96	534	5.64
1966	587	41.75	611	6.70
1967	660	49.30	543	6.36
1968	707	51.57	577	7.42
1969	545	44.49	613	8.42
1970	480	42.82	558	8.54
1971	602	51.00	608	9.43
1972	429	43.12	765	12.66

Source: Cotton Board, *Quarterly Statistics*; Singleton, *Lancashire*, p.120; *Cotton: Monthly Review of World Statistics, 1967–81*

TABLE 3
IMPORT PENETRATION OF THE UK DOMESTIC MARKET BY JAPAN, HONG
KONG, INDIA AND PAKISTAN COTTON CLOTH, 1950-61 (M SQ. YDS)

Date	Total	Japan	Total H, I and P	% of total H, I and P	H, I and P % of domestic consumption
1950	287	92	76	26.5	4.5
1951	377	86	109	28.9	6.0
1952*	180	71	11	5.9	0.9
1953	99	38	18	18.6	1.4
1954	268	52	153	57.0	8.9
1955	244	64	188	77.0	12.8
1956	306	32	198	64.7	13.7
1957	416	58	267	64.2	16.8
1958	387	42	249	64.3	17.4
1959	537	44	361	67.2	23.7
1960	728	53	394	54.1	23.2
1961	731	62	321	43.9	19.1

Notes: H= imports from Hong Kong.
I= imports from India.
P= imports from Pakistan.
* 1952 world recession in cotton textiles.

Source: Cotton Board, *Quarterly Statistics.*

In the United States the cotton interests complained that their industry was being crippled by the combined impact of government support schemes for raw cotton, which placed them at a disadvantage in the purchase of raw cotton in comparison with foreign competitors. In addition, they were threatened by imports of cotton goods first from Japan and later from Hong Kong and India.[6] Additionally, especially with regard to the industrial reconstruction of Japan and the tariff concessions granted in 1955, they believed that American foreign policy objectives worked against their increasingly obsolete industry and threatened 2.4m jobs.[7] These factors created discontent, which was vigorously and effectively articulated by the American Cotton Manufacturers' Institute (ACMI), which represented 80 per cent of the industry.[8]

In Britain in the 1950s and 1960s the reluctance of successive governments to protect the cotton industry in the face of Far Eastern and especially Commonwealth competition has been well documented[9] and needs only brief reiteration here. In striking contrast to experience elsewhere in the developed world and especially in the United States, British governments at best gave low priority to the protection of the cotton industry, whether against low labour cost imports or to allow for industrial regeneration. Instead of enhanced protection, they favoured the scrapping of obsolete and surplus capacity and the re-equipment of the remaining core of the industry.[10] At worst, as with the Anglo-Japanese Payments and Trade Agreement of 1954, their commercial policies worked directly against Lancashire and were formulated without consultation with the Cotton Board, which represented the industry.[11]

As far as all interests in Lancashire were concerned, the most galling aspect of government policy was its inflexibility regarding duty-free Commonwealth imports, a legacy of the Ottawa Agreements of 1932. The origins of these agreements lay in the Sterling area, based upon imperial preference, that was constructed after the abandonment of the gold standard in 1931. While British goods were to enter the Empire at preferential rates, the Ottawa Agreements laid down that all goods qualifying for Empire preference entered Britain duty free. In the 1930s the assumption had been that Empire imports would comprise predominantly of raw materials, but in the post-war period they included Commonwealth cotton goods. That these arrangements were not modified until 1972 placed Lancashire at a significant disadvantage in comparison with other developed economies. This is because whilst, as Table I has shown, British tariffs on foreign-produced goods were very much in line with those of both Europe and the United States, UK producers were alone in facing duty-free imports from Hong Kong, India and Pakistan, which were after all the most rapidly growing sources of cotton textile exports.

During the 1950s and 1960s all the evidence suggests that both Conservative and Labour governments were unwilling to yield to the Cotton Board's demands for a reversal or at least a modification of this policy. At the same time, any efforts by the Cotton Board to negotiate voluntary quotas with the cotton masters of Hong Kong, India and Pakistan in the 1950s were doomed without government support and achieved remarkably little.[12] Even when the Long Term Arrangement (LTA) was negotiated under the auspices of GATT in 1961 to allow for an orderly expansion of exports of cotton goods from the developing to the developed world, the British government was tardy in its use of it, much to the chagrin of Lancashire.[13] Against this background, the system of global quotas covering yarn, cloth and made-up goods, introduced in 1966, came too late to be of any significant benefit to Lancashire and did not stem the flow of imports.[14]

In the United States, in contrast to the relative impotence of the cotton interests in general and the Cotton Board in particular, the cotton textile lobby became extremely powerful after the Second World War. It did not succeed in reversing the public commitment of governments to world trade liberalisation, but it was successful in gaining a number of major concessions in terms of non-tariff protection. In addition, despite the commitment of the United States government to tariff reductions, which saw a series of tariff cuts to cotton goods in 1955, 1962 and 1971, the American cotton industry with *ad valorem* tariffs of 16 per cent and 23.8 per cent on yarns and fabrics respectively was, in 1974, amongst the most highly protected in the developed world. Certainly these rates were significantly higher than the 8.6 per cent and 14.3 per cent duties imposed by the European community.[15] Taking the whole of the period from 1950 to 1971, the contrast with Britain is even starker. In the first place, the effective rate of protection remained higher in the United States than in Britain, as Table 4 shows. In addition, of course, the United States industry was protected against the imports of such Commonwealth countries as India, Pakistan and Hong Kong. Moreover, although the cotton interests in the United States were not able to reverse government commitment to freer trade, they were able to obtain some moderation in tariff reductions. In the Kennedy Round, for example, 56 per cent of textile and textile products experienced no reductions or reductions of less than 50 per cent.[16]

TABLE 4
EFFECTIVE RATES OF PROTECTION FOR TEXTILES IN THE UNITED STATES AND
THE UNITED KINGDOM IN 1962 (%)

	United States	United Kingdom
Thread and yarn	31.8	27.9
Textile fabrics	50.6	42.2

Source: B.A. Belassa, 'Tariff Protection in Industrial Countries: An Evaluation', *Journal of Political Economy*, Vol.LXXIII (1965), p.57.

The United States cotton industry was, therefore, shielded from international competition by higher and more comprehensive tariffs after the Second World War than existed in Britain. In addition, American cotton manufacturers received more extensive non-tariff protection than was secured by the Cotton Board and were generally a more potent political force. As a result, they achieved far more wide-ranging government responses to their difficulties than was the case in Britain. In the 1950s, for example, Japanese import penetration, directly encouraged by tariff reductions introduced in 1955, was portrayed as the major threat to the health of the cotton industry, and the ACMI exerted sufficient pressure on its government to achieve an intergovernmental agreement in 1957. This placed a binding quota on Japanese imports of cotton goods with no guaranteed growth.[17]

This was just the start of a series of relatively successful campaigns to secure government support for the industry. These included the establishment of a Congressional sub-committee on the Domestic Textile

Industry in 1958, which was to 'conduct a full and complete study of all factors affecting commerce and production in the textile industry of the United States'. The so-called Pastore Committee concluded that, aside from achieving productivity gains, textiles had not experienced the dramatic post-war rise in prosperity achieved in other sectors. In addition, it suggested that so great was the decline in cotton textiles that both Congress and the Administration should review all policies contributing to that decline. Finally, it secured confirmation from the Office of Civil and Defense Mobilization that the cotton industry was 'an essential industry and an essential part of the nations' mobilization base'. Consequently, the Pastore Committee justified the need to maintain high levels of textile capacity and employment on the somewhat dubious grounds of national security. On this basis, it recommended the introduction of import quotas and the termination of the two-price raw cotton system.[18]

These recommendations were encapsulated in John F. Kennedy's Seven Point Plan for the cotton industry of 1961 and implemented in the same year. It was a plan which was infinitely more supportive of the domestic industry than the 1959 Cotton Industry Act had been in Britain. It was designed to facilitate the modernisation of the industry in a relatively secure external environment. Easily the most significant consequence for the cotton industry was the hastily convened international conference of representatives of developed and developing economies in Geneva which was promised under the plan. The idea was to reduce the disruption of markets in industrialised countries which the international spread of industrialisation caused. It resulted in the Short Term Arrangement, followed swiftly, in 1962, by the Long Term Arrangement (LTA), which allowed for a controlled growth of imports of five per cent per annum. However, where imports from one participating country threatened to disrupt the domestic market of another, restraint could be called for.[19]

The LTA, which was successively renewed until 1973, fell short of the ACMI's demands for non-tariff protection for all textiles. It did, however, mark a major and welcome step forward in the industry's quest for special treatment. Successive United States administrations had the opportunity to protect their national cotton industry behind the respectability of an international agreement. Kennedy had, therefore, found an international solution to a potentially embarrassing domestic economic and political problem.[20] For the cynical, it is instructive that with far lower levels of import penetration than occurred in Britain, as was shown in Table 2, the United States invoked the LTA far more frequently. Indeed, between 1962 and 1965, the United States took restrictive action against the cotton goods of Argentina, Brazil, Colombia, Mexico, Pakistan, the Republic of China, Hong Kong, India, Israel, Jamaica, Korea, Spain, Portugal, the Philippines,

Poland, Yugoslavia, Turkey, Japan, Greece and the United Arab Republic, covering a range of 49 categories of goods. By 1972 the United States had constraints on imports from 30 suppliers.[21] Since the seventh point of the Kennedy Plan used the alleged national security standing of the industry as a basis for special case pleading under trade agreements, leaving open the possibility of unilateral protective measures, the position of the cotton industry as a special case was secure.[22]

An important consequence of the LTA was that developing countries began to shift production towards synthetics, which were not covered by the agreement. This signalled the start of a new series of campaigns in the United States in the late 1960s and early 1970s, which, following the pattern of the cotton campaigns, culminated in a new international trade treaty, the Multifibres Arrangement (MFA), which was concluded late in 1973. As with LTA, the initiative and much of the political pressure for MFA came from the United States and followed renewed domestic pressure for protection against imports of synthetics first from Japan in 1969–71 and subsequently from East Asia.[23]

III

The explanation of precisely why cotton textile interests in Britain proved less successful in influencing governments than was the case in the United States is a complex issue. It involves the interaction of historical, cultural and politico-economic domestic forces, with changes in both the international balance of power and in foreign economic policy on either side of the Atlantic.

One possible explanation of the greater success of the United States' campaigns for cotton protection, as compared with those in Britain, is the legacy of nineteenth-century experience. It could simply be that with a history so closely linked to the development of the tariff,[24] the American cotton interests had much more experience in lobbying for protection than did their British counterparts, with their free trade traditions.

Certainly there were historical precedents for differences in bargaining power to be found in the inter-war period. In the 1920s and 1930s, British governments were prepared to make only marginal concessions to Lancashire, when their interests were damaged as a result of changing policy with regard to India. In the United States, on the other hand, Roosevelt was quick to concede to the demands of the cotton interests for enhanced protection against Japan, even though they came in 1936, just two years after the passage of the Reciprocal Trade Act, which was a first step towards trade liberalisation by the United States.[25] This pattern continued in the post-war period, especially after 1955, when in the United States the coalition of cotton apparel and textile interests emerged as a major political force that had to be neutralised every time successive governments, from Kennedy to Reagan, wanted to make any progress on its central objective of multilateral trade liberalisation. Yet to conclude that the superior bargaining power of United States cotton manufacturers was the result of greater and longer experience than was the case in Britain is to oversimplify the issues.

In studying the effectiveness of pressure groups in achieving import protection, economists have identified a number of significant influences. Of these, the most important determinants of success have been a relatively small number of firms in the industry,[26] combined with a high degree of geographic concentration and a rapid growth of import penetration. Against this background, it has also been predicted that pressure groups would be most likely to gain protection for an industry which is both highly labour intensive and which accounts for a high level of employment, whilst producing a commodity which makes up only a small proportion of consumers' budgets. Moreover, protection was most likely to be successful when only a small share of output was exported and where there were relatively low levels of foreign direct investment by firms in the industry.[27]

Some contrasting economic forces provide a partial explanation of why pressure groups in the United States were more successful in securing protection they were in Britain. In the first place, the United States cotton industry was historically far less export oriented than Britain's, a trend which continued in the post-war period, as Table 5 testifies. Moreover, in the 1950s, as Table 2 has demonstrated, although both were experiencing similar rates of growth of import penetration, in the United States cotton piece good imports started from a far lower base, so that the shock factor is likely to have been greater than in Britain.

These historical trends in market orientation in turn influenced attitudes towards foreign competition in the United States. As a consequence, even though import penetration was a fraction of the level in Britain, cotton manufacturers were simply noisier in their complaints than their British counterparts. High nineteenth-century tariff barriers meant that United States' cotton manufacturers had built up their industries under the assumption that the vast domestic market was their preserve. Cotton manufacturers remained firmly protectionist, and, in 1961, one former textile executive pointed out in a letter to the *New York Times*:

> We would welcome imports which were improvements on our own; our objection is to import of imitations of our own products coming in only because they are lower in price because they are made under cheaper foreign wages and standards ... We are looking for no temporary adjustment. Therefore we want permanent protection, whether by tariff or quota or both, that will maintain our American standards today, tomorrow and forever.[28]

TABLE 5
PROPORTION OF PIECE GOOD OUTPUT EXPORTED 1950–1972 (%)

Date	UK	US
1950	36.9	5.0
1951	37.4	7.0
1952	39.9	7.0
1953	36.7	5.6
1954	30.5	5.7
1955	31.2	4.9
1956	29.4	5.0
1957	28.0	5.9
1958	26.9.	5.4
1959	26.0	5.1
1960	25.3	4.7
1961	23.3	5.2
1962	21.4	4.5
1963	20.9	4.2
1964	19.3	4.4
1965	18.8	3.3
1966	16.9	3.8
1967	16.9	6.6
1968	19.0	7.7
1969	17.7	8.8
1970	17.8	8.9
1971	19.7	9.9
1972	15.5	13.5

Source: R. Robson, *The Cotton Industry in Britain* (London, 1957), p.358; Cotton Board, *Quarterly Statistics*; *Cotton: Monthly Review of World Statistics, 1965–72.*

Any infiltration or threat of incursion into the domestic market was, therefore, treated with alarm and outrage, and cotton manufacturers in the United States did not believe that foreign producers had an inalienable right to penetrate their markets. In 1961, for example, on the eve of the opening of the Geneva meeting on the proposed Long Term Arrangement on cotton textiles, the ACMI called for 'recognition that growth of the American textile market is not created for overseas manufacturers and that they have no vested right to any part of it'.[29]

Raymond Streat has observed that British manufacturers were far more gentlemanly than their American cousins in their cries for protection. This cultural difference may well have stemmed, in part at least, from contrasting historical influences on the market orientation of the industry.[30] However, apparent British restraint should not be exaggerated, for, as the campaign for protection gathered momentum, so it became more flamboyant, especially when orchestrated by Cyril Lord during the 1950s.[31]

If differences in the market orientation of the two industries were significant in influencing the culture of the industry and styles of campaigning, the impact of other economic forces on bargaining power was nothing like as conclusive. The relative labour intensity of the cotton industry in high-income economies made the industries of both the United States and Britain ideal candidates for successful campaigns for protection. However, since the American industry was more capital intensive than the British, this clearly does not explain differences in bargaining power. Secondly, lacking a national low labour cost alternative, such as the southern states of the United States, it is true that British firms were more inclined to undertake foreign direct investment than their United States counterparts. Yet there is little evidence that this was sufficient, in the period in question, to explain differences in bargaining power.[32]

High levels of economic and geographic concentration increase the effectiveness of pressure groups. In Britain the cotton industry continued, albeit to a somewhat reduced degree, to be concentrated in Lancashire, while in the United States the proportion of cotton textile manufacturing located in the southern states continued to increase. It has been suggested, however, that any collective action in Lancashire was hampered by the relatively small scale of firms and by the lasting influence of vertical and spatial specialisation, which made it difficult for the industry to speak with one voice.[33] Yet nothing so simple as differences in economic and geographic concentration explain the contrasting bargaining power of cotton industry pressure groups on either side of the Atlantic. This is because, even though levels of integration were lower in Britain than in the United States, concentration ratios in textiles were 44.2 and 34.5 respectively, making British levels marginally higher. More significantly in both cases, these were low relative to such sectors as automobiles, and therefore reflected a comparatively limited level of national bargaining power.[34]

Simple economic analysis clearly cannot explain why the cotton interests were so much more effective in influencing government policy in the United States than in Britain. Nor are cultural variations, which shaped attitudes to import penetration, the whole story. A full appreciation of the success or failure of interest groups in moulding government policy is dependent upon both the structure of the political system and wider policy objectives, both of which are in turn shaped by historical forces.[35]

IV

In the United States the political system is decentralised, with power divided between the President and Congress. Under this system, the majority party in Congress may differ from the Head of State. Its origins can be traced back to the early post-revolutionary period. Suspicious of concentrations of influence, America's founding fathers sought to divide power within the government and within society, an objective which was entrenched in the Constitution. As a consequence, the identity and legislative power of individual states was preserved, with control divided between federal and state governments. In turn, within the federal government, executive power was to rest with the President, whilst legislative power was to lie with Congress, as the guardians of state interests. Members of Congress, mindful of a desire for re-election, have been able to put local interests ahead of national ones. This has meant that they have tended to weigh up the likely local consequences of any policy initiative and vote accordingly, rather than necessarily along party lines. The Seventeenth Amendment of 1913, which required that Senators should be elected rather than being the placemen of the state legislatures, inevitably reduced the power of interest groups in United States politics, as is witnessed by voting patterns on the Smoot Hawley Tariff of 1930.[36] However, the power of the President continued to be moderated by Congress with its wide representation, whilst the threat of the presidential veto in turn has moderated the influence of Congress.[37]

There is also a complex committee structure in Congress which facilitates the legislative process and further reinforces the power of interest groups. In the United States, congressional committees are established by the legislature, not the President, so that Congress controls the membership. This committee structure means that Congress has had the opportunity of filling committees with sympathetic members and has frequently exercised this privilege.[38] Inevitably, those members of Congress who served on committees exerted most influence on the path of legislation.[39] It is interesting, therefore, to note that John Pastore, who chaired the Sub-Commitee on Domestic Textiles, was Senator of Rhode Island, whilst the first members were the Senators of South Carolina and New Hampshire.[40]

In terms of the formulation of foreign commercial policy, the United States Constitution divided executive and legislative power between President and Congress. Consequently, although presidential influence over commercial policy stemmed from responsibility for conducting foreign relations, under Article I, Section 8, Congress had the right to regulate foreign commerce and to raise duties and taxes.[41] This clear division of responsibility continued until the 1930s. The President directed foreign affairs, whilst taxation, including the raising of tariffs, remained the responsibility of Congress. With tariffs viewed essentially as an issue of domestic, as opposed to foreign, economic policy in a relatively isolationist economy, there was relatively little conflict of interest.

By authorising the President, for a three-year period, to make tariff cutting agreements with other countries, Roosevelt's 1934 Reciprocal Trade Act altered this balance. It passed the power to adjust tariffs from Congress to the executive.[42] This has meant that the President and the State Department have been able to take the initiative in formulating foreign economic policies, in line with broader strategic foreign policy objectives, such as the economic reconstruction of Europe and Japan. However, by retaining the right to veto a further three-year extension of this power, Congress has continued to monitor the process, giving due consideration to such issues as the implications of policy for domestic industry and employment.[43] This has meant that any post-war United States' President wishing to make any progress on trade liberalisation has required the support of Congress at the very time when the power of the southern bloc vote became a major source of political compromise.[44] In addition, the continued power of Congress has meant that campaigning commitments by potential presidents could not simply be empty promises to win votes. This was because, if undertakings were not ratified, congressional support could be withdrawn from major initiatives.

In such an environment, the cotton industry interest groups in the United States have been able to exert considerable influence over the political process. Moreover, the mergers during the 1940s and 1950s and the formation of such giant combines as the Burlington Mills Corporation, M. Lowenstein & Sons Inc, J. & P. Stevens and Textron, brought a growing unity of economic interest between north and south, which shared the damaging effect of import penetration in the 1950s and 1960s.[45] It proved to be a powerful mix, because the managers of the northern-owned southern mills were their one-time owners, who retained prominent positions in close-knit local elites and hence remained in regular and personal contact with Congressmen. So close were the ties between the two groups that, in the Second World War, the relationship between southern millowners and Democratic congressmen has been likened to incest. Such close ties meant that, mindful of their prospects for re-election, Southern Democrats were increasingly prepared between the mid-1950s and mid-1970s to abandon their historical and partisan allegiance to liberalism and vote in line with local interests. This meant that the ACMI's letter writing campaigns, as Table 6 indicates, significantly influenced voting patterns on the renewal of the Reciprocal Trade Act in the mid-1950s, a pattern which was reinforced during the 1960s.[46]

From the mid-1950s, the political strength of United States cotton interests to influence voting patterns was further enhanced by the formation of successful alliances with both the clothing and man-made fibres sections of the industry, all also located in the southern states. By the early 1960s, on the other hand, the ACMI was also able to compel the National Cotton Council, an association of previously free trade cotton growers, and the Textile Workers of America to join them. The result was a combination of

TABLE 6
VOTING PATTERNS ON MAJOR TRADE LEGISLATION, 1922–62

Textile District	Textile Employment	Vote by Representative			
		1922	1930	1955	1962
Georgia (4th district)	22,830	L	L	P	L
Georgia (7th district)	24,000	L	L	P	L
N. Carolina (9th district)	61,700	L	L	P	P
N. Carolina (10th district)	41,800	L	L	P	P
N. Carolina (11th District)	39,170	L	L	P	P
S. Carolina (3rd District)	36,300	L	L	P	L
S. Carolina (4th District)	51,000	L	L	P	L

Notes: L – Liberal P – Protection
Source: R. Bauer, I. deSolla Pool and L. Dexter, *American Business and Public Policy* (Chicago, IL, 1964), p.360.

sectors and interests which became a formidable political force representing the united interests of the declining North with the politically powerful south.[47]

The threat of the southern bloc vote has, therefore, been a critical feature of American trade negotiations in the 1950s and 1960s. Moreover, presidents needed the south to get elected in the first place, and the prospect of the southern bloc vote against major initiatives, of both strategic and electoral importance, was enough to ensure that the cotton interests secured major concessions.[48]

Kennedy's desire for tariff reductions, which culminated in the Trade Expansion Act of 1962, stemmed from a wish to neutralise the impact of the EEC common external tariff on United States business and agricultural interests. To achieve this wider objective, he had to carry the representatives of the cotton industry groups with him, a group of 128 congressmen, who, throughout the 1950s, had voted as a group against freer trade.[49] This could only be achieved by fulfilling promises made in his electoral campaign. In August 1960, as Democratic nominee, he had published a letter to Governor F. Hollings of South Carolina in which he acknowledged the need for an industry-wide remedy if rising unemployment was to be avoided in both the textile and apparel industries.[50] This became the foundation of his 1961 seven-point plan for textiles, which guaranteed the vital support of the ACMI for the Trade Expansion Act in 1962.[51] It was a resolution which freed normally protectionist Congressmen to vote for liberalisation. As a further reward, the cotton industry was faced with below average tariff reductions of 25 and 27 per cent respectively on cotton cloth and cotton yarn, as compared with the norm of 36 per cent and a maximum of 50 per cent.[52] The need to ratify electoral promises made to the textile coalition by prospective presidents remained a feature of 1960s and 1970s politics, whether presidents were Democrats or Republicans. Thus, in 1968, in an effort to secure the Republican nomination, Nixon promised to stem rising flows of textile imports. It was a promise which tied him into lengthy, frustrating and costly negotiations with the Japanese over imports of synthetics between 1969 and 1971, at the very time he was trying to improve US–Japanese relations.[53]

From being a marginal, often divided pressure group with a facility for lobbying Congress over protection, the United States cotton industry therefore emerged as a significant political force, capable of threatening major pieces of trade liberalising legislation unless concessions were granted. As a result of a combination of differences in the political system, structural arrangements in the industry and the wider macroeconomic objectives of governments during the 1950s and 1960s, this position simply was not replicated in Britain.

The British parliamentary system is far more centralised than in the United States, with power resting firmly with the Prime Minister, who is also leader of the government. In addition, the Prime Minister will also be the leader of the majority party in the House of Commons, where voting on all major policy issues will be along party lines. In Britain, therefore, executive and legislative power are united, with the executive dominating the legislative process.[54] Policy is, therefore made by the Prime Minister and the Cabinet and ratified by a parliament in which the government will be the majority party. Unlike congressional committees, whose membership may be the placemen of Congress, the composition of British Select Committees is determined by the executive without favour to local interest groups.

The system of government in Britain has limited the power of pressure groups to block major initiatives. In the twentieth century, the combination of centralised political power in a parliamentary system, with the vagaries of the timing of British elections, has meant that the impact of local, sectional interests has often been relatively limited. With the important exceptions of the City of London, with its close-knit networks of contact with the Treasury,[55] or the defence-related industries, with aspirations in accordance with government foreign policy, local or industrial interest groups have had a relatively marginal influence on economic policy formulation .

With respect to the cotton industry groups, their impact on policy was greatest around general elections. This was especially so if the outcome was uncertain, as in 1957–58, when there were nine marginal Lancashire constituencies and the cotton interests gained some concessions from the Conservative government.[56] During the rest of the 1950s, however, although first Churchill and then Eden were troubled by the complaints of Lancashire's parliamentary candidates, they simply were not a sufficiently large group to be politically significant during the life of the parliament. Lancashire was also politically divided, with Liberal MPs maintaining their historical support for free trade, especially in towns less affected by the coarse imports from the Commonwealth. In the 1958–59 session of the Bolton and District Works Managers' Association, for example, A.F. Holt, the Liberal MP for Bolton West, spoke in favour of free trade to a not unenthusiastic audience, whose livelihood lay at the finer end of the cotton industry.[57] In addition, it is worth noting that the cultural environment found in the southern states of the United States was quite unlike the relations which existed in Lancashire between MPs and millowners, where there was a considerable cultural divide between the majority in parliament and industrialists.

It was demonstrated in the case of the United States that the merger wave of the 1940s and 1950s significantly increased the political effectiveness of the cotton interests. In Britain the equivalent merger wave, which restructured the industry along vertical rather than horizontal lines and led to a significant rise in concentration, was delayed until the 1960s. The wave of amalgamations began in 1963 as a struggle for control of Lancashire's dwindling capacity between the major man-made fibres producers, Courtaulds and ICI. Within three years, what remained of the cotton industry was in the hands of four combines, Courtaulds, Viyella International, English Sewing Cotton and Carrington Dewhurst. Often portrayed as a last-ditch attempt to stem the decline of the Lancashire cotton industry by radical restructuring,[58] the amalgamations, which made the British cotton industry the most heavily concentrated in the world,[59] were also designed to increase its bargaining power with the government. Indeed, Sir Arthur Knight, Deputy Chairman of Courtaulds, admitted that this lay behind his company's acquisition of Fine Spinners & Doublers and the Lancashire Cotton Corporation, which he believed were essential if there was to be 'any prospect of influencing government attidudes over imports'.[60]

That the industry, in reality, exerted so little leverage and that tariff protection against the Commonwealth was not achieved until 1972 is a measure of the textile interests' limited bargaining power with the government, especially as compared with the United States. This was partly because the tight ties of ownership between the remnants of the Lancashire cotton industry and the combines did not lead to further geographic concentration, as had happened in the southern states of the United States. Moreover, neither Courtaulds nor Viyella International had their origins in Lancashire and their industrial interests were geographically scattered within Britain.[61] However, since Lancashire still remained a significant home of the remnants of the industry and hence a potential political power-base, this cannot be the whole story. More important in terms of explaining differences in bargaining power was the cross-sectoral alliance between the United States' man-made fibre producers and clothing industries and the cotton industry to form a formidable coalition of dynamic and declining industries. In Britain the man-made fibre producers became prominent owners of Lancashire so that this formidable display of collective unity between the strong and the weak was missing.

It is clear that differences in the development of the political systems of the United States and Britain meant that the relative power of interest groups to bend government policy in their favour varied. It is not, however, sufficient to conclude that the limited success of Lancashire's protectionist campaigns was entirely the result of a more centralised political system than prevailed in the United States. In any event, industries such as defence did receive preferential treatment by British governments in this period. It is clear, therefore, that differences in the wider economic and political objectives of the two governments had differing implications for the two industries in this period.

The United States' commitment to world trade liberalisation gave governments greater flexibility in responding to the demands for concessions by the cotton interests than did Britain's commitment to Commonwealth. More than anything, it was the centrality of the Commonwealth to British macroeconomic policy in the 1950s and 1960s which explains why both Tory and Labour governments were reluctant to increase the protection of the cotton industry. In the 1950s, therefore, Churchill feared that any concessions to Lancashire, especially with respect to India, might risk Indian tariff preferences on other British goods. Similarly, and perhaps surprisingly, the Labour Party was only slightly more amenable to the reversal of the policy on duty-free imports than the Tories, though they introduced a blanket surcharge of 10–15 per cent on all imports in 1964–66.[62] With a commitment to alleviating world poverty it would have been politically damaging and deeply contradictory to have introduced a tariff specifically against Commonwealth imports.[63] However, perhaps the most important policy impediment to enhanced protection for Lancashire against imports from Hong Kong, Pakistan and India was the vital role which Commonwealth sterling balances played in British macroeconomic policy regarding the sterling area in this period.[64]

During the Second World War Britain had relied on credits, mainly from Empire banks, to purchase imports. These were held in London as sterling balances amounting to £3,567m by 1945. By the end of 1957 trade patterns within the sterling area meant they had risen to £3,912m, a third of which were held by colonial banks, including, of course, those based in Hong Kong.[65] Any introduction of import restrictions on Commonwealth cotton goods would have provoked a withdrawal of these sterling balances and a major sterling crisis, and fundamentally undermined British economic policy. It was a constraint for which there was no equivalent in the United States, and it effectively meant that the United States position as the champion of trade liberalism was a far smaller obstacle to protection of the cotton industry than was Britain's commitment to the Commonwealth. It was, therefore, no accident that the introduction of duties on imported Commonwealth cotton goods was delayed until 1972, when the sterling area ended.[66]

Finally, all campaigns for protection should be placed in the context of wider considerations of international economic policy and diplomacy. In the world which emerged after 1945 it is impossible to ignore the fact that the shift in the international balance of power from Europe, and especially from Britain, to the United States was complete and that this had consequences for domestic policy formulation in the two countries. The considerable international political and economic power of the United States gave presidents the option of shifting domestic economic problems into the international arena, as Kennedy had done in 1961 and Nixon in 1973. The UK's diminished international prestige after 1945 meant that such actions simply were not options open to British administrations.

V

Singleton is undoubtedly correct to conclude that international shifts in comparative advantage made protection a waste of resources after 1945.[67] Yet, despite an international liberalisation of world trade, at the prompting of the United States following the Second World War, textile protection has remained a fact of life, and nowhere more prominently than in America. This was patently not so in Britain, where the political power of Lancashire, in reality never that significant, was eroded further after the Second World War as the industry declined. British governments, therefore, remained relatively unmoved when the objective of Commonwealth development led to competition in both foreign and domestic markets. The cotton industry in the United States did not reverse its government's commitment to internationalism any more than British interests undermined British commitment to Commonwealth trade and development. However, in contrast to the position in Lancashire, American cotton manufacturers were able to secure government concessions for the industry and be confident of government support when their domestic markets were threatened. Moreover, the international standing of the United States meant that its government was in a position to influence the direction of international agreements for textiles in ways which favoured American cotton interests.

In addition, cotton manufacturers could be confident that such agreements would be interpreted in the most favourable possible way.

This analysis of campaigns for protection of the British and United States cotton industries since 1945 has confirmed the importance of comparing the political and institutional environment surrounding business in a number of ways. In the first place, it has shown how critical has been the influence of national differences on the development of political institutions in shaping the bargaining power of interest groups. In the second, implicit in the discussion has been the long-term historical implications of institutional development for the cotton industries in Britain and the United States. Thus, whereas Lancashire's dramatic expansion had been inseparable from the Empire, and especially India, the rise of the cotton industry in the United States was just as closely associated with the tariff. These trends had profound implications for the two industries in the changed world after 1945. It left Lancashire with the legacy of the Ottawa Agreements, at a time when British governments were anxious to promote Commonwealth development. In the United States, on the other hand, past associations with protection continued to work in the cotton industry's favour, despite changing national policies. Finally, differences in the institutional environment were among a range of factors which affected the structure of the two industries and their ability to survive after 1945.

It is not intended to suggest that the relative weakness of protection of cotton textiles was the only explanation for the demise of cotton manufacturing in Lancashire in the late twentieth century. Equally, it should not be concluded that there was an economic case for protection. However, the relative success of cotton manufacturers in the United States in campaigns for protection in the 1950s and 1960s, as compared with their Lancashire counterparts, undoubtedly had bearing on their respective industrial profiles. Clearly, the prevalence of obsolete machinery, in comparison to the United States, goes some way towards explaining why the Lancashire cotton industry declined so rapidly. However, if set alongside two decades of inter-war decay and depressing market trends, during and after the Second World War, the resistance of British governments to pleas for protection represented the final straw.[68] There was simply, as Singleton has shown, little incentive to invest in productivity enhancing technology in a deeply uncertain and depressing market environment.[69] Indeed, it has been argued that European cotton industries displayed similar structural and technical weaknesses as Britain in the 1950s, but were protected and imposed import restrictions which breached GATT and allowed for successful modernisation.[70]

In the United States, on the other hand, not only had wartime and post-war trends been more favourable to the cotton industry than was the case in

Britain, but the growing awareness of their political power, especially after 1960, and relatively high tariff and non-tariff barriers encouraged investment by cotton manufacturers.

It has been suggested that before 1945 the relatively high level of protection afforded to American industry generally helped to give it its distinctive characteristics of high productivity, capital intensity and standardisation.[71] In the case of the cotton and related textile industries there is ample evidence of these characteristics, at least in Massachusetts and the southern states. In the post-war period, the enjoyment of relatively high levels of protection reinforced these trends. It meant that although the United States' tastes became increasingly sophisticated, the size of the domestic market allowed continued standardisation. Larger and highly rationalised mills therefore produced a limited array of fabrics.[72] After 1961 the combination of still relatively high tariffs and the active use of the LTA by successive administrations encouraged a wave of productivity-enhancing investment which reinforced existing trends in the industry.[73] Conversely, it was argued by the United States Department of Commerce in the 1960s that it was vital that the disruptive effects of unexpected imports be avoided, because the psychological effect of being unable to predict market changes would reduce levels of investment.[74]

Ironically, however, the long-term consequences of the protection of the American cotton and textile industries may be less encouraging. In the first place, productivity enhancement has led to a rise in unemployment during the 1970s and 1980s. Moreover, the reinforcement of trends towards standardisation have meant that, with the doubling of imports between 1973 and 1985, many United States firms have looked for overseas markets and found it difficult to move over from production-oriented methods to those geared towards a range of markets. As a consequence, between 1981 and 1984 alone there have been 231 plant closures and numerous southern towns have become ghost towns.[75]

Ironically, the analysis of the implications of differing political institutions must also bring into question the notion that Lancashire's decline was principally the result of institutional rigidities. Certainly, differing historical experience does help to explain why Lancashire's post-war decline came earlier and was more precipitous than occurred in the United States. However, it was not simply the case (as Lazonick has suggested) that varying economic forces had created two industries with contrasting organisational and technological structures, and consequently differing capacities for change.[76] There were significant long- and short-term differences in the investment environment faced in the United States and Britain. In addition, it has been demonstrated that long-term political and cultural influences were every bit as important to the formulation of business strategy as the legacy of past forms of capitalism. Combined with twentieth-century changes in the balance of international power, these influences meant that United States cotton manufacturers had greater power to mould commercial policy in their favour than was the case for Lancashire's cotton interests.

NOTES

I should like to thank the participants at the conference held at Lancaster University in May 1996 on 'Evolutionary and Institutional Theory and Business History' for their helpful comments. Thanks are also due to two anonymous referees and to Geoff Jones, Marguerite Dupree, Steve Toms and Mike French for their written comments. The usual disclaimers apply.

1. D.B. Keesing and M. Wolf, *Textile Quotas against Developing Countries* (London, 1980), p.44; R.A. Pastor, *Congress and the Politics of United States Foreign Economic Policy, 1929–1976* (Berkeley, 1980), p.29.
2. H.S. Hunsberger, *Japan in United States Foreign Economic Policy* (Washington, 1961); R.B. Brandis, *The Making of Textile Trade Policy, 1935–81* (Washington, 1982); M. Dupree, 'Struggling with Destiny: The Cotton Industry, Overseas Trade Policy and the Cotton Board', *Business History*, Vol.32 (1990), pp.106–8.
3. R.P. Dore, 'Adjustment in Process: A Lancashire Town', in J.N. Bagwhati (ed.), *Import Competition and Response* (Chicago, 1982), pp.312–17; Dupree, 'Struggling', 106–28; J. Singleton, *Lancashire on the Scrapheap: The Cotton Industry, 1945–1970* (Oxford, 1991), pp.114–39.
4. Singleton, *Lancashire*, pp.118, 123.
5. Ibid., pp.115–16; H.B. Lary, *Imports of Manufactures from Less Developed Countries* (New York, 1968), p.83.
6. V.K. Aggarwal with S. Haggard, 'The Politics of Protection in the US Textile and Apparel Industries', in J. Zysman and L. Tyson (eds.), *American Industry in International Competition* (Ithaca, NY, 1983), pp.259–60; R. Robson, *The Cotton Industry in Britain* (London, 1957), pp.262–3.
7. Hunsberger, *Japan*, pp.258, 310; Brandis, *Making of Textile Trade Policy*, pp.8–10.
8. Aggarwel with Haggard, 'Politics', pp.259–61; R. Bauer, I. de Sola Pool and L. Dexter, *American Business and Public Policy* (Chicago, IL, 1964), p.10.
9. Dupree, 'Struggling', pp.106–28; J. Singleton, 'Showing the White Flag: The Lancashire Cotton Industry, 1945–65', *Business History*, Vol.32 (1990), pp.129–49.
10. C. Miles, *Lancashire Textiles: A Case Study of Industrial Change* (Cambridge, 1968), pp.46–54.
11. Dupree, 'Struggling', pp.119–20.
12. Ibid., pp.110–28; Singleton, *Lancashire*, p.136; Cotton Board, *The Cotton Industry and Unlimited Imports* (Manchester, 1956).
13. J. Tomlinson, *Government and Enterprise since 1900* (Oxford, 1994), p.352; Singleton, *Lancashire*, pp.135–7; A. Knight, *Private Enterprise and Public Intervention: The Courtaulds Experience* (London, 1974), p.110; Textile Council, *Cotton and Allied Trades: A Report on Present Performance and Future Prospects* (Manchester, 1969), pp.128; GATT, *A Study on Cotton Textiles* (Geneva, 1966), p.83; Federation of Master Cotton Spinners' Associations Ltd, *Annual Report* (London, 1965), p.97.
14. Singleton, *Lancashire*, p.139; Caroline Miles, 'Protection of the British Textile Industry' in W.M. Corden and G. Fels (eds.), *Public Assistance to Industry: Protection and Subsidies in Britain and Germany* (London, 1976), p.197.
15. Keesing and Wolf, *Textile Quotas*, p.44.
16. J.W. Evans, *The Kennedy Round in American Trade Policy: The Twilight of GATT?* (Cambridge, MA, 1971), p.284.

17. Brandis, *Making of Textile Trade Policy*, p.11.
18. Ibid., pp.16–18.
19. Ibid., pp.20–26; W.H. Simpson, *Some Aspects of America's Textile Industry* (Columbia, OH, 1966).
20. Aggarwal with Haggard, 'Politics', p.377.
21. GATT, *A Study*, p.83; Simpson, *Some Aspects*, p.29; R. Anson and P. Simpson, *World Textile Trade and Production Trends* (London, 1988), p.109.
22. Aggarwal with Haggard, 'Politics', p.279.
23. I.M. Destler, H. Fukui and H. Sato, *The Textile Wrangle* (Ithaca, NY, 1979); Brandis, *The Making*, p.44; Keesing and Wolf, *Textile Quotas*, p.39.
24. S. Ratner, *The Tariff in American History* (New York, 1972).
25. Bauer, de Sola Pool and Dexter, *American*, pp.25–6.
26. Olson, *Logic*.
27. Anderson and Baldwin, 'Political', p.14.
28. Letter from Donald Comer, former textile executive, *New York Times*, 24 March 1961, quoted Hunsberger, *Japan*, p.363.
29. Brandis, *Making of Textile Trade Policy*, p.24.
30. *Cotton Board Trade Letter*, 1949, p.3.
31. M. Dupree, *Lancashire and Whitehall: The Diary of Sir Raymond Streat, 1931–57* (Manchester, 1987), Vol.2, p.885.
32. F. Clairmont and J. Cavanagh, *The World in their Web: Dynamics of Textile Multinationals* (London, 1981), p.139; Knight, *Private*, p.55.
33. C. Wurm, *Business Politics and International Relations: Steel, Cotton and International Cartels in British Politics, 1924–39* (Cambridge, 1993), p.198.
34. R.L. Nelson, *Concentration in the Manufacturing Industries of the United States: A Mid Century Report* (New Haven, CT, 1963), p.37; L. Hannah, *The Rise of the Corporate Economy* (London, 1983), p.144. It should be noted that the United States concentration ratio is a four-firm ratio for 1954 and the United Kingdom one is a five-firm ratio for 1957).
35. Davis and North, *Institutional Change*.
36. Ibid., p.67; C.M. Callahan, J.A. McDonald and A.P. O'Brien, 'Who Voted for Smoot-Hawley', *Journal of Economic History*, Vol.54 (1994), pp.683–90.
37. Ibid., p.62; J.D. Lees, *The Political System of the United States* (London, 1969), pp.36, 189.
38. Rowley *et al.*, *Trade Protection*, pp.97–8; Lees, *The Political System*, p.135.
39. Baldwin, *The Political Economy*, p.50.
40. Brandis, *Making of Textile Trade Policy*, p.16.
41. P.B. Feller and A. Carlisle Wilson, 'United States Tariff and Trade Law: Constitutional Sources and Constraints', *Law and Policy in International Business*, Vol.8 (1976), pp.106–7; Rowley *et al.*, *Trade Protection*, p.124.
42. Bauer *et al.*, *American Business*, p.26.
43. Baldwin, *The Political Economy*, pp.34–5.
44. Pastor, *Congress*, p.53; T.M. Moe, 'Politics and the Theory of Organization', *Journal of Law, Economics and Organization*, Vol.7 (1991), pp.106–29.
45. J.W. Markham, 'Integration in the Textile Industry', *Harvard Business Review* (Jan. 1950), pp.83–5; Simpson, *Some Aspects*, pp.57–9.
46. Bauer *et al.*, *American Business*, pp.359–62; J.K. Galbraith, *A Life in Our Times* (London, 1981), p.149; Baldwin, *Political Economy*, pp.15–29.
47. Aggarwal with Haggard, 'The Politics', pp.257, 274–7; Robson, *Cotton Industry*, p.45; T.W. Zeiler, *American Trade and Power in the 1960s* (New York, 1992), p.76.
48. Brandis, *Making of Textile Trade Policy*, p.17; I.M. Destler, H. Fukui and H. Sato, *The Textile Wrangle* (Ithaca, NY, 1979); Keesing and Wolf, *Textile Quotas*, p.39.
49. Baldwin, *Political Economy*, pp.15–35; Pastor, *Congress*, p.63.
50. Brandis, *Making of Textile Trade Policy*, p.17.
51. Pastor, *Congress*, p.109.
52. Brandis, *Making of Textile Trade Policy*, p.33.
53. Destler *et al.*, *Textile Wrangle*, pp.69–71.
54. S. Krasner, 'US Commercial and Monetary Policy: Unraveling the Paradox of External

Strength and Internal Weakness', in P. Katzenstein (ed.), *Between Power and Plenty: Foreign Economic Policies of Advanced Industrial States* (Madison, 1978), pp.57–61.
55. P.J. Cain and A.G. Hopkins, *British Imperialism: Crisis and Deconstruction, 1914–1990*, (London, 1993), pp.265–7.
56. Miles, *Lancashire Textiles*, pp.46–54.
57. Bolton and Distirct Textile Works Managers' Association, 1958–59, Address by Mr A.F. Holt MP, 'Free Trade ... Not Protection', pp.135–7. I am grateful to Steve Toms for drawing my attention to this speech.
58. W. Lazonick, 'The Cotton Industry', in B. Elbaum and W. Lazonick (eds.), *The Decline of the British Economy* (Oxford, 1986), p.37; Singleton, *Lancashire*, pp.209–28.
59. Anson and Simpson, *World Textile*.
60. Knight, *Private*, p.49.
61. D.C. Coleman, *Courtaulds: An Economic and Social History*, Vol.2 (Oxford, 1969), pp.24–36; Singleton, *Lancashire*, p.221.
62. Federation of Master Cotton Spinners' Associations, *Annual Report* (1966), p.21.
63. Brian Lapping, *The Labour Government, 1964–1970* (London, 1970), p.76.
64. Dupree, *Streat Diary*, Vol.2, p.xxiv; P.W. Bell, *The Sterling Area in the Post-War World: Internal Mechanism and Cohesion* (Oxford, 1956).
65. A.R. Conan, *The Rationale of the Sterling Area* (London, 1961), p.55.
66. Cain and Hopkins, *British Imperialism*, p.285.
67. Singleton, 'Showing the White Flag', pp.129–49.
68. Dupree, 'Struggling', pp.123–5.
69. Singleton, *Lancashire*, pp.141–67.
70. B. Bardan, 'The Cotton Textile Agreement, 1962–72', *Journal of World Trade Law*, Vol.7, pp.8–35.
71. R.P. Nelson and S.G. Winter, *An Evolutionary Theory of Economic Change* (Cambridge, MA, 1982), p.139.
72. B. Toyne *et al.*, *The United States Textile Mill Products Industry: International Challenges and Strategy for the Future* (Columbia, 1983), pp.8–21.
73. P. Isard, 'Employment Impacts of Textile Imports and Investment: Vintage Capital Model', *American Economic Review* (1973), pp.402–15.
74. Bardan, 'The Cotton Textile'.
75. J. Gaventa and B.E. Smith, 'The De-industrialization of the Textile South: A Case Study', in J. Leiter *et al.* (eds.), *Hanging by a Thread* (Ithaca, NY, 1991), pp.183–5.
76. Lazonick, 'The Cotton Industry'.

Institutional Economics and Business History: A Way Forward?

MARK CASSON
University of Reading

The institutional theory of the firm, derived from Coase and developed by Williamson and others, has only partially fulfilled its early promise.[1] It has succeeded in explaining where the boundaries of the firm are drawn, but has failed to relate these boundaries to what goes on inside the firm. As the firm grows and diversifies, its boundaries shift and its internal organisation changes. But the sources of this growth, and the consequences for internal organisation, have received little attention so far. It is to address these omissions that modern theories of entrepreneurship and organisational capabilities have been developed.[2] Although these theories are institutional too, in a general sense of the word, they are not concerned so exclusively with transactions costs as is the Coasian theory of the firm.

To provide a comprehensive theory of the firm, these different approaches must be integrated. Since all the theories are in some sense institutional, it is possible to effect the integration without too much difficulty. This can be done using the concept of information cost. Information costs can be viewed as a generalisation of transaction costs. Information costs relate to the costs of collecting, communicating and memorising information. They also include the costs of calculation, and the costs of forming the judgements required for a decision. Many transaction costs are, in fact, information costs, but most information costs are not transaction costs. Transaction costs are incurred when other people behave in a selfish, dishonest or opportunistic manner. Transaction costs tend to be information costs because the rational response to dishonesty is to collect more information about the people concerned. Many information costs are not transaction costs, however, because a great deal of the information collected by the firm is not required to combat dishonesty, but to improve overall business strategy instead. For example, transaction costs are incurred chiefly in the negotiation and enforcement of contracts, where the withholding of relevant information by other people is a serious problem. Transactions costs reflect a lack of trust between the people concerned. Information costs, by contrast, are incurred chiefly in monitoring competitors, in forecasting market demand, and in the appraisal of investment decisions. The costs of collecting the relevant information on prices, costs, consumer fashions, and so on, have to be incurred whether other people are honest or not.

Because the theory of information costs is, relatively speaking, still in its infancy, it is unfamiliar to many scholars. There is therefore a tendency for business historians (and others) to invoke the concept of transaction cost when it is really the concept of information cost that they require. It is an opportune moment to distinguish more clearly between information costs and transaction costs, because the handling of information is receiving much more attention from business historians than it did in the past. Following pioneering work by Beniger and Yates, a number of symposia have appeared.[3]

The concept of information costs is particularly useful to historians in three respects. The first is in understanding changes in the internal organisation of the firm.[4] The organisational structure adopted by a given firm can be analysed as a rational response to information costs. As information costs decline over time, so organisational structures will evolve to facilitate a greater use of the cheaper information. The managerial division of labour will advance, and more sophisticated structures will emerge. The second respect concerns the explanation of success and failure amongst firms. Entrepreneurs who found firms with the ambition of employing others implicitly believe that they have lower information costs than those people. The entrepreneurs whose costs really are low will tend to be the most successful; their firms will not only survive, but grow faster than others.[5] Low information costs are typically reflected in high intelligence, breadth of vision and, above all, in social skills – for most commercially sensitive information is obtained through informal contacts with people who do not necessarily realise themselves the significance of what they have to say. The theory of information costs thereby relates the success of the firm to the personal qualities of the entrepreneur.

Thirdly, information costs are useful in analysing interorganisational collaboration. This encompasses both collaboration amongst firms – for example, between producers, retailers and brand owners within the distribution channel for a product – and collaboration between different types of organisation – as when firms, banks and government collaborate in promoting an export industry. This third area of application is the main focus of this essay.

Finally, it should be noted that there is not just one way of incorporating information costs into economic discourse, but several.[6] The approach adopted here is firmly embedded in the 'rational action' approach to economic modelling.[7] It is assumed that individuals can value information they do not have by forming an expected value of what it would be worth if they had it. This expected value is calculated using subjective probabilities of what the information might turn out to be. The value of the information derives from the fact that better decisions can be made with the information than without it, so that fewer mistakes will be made. Because information is costly, it does not follow that all the information required for a perfect decision will be collected; on the contrary, some information will normally be ignored. Information is collected by a rational individual only so long as its expected value exceeds its cost. It is the outcome of this decision that determines what information is collected, and by whom. Such decisions, when applied to different information sources, determine the organisational structure used to process the information.

This approach makes no concessions to those writers, like Simon and Williamson,[8] who subsume information cost under 'bounded rationality'. Boundedly rational behaviour, according to the view presented here, is best understood as a rational response to information costs, and not as an irrational response to a degree of complexity with which people simply cannot cope. The 'rational action' approach suggests that the incidence of bounded rationality varies according to magnitude of information costs. When information costs are high, behaviour is boundedly rational because it is rational to economise on information by risking more mistakes, and when information costs are low, behaviour is less boundedly rational because it is rational to make greater use of information, so that fewer mistakes are made. These propositions differentiate the 'rational action' approach from the more usual approach, which tends to invoke bounded rationality as an *ad hoc* explanation of behaviour whenever the argument appears to require it.

II

The theory of information costs offers a vision of the economy as a cybernetic system. This vision counterbalances the more conventional view of the economy as a system of material flow. The focus is on the handling of the abstract commodity of information, rather than on the handling of physical commodities themselves.

This vision is inspired by the work of Hayek, Richardson and Marschak.[9] Although each of these writers has a different emphasis, they all perceive economic institutions as mechanisms for allocating decision-making responsibilities and for structuring information flow. They interpret the pattern of institutions existing at any given time as a rational response to the social need to economise on information costs. As information costs change, so does the institutional structure of the economy. In particular, as technological progress drives down communication costs over longer distances, so institutions adapt by increasing the geographical scope of their activities. This institutional evolution, in its turn, supports a higher level of economic development.

The role of information in the co-ordination of economic activities was first emphasised by Hayek, who explained how the market system motivates entrepreneurs to search out information for their private use. This information is then communicated to other people indirectly in the form of price quotations. In this way everyone becomes aware of the relative scarcities of different products. Each individual who scans price information therefore receives sufficient guidance to make decisions which are in harmony with those of other people.

Richardson too emphasised the importance of information to the co-ordination process. He was concerned with the general issue of how a complex economic system is co-ordinated, and in particular with the co-ordination of individual investment plans in related activities. He showed how informal structures of inter-firm collaboration may emerge to fill the gaps in knowledge flow that would otherwise distort the decisions of firms. The application of Richardson's ideas to business strategy has recently been elaborated by Kay.[10]

It was not until Marschak, however, that a systematic account of the role of information in the economy was provided. Marschak approached information from a decision theory perspective. This is very useful, because 'economic man' is basically 'man the decision-maker'. Thus a full analysis of the role of economic information must consider the impact of information on decisions of every kind. This perspective emphasises the economic value of information. Better information leads to better decisions, on account of both better individual judgement and better co-ordination of different individual decisions. Better decisions lead, in turn, to better use of resources, and hence to higher social welfare.

The vision of the economy as an information system is in sharp contrast to the materialistic vision of the economy found in standard economic textbooks. A typical textbook summarises the economy in terms of a 'wheel of wealth' (or 'wheel of income'), in which households supply factors of production to firms, who use them to produce goods which households themselves consume.[11] Markets co-ordinate the flows of factors from households to firms and the flows of products from firms to households.

This account is a travesty of the way that the economy actually works. It equates the firm with a producer, ignoring the fact that many firms are actually responsible for the organisation of the market process itself.[12] Firms create markets by innovating new products. They engage in arbitrage and speculation, integrating markets over space and time. Retailers and wholesalers hold inventories which help to buffer fluctuations in supply and demand. Advertising agencies help to disseminate information on product quality. Banks handle specialised information on the debts that are created when payments cannot be fully synchronised with the delivery of products. A simple way of summarising these points is to say that firms are specialised intermediators. In a very general sense firms intermediate between households as factor owners and households as consumers.

The materialistic view of the economy suggests that the essence of intermediation is production. It is the need to combine different factor inputs in given proportions, and in quantities sufficient to exploit economies of scale, that calls for intermediation by the firm. The cybernetic vision of the economy suggests that the essence of intermediation is the organisation of trade instead. This type of intermediation is effected by market-making firms. Trade requires people to make contact with each other, to communicate their wants, and explain what they offer in return, to negotiate a price and to monitor the fulfilment of their contracts. The costs of these activities can be reduced through intermediation. Market-making intermediation is thus a value-adding activity; indeed, it is one of the most important sources of added value in the entire economy.

The link between intermediation and information costs is very simple. Intermediators take responsibility for handling much of the information flow that is needed to make the economy work. They are specialised bearers of information costs. It is their decisions on how to structure information flow that governs the efficiency with which the economy operates. Competition between intermediators tend to select in favour of those who are most successful at minimising information costs whilst maintaining an adequate quality of decision making. It is these firms that grow most quickly. Their success resides in the owner's flair for spotting opportunities for intermediation, and the owner's skill in choosing an appropriate organisational structure.

III

The market-making intermediator improves communications between buyers and sellers by acting as a hub. Five key tasks of a market-making intermediator are listed in Table 1. All five tasks incur information costs, but only two of them – negotiation and enforcement – involve transactions costs in the sense defined above. In the other three cases the over-riding concern is that information is accurately recorded, and is stored and retrieved in an efficient way. The search function requires the intermediator to elicit the names and addresses of potential customers through advertising; the specification function requires him to carry out market research to ensure that the product specification matches customer requirements; and the

TABLE 1
THE PRINCIPAL TASK OF A MARKET-MAKING INTERMEDIATOR

Market-making activity	Obstacles to transaction	Intermediator's task	Need to assure quality of information
Ex ante			
1. Search	No contact between buyer and seller	Take initiative in seeking out buyer and sellers. Advertisement.	No
2. Specification	No knowledge of reciprocal wants	Publish catalogues and brochures. Arrange retailer displays, etc.	No
3. Negotiation	No agreement over price	Take hard line to simplify negotiation process. Build reputation for competitive prices.	Yes
Ex post			
4. Completion	No coincidence over place and time of delivery	Inventory holding. Planning of logistic of delivery to households or business premises.	No
5. Enforcement	No confidence that goods correspond to specification, or that restitution will be made for default on payment or delivery	Monitor suppliers. Monitor retailers. Create reputation through brand name. Require buyers to pay in advance and pay suppliers in arrears.	Yes

Source: Adapted from M.C. Casson, *The Entrepreneur: An Economic Theory* (Oxford, 1982).

completion function requires that deliveries to customers are optimised with respect to packing procedures and vehicle routes.

If intermediation is so important, why has it been so neglected? The key lies in the abstract nature of information. There are two related aspects of this. First, information handling has few physical manifestations, and so leaves little evidence behind. There is not much to observe when a person is thinking, and it is therefore easy to dismiss the communication of information through conversation as a purely social activity. In fact, though, the handling of information is of vital strategic significance, because without the collection of information most decisions would be seriously wrong. Even when information is collected there is a risk of error, but the risk is lower than it would be if no information had been collected at all.

By contrast to information handling, the handling of material product can generate dramatic effects. In the medieval economy the role of the intermediator was fairly clear: the colourful novelties of the market-place focused attention on the role of the merchant in transporting goods from distant and exotic locations. But with the coming of the industrial revolution, transportation became much easier and attention switched to the process of production itself. The blast furnaces that lit up the night sky encouraged the belief that the accumulation of fixed capital now held the key to economic success. The accumulation of information, particularly about export opportunities, was no less important, but was almost entirely ignored by commentators of the day. As a result, economists of the nineteenth century became fixated with production instead of market-making intermediation and with the flow of materials rather than the flow of information. It was a view of the economy that fitted, in a superficial way, the scientific materialism of the age.

The second aspect of information that accounts for the neglect of market-making intermediation is the popular view that information is a free good. The principal cost of gathering information is the opportunity cost of the time spent in investigation. Since no expenditure of materials is involved, information appears to be costless to the uninitiated. Likewise, the communication of information seems to be practically costless too. Even with long-distance communication, public access to posts, telegraphs and telephones means that the communication costs are likely to be quite small. The importance of face-to-face meetings for the communication of tacit information, and the consequent opportunity costs of travel, are easily ignored.

This populist view of information suggests that intermediators have no right to profit from the information that they acquire.[13] If information is scarce it is because the intermediators have created the scarcity themselves by keeping secret information that should have been shared. Intermediators, in other words, are monopolists. According to this view, the value added by intermediators is not the opportunity cost of scarce resources (such as the time devoted to investigation and communication), but pure monopoly rent. This ignores the fact that if intermediation were purely a question of monopoly rent then in the long run payments to intermediators would be eliminated by competition. In practice, long-run payments for intermediation are quite high, and often exceed the cost of production. This reflects the fact that intermediation involves significant resource costs and is a major component of the service sector of the economy.

IV

In the absence of intermediation it is difficult for any trade to take place. Trade is set up by contact between a buyer and seller, as illustrated in Figure 1. The physical flow of product is indicated by the thick black line connecting the two square boxes. At the top of the figure the left-hand box represents the muscle power of the worker, W, and the right-hand box the physical consumption of the product, C. The thin line represents the flow of information between the worker and the consumer. In contrast to the flow of product, which proceeds in one direction only, the flow of information is

FIGURE 1
A SIMPLE PATTERN OF INTERMEDIATION

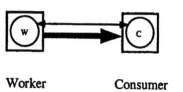

Worker   Consumer

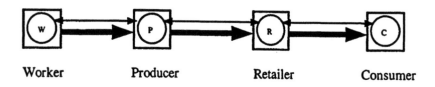

Worker   Producer   Retailer   Consumer

a two-way affair. To distinguish clearly between the roles of individuals as decision makers and as physical agents, their mental activities are represented by circles instead of squares. The thin lines of information flow connect the circles and the thick lines of material flow connect the squares.

The top part of the figure shows that in the absence of intermediation workers and consumers would have to deal directly with each other. The intermediation shown at the bottom of the figure helps trade to proceed more easily. The producer, P, intermediates by hiring workers, and then passes on the product to a retailer, R, who distributes it to the consumer. There are, however, certain limitations of this arrangement, which explain why only variants of it are normally observed in practice.

The first point is that neither of the intermediators is fully specialised in handling just information. A typical role for a pure information specialist is illustrated in the top part of Figure 2. The market is set up by the entrepreneurial brand owner, N, who has carried out market research and designed a product which he believes customers will prefer to established alternatives. The brand owner is essentially a specialist in the search and specification functions described above. He also handles information at higher level of aggregation than other people, as described below.

The brand owner sub-contracts production to the producer, P; he buys the product from P at a pre-determined price and sells it to the retailer, R, at a recommended retail price less a discount. He advertises the recommended price, along with the desirable product characteristics, to the customers, C. By buying from the producer and re-selling to the retailer he ensures that adequate supplies are always available to meet demand. Whilst the producer intermediates between the worker and the retailer, and the retailer

FIGURE 2
MORE COMPLEX PATTERNS OF INTERMEDIATION

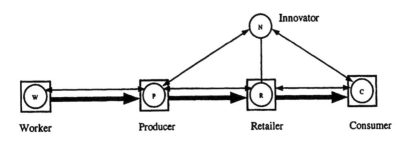

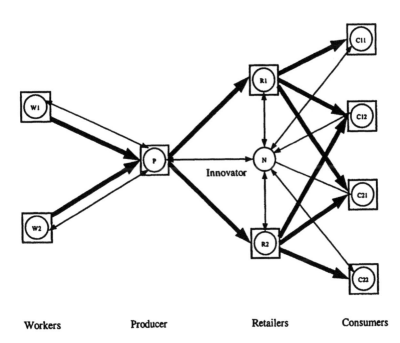

intermediates between the producer and the final customer, the brand owner, by intermediating between the producer and the retailer, co-ordinates the entire distribution channel linking the worker to the final consumer.

This contractual arrangement allows the brand owner to extract entrepreneurial rent from his product innovation without getting involved in handling the product at all. The rent is equal to the excess of the discounted price which the retailer pays over the price that the producer receives for his output. It introduces a further stage into the intermediation of information flow, but not into the physical flow of the product.

This additional stage of intermediation facilitates the input of additional information by the brand owner. The additional information is more general and more long term than the information handled by the producer and the retailer. The brand owner is not concerned, as the retailer is, with the identity of individual customers, nor with their demand for the product at any particular point of time. His geographical focus is wider too. This is illustrated in the lower part of Figure 2, where the brand owner intermediates between different local retailers on the one hand and the producer on the other. This configuration is common wherever there are significant economies of scale in production at the plant level, and the product is easy to transport. If, in addition, information is easy to communicate over long distances then the brand owner may broadcast information on the product nationally or internationally, encouraging people to inspect the product and take delivery through regional or local retailers. This is illustrated in the figure by the information radiating out from N to all the customers, C. Note also that the market areas of the retailers overlap at the margin. Setting recommended retail prices helps the brand owner to prevent the dissipation of his monopoly rents through price competition between the retailers. He needs to ensure that competition between R1 and R2 for the custom of C12 and C21 does not reduce the price too far below the maximum that C11 and C22, who are captive customers of their respective retailers, are willing to pay.

V

The second limitation of the structure shown in Figure 1 is that distribution of the product involves only a single stage. But, just as manufacturing can be broken down into successive physical stages, so distribution can be broken down into several stages too. The top part of Figure 3 shows how the export of a product involves transhipment at two ports – indeed, the sequence would be even more elaborate if land transport to and from the ports were shown, together with the voyage of the ship. Intermediation between successive stages of overseas distribution has a long tradition in international trade. A typical arrangement, involving both an export merchant and an import merchant, is shown in the figure. These merchants, like the brand owner discussed above, do not actually handle the product. What they handle are claims to the product. They negotiate the prices of the claims and do their best to see that the claims they hold are fully enforced.

The figure illustrates the important point that multi-stage distribution leads to multi-stage intermediation by market makers too. This point is of considerable significance for the analysis of vertical integration. For it shows that vertical integration applies not only to multi-stage material flow, but to multi-stage information flow as well. Vertical integration of information flow has specific implications. Suppose, for example, that the intermediators X and M in Figure 3 merged to form a vertically integrated multinational trading firm. In the course of distribution the product would pass through a sequence of independently owned physical facilities whilst still remaining under the effective control of the multinational firm. The process would begin with production being subcontracted to the independent producer, P. P's output would then be passed on to an independently owned warehouse at the exporting port, H1. Following its voyage, it would be collected from another independently owned warehouse in the importing country, H2, for delivery to the independent foreign retailer, R, for sale to the final customer. Throughout its transit from the factory to the shop the product would remain the property of the multinational firm, even though all the premises that it passed through were independently owned.

FIGURE 3
INTERMEDIATION IN INTERNATIONAL TRADE

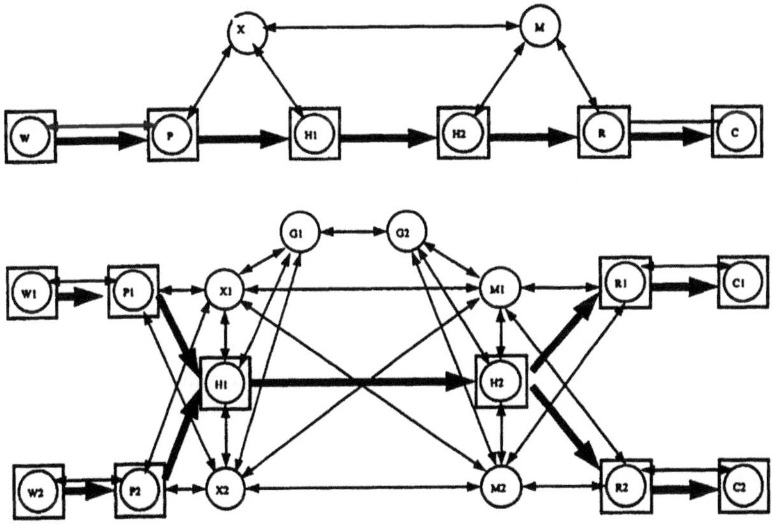

The final limitation that needs to be addressed is the implicit assumption that each stage of intermediation is dominated by a single firm. This need not, of course, be the case. Competition between intermediators is certainly possible, although it often takes the form of oligopolistic competition, in which each intermediator enjoys the loyalty of a significant proportion of total customers. Alternatively, it takes the form of monopolistic competition in which each intermediator either trades in a different variety of product or offers a distinctive quality of service. In such cases, 'the market' often refers, in common parlance, to the set of competing intermediators. The market does not signify an impersonal collection of buyers and sellers trading directly with each other, as suggested by conventional economic theory, but rather a collection of intermediating firms instead.

The role of competition in an export market is illustrated in the lower part of Figure 3. There are two export merchants in country 1 (on the left) and two import merchants in country 2 (on the right). Each importer is prepared to deal with either exporter. Each exporter is in turn willing to procure output from either of the producers, P1, P2. Likewise, each importer is willing to deal with either of the retailers, R1, R2. Between them the competing export and import merchants constitute the 'market', as considered from an institutional point of view. Each side of the market derives some reassurance over the price demanded by the other side from the fact that those on the other side are competing with each other.

VI

The fact that the intermediating firms compete for custom does not mean that they do not share a common interest as well. For example, the retailers who compete on the high street of one town have a common interest in promoting that town as a shopping centre, in competition with neighbouring towns. Indeed, the more intensively they compete, the lower their prices are likely to be, and the more they stand to gain from advertising that fact to a wider population. The greater the intensity of competition in selling to people once they arrive in town, the greater the gains from co-operation in getting them to come there in the first place. Conversely, although individual shopkeepers in one town have little to fear from individual shopkeepers in another town, each may nevertheless join with its local competitors to advertise against the firms in the other town. Everyone co-operates with their closest rivals in order to compete more effectively as a group.

Special co-operative bodies, such as industry trade associations and local industrial development councils, often emerge for such purposes. These bodies 'intermediate' between the intermediators. They represent a higher level of intermediation than do the ordinary firms that belong to these associations. Another example of group interest amongst intermediators is the establishment of a code of practice under which local trade takes place. Each town may have its own 'rules of the game' where competition is concerned. There may even be a special building where these rules prevail.[14] In this case the market may become a distinct spatial and architectural entity. Local self-regulation is particularly noticeable in financial markets. Each market attempts to create a reputation for integrity, confidentiality, liquidity, and so on. Competing intermediators co-operate to promote the interests of their market, and, indeed, may agree to promote the intensity of competition between them as their chief selling point. The more frequently they co-operate, the stronger the social ties between them become. The City of London, for example, transacts impersonal global business through highly personal connections between specialist intermediators who not only know each other personally, but belong to the same clubs, and in some cases went to the same school as well.[15]

Intermediators can also make common cause in obtaining special privileges. One of the main problems in liberalising services under recent GATT rounds was the difficulty of overcoming lobbying by local intermediators fearful of seeing their markets being taken over by more professional foreign firms. Indeed, because of their skills in handling information, intermediators are likely to be particularly effective in defending their collective interests against outside competition. It is surely no accident that intermediators such as shopkeepers and estate agents are so strongly represented on town councils and other bodies that regulate local affairs.

VII

Intermediation is a very general principle which can manifest itself in many different forms. For example, a government may be thought of as an intermediator between its citizens, supplying defence, law and order, and other 'public goods' through state organisations.

Forms of intermediation differ according to the kind of information in which they deal. A core activity of government is the collection of military intelligence on the policies of rival states. It also requires a police force and judiciary to investigate crimes within its territory, and to convict the perpetrators. Governments therefore tend to specialise in handling highly confidential information – their aim is to discover other people's secrets without them being aware of the fact. This form of specialisation leads to a distinctive culture of secrecy in government bureaucracies.

Ordinary firms, by contrast, concentrate on collecting commercial information. Here, too, there is an element of secrecy, but the secrecy lies rather in the identification of an opportunity for intermediation than in the way in which it is implemented or exploited. Firms normally disseminate much more information than do governments because they must advertise their product and keep in regular contact with their customers and suppliers. Despite these differences, however, institutions of different types still have a lot in common. In general, intermediators are people or institutions with high reputation who intermediate between those with less reputation than themselves. Intermediators need a reputation for integrity because they do their work by allowing other people to place their trust in them when, for whatever reason, they cannot really trust other people instead.

Some co-ordination tasks are so complex that different types of intermediator must join forces to deal with them. The challenge of rapid economic development – through 'catch up' industrialisation, for example – often throws up challenges of this kind. Infant industry protection is a case in point. This frequently leads to firms and governments interacting closely to implement an interventionist industrial policy.[16]

The lower part of Figure 3, previously described, illustrates a situation where the governments of both exporting and importing countries have intervened in trade. The government of country 2, G2, has decided, in response to pressure from domestic industry, to protect local producers by levying duties at the port of entry, H2. This raises the effective price that the import merchants, M1, M2, are obliged to pay. This in turn reduces the prices they are willing to offer to the export merchants, X1, X2. The government of country 1, G1, is concerned, however, that falling exports may lead to higher unemployment, and a consequent increase in the social security bill. The government, G1, therefore intervenes to offer export subsidies at the port, H1. This encourages the export merchants, X1, X2, to accept the lower prices offered by M1 and M2. The result of this is a net transfer of income from the government in country 1 to the government in country 2, but little change in the level of trade. Government G1 may then approach government G2 with a view to negotiating a reduction in the tariff, in return, perhaps, for some concession on another issue.

The government–industry interactions are illustrated in the figure by the lines connecting X1 and X2 to G1, and by the lines connecting M1 and M2 to G2. Intergovernmental interactions are indicated by the line connecting G1 and G2. These lines represent the flows of information generated by a division of labour in intermediation between different kinds of institution.

Another aspect of the division of labour in intermediation concerns the use of currency to simplify transactions. Currency, in the form of circulating note and coin, allows people to trade without a 'double coincidence of wants'. The homogeneity of currency promotes the use of deposits held with clearing banks. It also encourages the growth of foreign exchange banking to support international trade. The role of banks in international trade is illustrated in Figure 4. The figure illustrates a two-way material flow, with exports from country 1, produced by P1 and retailed by R1, being exchanged for imports from country 2, produced by P2 and retailed by R2. The exports and imports are not directly bartered. Instead, currency is used as a medium of exchange. A variety of arrangements is possible. In one of the simplest, foreign exchange earned by the exporting merchant in country 1, X1, is recycled through the bank, B1, to the importer, M2, who uses it to pay for imports from country 2. The exporter in country 2, X2, deposits his funds with the bank, B2, who passes them on to the importer, M1, who then uses them to pay the exporter in country 1. The flows of information required to support these currency transactions are indicated in the figure by the lines connecting B1 to X1 and M2, and B2 to M1 and X2.

FIGURE 4
ROLE OF BANKS IN INTERNATIONAL TRADE

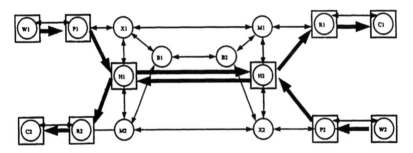

VIII

The importance of intermediation by merchants and entrepreneurs has been recognised by neo-Austrian economists such as Kirzner, but what is lacking in their treatment of it is any theory of the organisation of the firm.[17] Neo-Austrians believe that the ability to intermediate is fairly widespread whereas it seems that, as Schumpeter suggested, the number of people who can intermediate successfully is strictly limited.[18] This is certainly true of the pure intermediation exemplified by N in Figure 2 above. The pure intermediator requires not only the ability to recognise a market opportunity, but the competence and integrity to exploit it fully. Pure intermediation, such as the management of a brand, is a very information-intensive activity.

The amount of information that an intermediator needs to handle depends crucially upon the volatility of the market environment in which he operates.[19] Furthermore, the pattern of this volatility affects the structure of his organisation in significant ways. The more independent sources of volatility that there are, the wider the range of information that must be synthesised before a decision is taken. The amount of information often exceeds the capability of a single person. To intermediate efficiently it is necessary to create a division of labour in information handling and to structure the flow of information within the system.[20] The intermediator, in other words, requires an organisation.

General information may be handled by one group of people and specific information by another. Those who handle specific information may be asked to report unusual information to those who handle general information, in case this unusual information is a symptom of a general change. Some people may specialise in handling information using routines, whilst others may specialise in improvisation. Routines work best where a high proportion of the situations that arise belong to a small number of regularly recurring types. Improvisation is most appropriate in the opposite case, where each situation is unprecedented and unique.[21]

Communication costs impose a tax on an interpersonal division of labour in the synthesis of information. The higher internal communication costs are, the lower the degree of specialisation will be. Steps can, of course, be taken to reduce communication costs; for example, by establishing a common language and common culture within the firm. Such standardisation reduces the marginal cost of communication, though against this must be set the fixed costs of creating the standards in the first place.

Communication costs affect the way that information is synthesised as well. Some information is particularly costly to communicate because it is 'tacit' information which cannot be properly understood unless the context is clear.[22] If the context is unclear then a lot of effort must be made to explain it. It is therefore advantageous, in most organisations, to specialise authority on the person who collects the most tacit information, since this affords the greatest savings in communication costs.

Within any organisation the most tacit information is likely to come from external sources. Internal sources are more likely to generate explicit information. The information generated by internal specialists is therefore more likely to be explicit than the information generated by the person responsible for scanning the external environment. This suggests that an efficient organisation involves internal specialists reporting information to, and taking orders from, the person who handles the external relations of the firm. This authority relation creates a hierarchical structure in which the executives report information to a superior who hands down orders which incorporate his own tacit information on the environment of the firm.[23]

No intermediator can stick to the same organisational structure for ever, though. As new market opportunities emerge, so old ones disappear; this is part of the 'creative destruction' effected by innovation. If a firm is to survive it must continue to monitor its external environment for changes affecting the market as a whole. These changes are only intermittent, of course, but when they occur they are often large, and have profound implications for the firm. They may suggest diversifying into new markets, or quitting declining markets and 'refocusing' on other areas instead. An entrepreneur cannot afford to monitor such changes continuously, but he cannot afford to neglect them either. The key to the continued growth of the firm is a commitment to monitor persistent changes on a regular basis and to restructure the organisation when required so that the procedures are adapted to new circumstances. An 'inward looking attitude' and an excessive respect for the traditional way of doing things are inimical to continued success.

It is not only external shocks that create a need to change the organisational structure of the firm. As a firm grows by exploiting a given market opportunity more thoroughly (for example, over a wider geographical area), so the founder is likely to become increasingly overwhelmed by detail. For example, he may have begun by cultivating key customers, only to discover that they have recommended him to so many other people that he can no longer provide the personal service that his initial customers valued so much. Only by delegation can the organisation grow. But delegation poses problems to those not well versed in the principles of organisational design. It is difficult to define new jobs, to select appropriate people, and to know how much trust to place in them. Delegation is particularly difficult for autocrats and, in larger firms, for those who favour a 'familistic' style of management.

The implication is that successful firms must grow by achieving an appropriate balance between flexibility and routine. Detail is routinised as far as possible, but there is freedom to improvise as well. As the firm grows, and as its environment evolves, so its organisational structure must change. In the early stages of growth, this means replacing improvisation with routine. In the later stages of growth it means avoiding over-centralised and autocratic management, and adopting a consultative style instead. A large and diversified firm is subject to so many changes in different persistent factors that one chief executive cannot expect to monitor them all, and so he must share this responsibility with other members of the management team.

X

The theory of information costs has implications for all fields of business history. It suggests that firms are founded by entrepreneurs who have a comparative advantage in handling certain kinds of information, which enables them to identify new opportunities for intermediation. As the firm grows the founder must develop new organisational skills, or hire managers who have them. If he does neither then he must step aside and sell out to new owners instead. Organisational renewal is a feature of all successful firms. It is a regular, though not continuous process. It consists in updating organisational structures in response to the general growth of the firm, and to intermittent changes in its environment.

The focus on intermediation rather than production means that the theory is well adapted to analysing the organisation and growth of firms in the service industry. The control of information is vital in sectors such as transportation, retailing and banking. A focus on information rather than material flow helps to explain the contribution of the telegraph to the development of railways, the contribution of the postal service and the telephone to mail-order retailing, and the contribution of electronic databases to banking.

The emphasis on information also helps to explain the paradox of so-called 'hollow firms', which carry out no production of their own, but merely engage in trade. Such were the chartered trading companies of the seventeenth and eighteenth centuries and the managing agencies of the nineteenth century.[24] The entire rationale of these firms resides in their ability to minimise information costs; to analyse them solely in terms of transaction costs inevitably generates a highly distorted view.

Perhaps the most striking application of the theory of information costs, however, lies in the interpretation of changes in the pattern of intermediation over time. There is a large descriptive literature in both business history and economic history which tracks changes in patterns of intermediation over time. Market-making intermediation has developed from self-employed merchants who attended periodic local fairs and markets, through regulated trading companies, chartered trading companies and free-standing foreign investment companies to the major multinationals of modern times.[25] Important milestones in this process have been the consolidation of European merchant networks and trade diaspora in the seventeenth century, the emergence of urban shopping centres in the eighteenth century, the evolution of regional networks of middlemen supporting the factory system in the nineteenth century, and the movement towards vertical integration of mass marketing and mass production around the turn of the twentieth century.[26] Each transition has been charted and interpreted by a particular school of historians, but few have attempted to analyse all these transitions using the same conceptual scheme. It may be suggested (it would be premature to claim more) that the insights into intermediation offered by the information cost approach may help to provide a systematic account of this phenomenon.

The basic idea is that changes in the organisation of trade are driven by changes in the pattern of intermediation, and that these changes in turn represent a rational response to changes in information costs. From a long-run perspective two particular trends in information costs are relevant: a general decline in information costs as a whole, and a specific decline in the distance-related component of information cost. The first of these has promoted a general growth in the amount of information that is brought to bear on economic co-ordination. It has induced a more sophisticated division of labour in information processing which is associated with a more sophisticated pattern of intermediation. In particular, falling costs of search and specification have increased the number of different varieties of differentiated products that can be traded, and this has increased the number of market niches that intermediators can occupy. At the same time, the decline in the distance-related component of information costs has induced geographical rationalisation in intermediation, so that fewer intermediators occupy any given product niche. Each intermediator serves a wider market area than before. The decline in distance-related information costs has other implications for intermediation, such as the increasing agglomeration of intermediation in just a few metropolitan cities, regions or conurbations where information on many different subjects from many different sources can be readily combined (an early example of this trend is business networking in seventeenth-century Amsterdam[27]).

Superimposed upon these general changes have been other changes specific to particular industries. When an industry is new, the technology is experimental, and the market is growing through word-of-mouth diffusion, information costs tend to be relatively high. There is considerable demand for intermediation, but no single intermediator possesses a 'big picture' of the industry as a whole. Intermediators therefore have to deal with other intermediators who know about parts of the industry that they do not. At this early stage of the industry life cycle, the product may have to pass through the hands of many intermediators on its way to the final customer, and many margins may therefore be added to the cost to arrive at the final price. But as the industry matures, so technology standardises and information diffuses between the intermediators in the industry. The standardisation of technology affords an opportunity for driving down cost through economies of scale in production. These economies can be reinforced by economies of scale in marketing too.

To make the product really cheap, and expand the market to its maximum size, it is necessary to eliminate the multiplicity of intermediation. This process is assisted by the diffusion of information, which allows one set of intermediators to acquire enough knowledge of other parts of the industry to take over the work of other intermediators as well. Upstream intermediators may attempt to take over downstream intermediators, whilst the downstream intermediators may counter with takeover bids of their own. The intermediators who possess the scarcest knowledge – knowledge that does not readily diffuse – will tend to win. They will rationalise the industry by reducing the number of independent stages of intermediation, producing a 'leaner' structure in the production and distribution channel. By this stage the organisation of the industry has become mature.

The testing, and subsequent refinement, of these hypotheses provides a substantial agenda for historical research. Although the uniqueness of historical circumstances will always confound the generalisations deduced from any theoretical scheme, the scheme proposed here should be sufficiently flexible to accommodate many of the unexpected results thrown up by archival work. The concept of information costs is an extremely parsimonious one, and can be refined in several ways. The schematic diagrams are also a very flexible tool of analysis, and can be adapted to analyse a wide range of different historical circumstances.

NOTES

I am grateful to Andrew Godley, Eric Jones, Lien Luu and Mary Rose for discussions on this paper, and to Mira Wilkins and an anonymous referee for their comments on an earlier version of this paper.

1. R.H. Coase, 'The Nature of the Firm', *Economica* (New Series) Vol.4 (1937), pp.386–405; O.E. Williamson, *Markets and Hierarchies: Analysis and Anti-Trust Implications* (New York, 1975).

2. M.C. Casson, *The Entrepreneur: An Economic Theory* (Oxford, 1982); R. Nelson and S.G. Winter, *An Evolutionary Theory of Economic Change* (Cambridge, MA, 1982).

3. J. Beniger, *The Control Revolution: Technological and Economic Origins of the Information Society* (Cambridge, MA, 1986); J. Yates, *Control through Communication: The Rise of System in American Management* (Baltimore, MD, 1989). The symposia include L. Bud-Frierman (ed.), *Information Acumen: The Understanding and Use of Knowledge in Modern Business* (London, 1994); N.R. Lamoreaux and D.M.G. Raff (eds.), *Coordination and Information: Historical Perspectives on the Organization of Enterprise* (Chicago, IL, 1995); P. Temin (ed.), *Inside the Business Enterprise: Historical Perspectives on the Use of Information* (Chicago, IL, 1991).

4. R.N. Langlois and P.L. Robertson, *Firms, Markets and Economic Change* (London, 1995); M. Wilkins, 'Defining a Firm: History and Theory', in P. Hertner and G. Jones (eds.), *Multinationals: Theory and History* (Aldershot, 1986), pp.80–95.

5. E.T. Penrose, *The Theory of the Growth of the Firm* (Oxford, 1959).

6. See, for example, M.H. Boisot, *Information Space: A Framework for Learning in Institutions, Organizations and Culture* (London, 1995).

7. M. Blaug, *The Methodology of Economics, or How Economists Explain* (Cambridge, 1980).

8. H.A. Simon, *Administrative Behaviour* (New York, 1947); Williamson, *Markets and Hierarchies*.

9. F.A. von Hayek, 'Economics and Knowledge', *Economica*, New Series, Vol.4 (1937), pp.33–54; G.B. Richardson, *Information and Investment* (Oxford, 1960); J. Marschak, *Economic Information, Decision and Prediction* (Dordrecht, 1974).

10. J.A. Kay, *Foundations of Corporate Success: How Business Strategies Add Value* (Oxford, 1993).

11. See, for example, M. Parkin and D. King, *Economics* (London, 2nd edn. 1995).

12. D.F. Spulber, 'Market Microstructure and Intermediation', *Journal of Economic Perspectives*, Vol.10 (1996), pp.135–52.
13. P. Guillet de Monthoux, *The Moral Philosophy of Management: From Quesnay to Keynes* (Armonk, NY, 1993).
14. See Caunce in this volume.
15. G. Jones, *British Multinational Banking* (Oxford, 1993).
16. See Rose in this volume.
17. I.M. Kirzner, *Competition and Entrepreneurship* (Chicago, 1973).
18. J.A. Schumpeter, *The Theory of Economic Development* (trans. R. Opie) (Cambridge, MA, 1934).
19. M.C. Casson, *Information and Organization: A New Perspective on the Theory of the Firm* (Oxford, 1997).
20. M.J. Carter, 'Information and the Division of Labour: Implications for the Firm's Choice of Organisation', *Economic Journal*, Vol.105 (1995), pp.385–97.
21. F.H. Knight, *Risk, Uncertainty and Profit* (Boston, MA, 1921).
22. B. Kogut and U. Zander, 'Knowledge of the Firm, Combinative Capabilities and the Replication of Technology', *Organization Science*, Vol.3 (1996), pp.383–97.
23. M.C. Casson, *The Organization of International Business* (Aldershot, 1995), pp.73–5.
24. A.M. Carlos and S.J. Nicholas, 'Giants of an Earlier Capitalism: The Chartered Trading Companies as Modern Multinationals', *Business History Review*, Vol.62 (1989), pp.399–419; C. Harvey and J. Press, 'Overseas Investment and the Professional Advance of British Metal Mining Engineers, 1851–1914', *Economic History Review*, Vol.42, pp.64–86; G. Jones, 'Diversification Strategies and Corporate Governance in Trading Companies: Anglo-Japanese Comparisons since the late Nineteenth Century', *Business and Economic History*, Vol.25 No.2 (1996), pp.103–18.
25. M. Wilkins, *The History of Foreign Investment in the United States to 1914* (Cambridge, MA, 1989).
26. R.B. Westerfield, *Middlemen in English Business, Particularly between 1660 and 1760* (New Haven, CT, 1915); H.-C. Mui and L.M. Mui, *Shops and Shopkeeping in Eighteenth-Century England* (London, 1989); P. Hudson, 'The Regional Perspective', in P. Hudson (ed.), *Regions and Industries: A Perspective on the Industrial Revolution in Britain* (Cambridge, 1989), pp.5–38; A.D. Chandler, Jr, *The Visible Hand: The Managerial Revolution in American Business* (Cambridge, MA, 1977).
27. W.D. Smith, 'The Function of Commercial Centres in the Modernisation of European Capitalism: Amsterdam as an Information Exchange in the Seventeenth Century', *Journal of Economic History*, Vol.44, pp.985–1005.

Abstracts

Transaction Costs and the Theory of the Firm: The Scope and Limitations of the New Institutional Approach, *by S.R.H. Jones*

The new institutional approach to the theory of the firm represents a welcome advance over neoclassical theory in that, instead of treating the firm merely as a device to explain equilibrium under different market structures, it delves into the workings of the firm in an effort to understand why enterprises undertake the activities they do and how they grow over time. The theoretical framework for much of the new approach was developed by Oliver Williamson, who argued that firms evolved not because of technological non-separabilities but to economise on transaction costs. The object of this essay is to demonstrate that Williamson's comparative static methodology is ill-suited to explaining how firms actually evolve. It argues that far greater insights are provided by capability- or resource-based theories of the firm, which combine the concepts of transaction costs and firm-specific advantage in order to show that the boundaries of the firm are in fact determined by the non-separability and tacit nature of knowledge that lies at the heart of every enterprise.

Complexity, Community Structure and Competitive Advantage within the Yorkshire Woollen Industry, c.1700–1850, *by S.A. Caunce*

The Yorkshire wool textile area was a classic dynamic industrial district between 1700 and 1850. It played a full part in the development of the new technology associated with the industrial revolution, but this was only one element in the wresting of competitive advantage from the traditional leaders of the industry in England. The woollen sector in particular showed strong continuity with the past in its business structures and institutional framework, and this helped to get communities to push for change rather than fighting it. Moreover, West Yorkshire had an extremely complex economy which, in conjunction with an open and varied social structure, created the ideal landscape for evolutionary processes to work themselves out. It is also argued that this complexity allowed the links between clothiers and merchants to act as information processing systems analogous to neural networks, and that they were capable of generating apparently intelligent strategic action at the system level without requiring central control or deliberate co-ordination.

Invisible, Visible and 'Direct' Hands: An Institutional Interpretation of Organisational Structure and Change in British General Insurance, *by Oliver M. Westall*

This essay uses ideas drawn from institutional and evolutionary economics to explore three different approaches to the organisation of insurance operations in Britain since the eighteenth century: the market-based approach used by Lloyd's; the hierarchical approach developed by insurance companies from the nineteenth century; and the 'direct' approach introduced in the last few years. It argues that these ideas open up the 'black box' of internal operation to economic analysis and relate these to broader strategic change in the business, thus providing a better understanding of its long-term developments by showing how technological innovations have resolved previously intractable difficulties that have channelled the direction of organisational change.

Consultancies, Institutions and the Diffusion of Taylorism in Britain, Germany and France, 1920s to 1950s, *by Matthias Kipping*

This essay compares and analyses the evolution of Taylorist consultancies in the three major European economies. It shows that institutions established by the business community, often with government support, can provide an alternative channel for the dissemination of new management methods. Unlike private consultancies, they immediately benefit from a high level of trust, facilitate inter-firm comparisons, and ensure a relatively uniform application of these methods. This was the case in Germany where institutions such as the REFA and RKW trained a large number of work study engineers and collected benchmark data. In Britain on the other hand, the diffusion of scientific management relied much more on consultancies. Institutions served at best as intermediaries for the establishment of a trust-based relationship and provided some sort of quality control. In France, institutions had ambitions similar to the German 'model'. But they were weakened by splits and competition among themselves and thus left sufficient room for the development of consultancy activities.

Financial Reconstruction and Industrial Reorganisation in Different Financial Systems: A Comparative View of British and Swedish Institutions during the Inter-War Period, *by Hans Sjögren*

This essay provides a comparative perspective on the process of financial reconstruction and industrial reorganisation in the large-firm sector in inter-war Sweden and the UK. The behaviour of private banks is analysed during a period when their bargaining power is likely to have been transferred from the distressed firm to any of the external investors. In the UK and Sweden investors have traditionally been viewed as having respectively an arm's length approach towards industry and a control-oriented one. The hypothesis here is that the two financial systems were more similar than has conventionally been assumed. Besides protecting their claims, creditors in both countries became involved in the rationalisation of production which followed. This empirical study is limited to 24 large firms. However, the evidence suggests that whilst the Swedish system contained elements of the arm's length approach, the British investor's involvement in industrial transformation featured elements of control-orientation.

Post-War Strategic Capitalism in Norway: A Theoretical and Analytical Framework, *by Sverre Knutsen*

This essay provides an institutional approach to the analysis of the Norwegian state's effort to promote industrial development between 1950 and 1980. It explores the extent to which national financial systems influence the ability of governments to intervene in industrial policy. It also explores the extent to which both the governance structures and investment strategies of Norwegian firms have been influenced by government policy. It demonstrates that the financial system is indeed a critical factor in the effective implementation of industrial policy in the period in question.

The Politics of Protection: An Institutional Approach to Government–Industry Relations in the British and United States Cotton Industries, 1945–73, *by Mary B. Rose*

Internationally, the establishment of the GATT marked the beginning of a shift to greater trade liberalism. Against this background the governments of developed economies have generally treated textiles as a special case. This essay focuses on the differing level of political bargaining power exerted by the cotton industry interest groups in Britain and the United States, in their quest for protection, since 1945. It demonstrates that, to understand why pressure groups in the United States gained more concessions than those in Britain, it is necessary to consider the differing institutional and political environments in which they operated and the historical forces which shaped them.

Institutional Economics and Business History: A Way Forward?, *by Mark Casson*

Analytical business history requires a synthesis of theories of transaction cost, entrepreneurship and firm-specific competence. These theories can be integrated using the concept of information cost. Economies of information cost explain the emergence of market-making intermediation in capitalist economies. Economists have been so preoccupied with production that they have ignored the role of market-making intermediation, despite the fact that market-making intermediation has a crucial impact on the strategy and organisation of the firm. This essay charts the historical emergence of market-making intermediation, and analyses its effects using a diagrammatic technique specifically developed for this purpose. It is suggested that the concept of information cost, and the techniques of analysis allied with it, offer a useful way forward for business historians.

Index

Titles of Related Interest

BANKS, NETWORKS AND SMALL FIRM FINANCE
Edited by Andrew Godley and Duncan M Ross

This volume results from the observation that small firms often experience considerable difficulty in raising funds for expansion or investment. The essays explore a variety of alternatives in which networks are substituted for market transactions. They focus on the role of trust engendered by historical, cultural and geographical proximity, explore the possible conflicts of interest arising from business and social relationships and discuss the ways in which informal information can reduce the costs involved in sorting, screening and monitoring borrowers.

130 pages   1996   0 7146 4266 5 paper

NORDIC BUSINESS IN THE LONG VIEW
On Control and Strategy in Structural Change
Edited by Kersti Ullenhag

The essays highlight developments in Nordic business from the early 19th century up to the 1980's. Six cases are Swedish and the seventh is Danish.

110 pages   1993   0 7146 4524 9 cloth

ORGANISATIONAL CAPABILITY AND COMPETITIVE ADVANTAGE
Edited by Charles Harvey and Geoffrey Jones

This book examines the issues of competitive advantage and organisational capability in a comparative and historical perspective. It includes essays on the US, UK and Japan by a team of prominent business historians.

204 pages   1993   0 7146 3457 3 cloth

LABOUR AND BUSINESS IN MODERN BRITAIN
Edited by Charles Harvey and John Turner

The recent study of industrial relations history has been transformed, but much of the advance has been theoretical. This volume applies the state of the art in theoretical developments to the real work of analysing what went on in the factories, workshops and sweatshops of Britain within the last 100 years.

120 pages   1989   0 7146 3365 8 cloth

BUSINESS HISTORY
Concepts and Measurement
Edited by Charles Harvey
A collection of important original research by scholars which demonstrate the wide applicability of economic ideas and statistical methods to business history.
144 pages   1990   0 7146 3366 6 cloth

INTERNATIONAL COMPETITION AND INDUSTRIAL CHANGE
Essays in the History of Mining and Metallurgy 1800–1950
Edited by Charles Harvey and Jon Press
Presents key issues in the history of mining and metallurgy.
168 pages   1990   0 7146 3410 7 cloth

INTERNATIONAL COMPETITION AND STRATEGIC RESPONSE IN THE TEXTILE INDUSTRIES SINCE 1870
Edited by Mary B Rose
Drawing on the expertise of leading textile scholars in Britain and the United States, this book of essays focuses on the problem of and responses to foreign competition in textiles from the late nineteenth century to the present day.
194 pages   1991   0 7146 3412 3 cloth

BANKS AND MONEY
International and Comparative Finance in History
Edited by Geoffrey Jones
This volume assembles an international team of leading banking historians from the United States, Switzerland, Germany, Sweden, Britain and New Zealand to explore key themes in financial and banking history in a comparative perspective. Although there is particular emphasis on the theme of banking and industry, other topics are covered, including the issue of paper currency in Britain and its North American colonies in the eighteenth century, corporate finance and financial elites.
198 pages   1991   0 7146 3444 1 cloth

CAPITAL, ENTREPRENEURS AND PROFITS
Edited by R P T Davenport-Hines
Selected from the best of the articles published in the first thirty years of the journal *Business History,* the essays in this volume focus on such themes as marketing, pricing, the provision of financial services, investment decisions and diversification policy in nineteenth century manufacturing and the anatomy of Britain's business elite since 1860.
374 pages   1990   0 7146 3386 0 cloth